# PRODUCTIVE
# CHRISTIANS IN AN AGE OF GUILT-MANIPULATORS
## A BIBLICAL RESPONSE TO
# RONALD J. SIDER

## BY DAVID CHILTON

INSTITUTE FOR
CHRISTIAN ECONOMICS
TYLER, TX 75711

PUBLISHED BY THE INSTITUTE FOR CHRISTIAN ECONOMICS
P. O. BOX 8000, TYLER, TEXAS 75711

ISBN 0-930464-00-1

PRINTED IN THE UNITED STATES OF AMERICA

*This book is dedicated to*
**Pat Robertson**
*a "productive Christian" who
is leading God's people to victory.*

## ACKNOWLEDGMENTS

*A number of people have contributed in various ways toward this study. The manuscript was prepared with the generous help of good friends: Liz Allor, the Rev. and Mrs. Harold Chilton, Amy Craig, Janet Larson, Debbie Miani, Brian Peelle, Bob Pegram, Jayn Porter, Darlene Weaver, Marcelle Williams and Jackie Williamson. Very special advice and assistance was given by James B. Jordan. Dr. Gary North's editorial skills brought greater clarity to the exposition, and he has been gracious in many ways. David Thoburn and his typesetters have a combination of speed, precision and patience that is probably unequalled.*

*Finally, I wish to thank my wife, Darlene, whose love, godliness and wisdom are daily reminders of Proverbs 31. Without her counsel and encouragement, the work would not have been accomplished; and it is for her, and for Nathan and Jacob, that it was written.*

# TABLE OF CONTENTS

## PART I

# PREFACE TO THE SECOND EDITION

by Gary North

Perhaps the most striking feature of the picture [*of the shift in perspective of capitalists: from the long-run, multi-generation view of the founder of a family business to a short-run, one-lifetime outlook of the corporation man—G. N.*] is the extent to which the bourgeoisie, besides educating its own enemies, allows itself in turn to be educated by them. It absorbs the slogans of current radicalism and seems quite willing to undergo a process of conversion to a creed hostile to its very existence. Haltingly and grudgingly it concedes in part the implications of that creed. This would be most astonishing and indeed very hard to explain were it not for the fact that the typical bourgeoisie is rapidly losing faith in his own creed. . . . They talk and plead—or hire people to do it for them; they snatch at every chance of compromise; they are ever ready to give in; they never put up a fight under the flag of their own ideals. . . . The only explanation for the meekness we observe is that the bourgeois order no longer makes any sense to the bourgeoisie itself and that, when all is said and nothing is done, it does not really care.

Joseph Schumpeter (1942)[1]

Schumpeter blamed the rise of the "limited-liability" corporation and the parallel decline of the family-run business as the primary causes of this decline of faith. He should have looked more carefully. The decline of faith in a providential world run by a personal God was equally responsible. The rise of *Darwinism,* with its world devoid of cosmic purpose, undercut Christian civilization in Protestant nations, where Darwinism became the ruling idea by 1900 among intellectuals. Also, he should have recognized the two-pronged attack by Darwinism on the idea of God's providence. The first prong was its denial of planning and design in the advent of our world — its assertion of cosmic impersonalism. The second prong was visible from the beginning of Darwinism: the assertion of a new sovereignty, a new source of cosmic purpose: *Man, the new predestinator.* And more specifically, man's agent of predestination: *the planning State.* [2]

The humanists long ago abandoned faith in any version of the doctrine of creation by God. They captured the institutions of higher learning very early in this battle for the minds of men. Thus, as Christian denominations and Christian colleges began to seek "academic respectability," they made it a requirement that their professors (and in some cases, candidates for admission to theological seminaries) earn academic degrees from these humanistic institutions. It was as if Martin Luther had required all candidates for the Protestant ministry to earn advanced degrees in Roman Catholic universities before becoming ordained. Can you imagine the Apostle Paul requiring that all candidates for a preaching ministry first attend "Athens University" for their bachelor degrees, and then journey to "Pharisee Theological Seminary" in Jerusalem for advanced training?[3] Yet this is precisely what modern denominations frequently require, and virtually all Christian colleges and "universities," so-called. *They demand academic certification by Satan's institutions.*[4] To say that Christians suffer from a crippling academic inferiority complex is putting it mildly.

The result has been, universally, the teaching of Darwinism in seminary and Christian college classrooms. Sometimes this has been blatant, as in the case of the "prestige" divinity schools associated with humanistic "major" universities—the big-name schools that our little backwater Christian seminaries love to send their young men to, and then bring them back to teach, all nicely certified. You can almost hear the president of the denominational college or seminary introducing Professor Smith to some high-rolling donor: "Yes, sir, Dr. Smith here went to Harvard Divinity School, and actually survived with his faith intact!" But he *didn't* survive with his faith intact. And neither will his students at Laodicea Theological Seminary. The Darwinism he teaches will be "warmed-over" Darwinism—debased, inconsistent Darwinism from the point of view of the prestige humanist schools of higher learning—but Darwinism nonetheless. His version may be called "liberation theology." It may be called "socially concerned Christianity." It may not be tinged with outright Marxism. But it *will* be Darwinism: *faith in the predestinating State.*

**THE SIDER PHENOMENON**  In seminary after seminary, Dr. Ronald Sider is being invited to preach (pitch?) his version of the predestinating State. He is being received enthusiastically, in much the same way that "Father" Groppi, the now-defrocked Roman Catholic priest (who is a bus driver in Milwaukee today) was received on Christian college campuses in the late 1960's. Groppi was a master guilt-manipulator with a turnaround collar—a radical proponent of race war and revolution who was defrocked by the Roman Catholic Church only when he decided to get married.[5] The Church's hierarchy tolerated his economics and political theory, but marriage was just a bit too much. His appearances were always marked by wildly enthusiastic crowds at Protestant and State-supported colleges.

Why did this Roman Catholic verbal revolutionary receive warm welcomes by Protestant faculty members and humanist faculty members? Because Groppi was preaching a popular brand of humanism in 1969 and 1970—the "pre-Kent State" humanism of *college radicalism without personal risks*—which his listeners shared.[6] (The confrontation between the National Guard and the students at Kent State University in Ohio ended the college violence of the 1964-70 era, as an old-time New Deal liberal college classmate of mine predicted it would the week of the shootings. "Too risky for them now," he said. "They might get their ***** shot off." The following semester, all over the world, campus violence ceased, and a dozen years later, it is still quiet.)

The market for *soft-core radicalism* revived on the Christian college circuit in the late 1970's. There was a real "need" for a quiet, self-effacing, kindly preacher of class conflict and socialist wealth-redistribution. The schools are still staffed by Darwinists, and their faith is still intact. They trust the predestinating State, not the free market economy. But they needed a spokesman who was uniquely gifted to "sell the ideological product" on the post-Kent State campus. Where there is demand, the free market will eventually respond. The market produced the supply: Sider.

*Rich Christians in an Age of Hunger* is only one of a series of books designed to call into question the ability of free market institutions, coupled with Christian charity, to achieve the economic goals of the kingdom of God. The Christian Reformed Church's Task Force on World Hunger released its report, *And he had compassion on them: The Christian and World Hunger* (1978). Its thesis is as bad as its cover's typography: not enough capital letters, and not enough capitalism. World Vision produced Stanley Mooneyham's *What Do You Say to a Hungry World?* (1975). (What you say is what David Chilton's book is all about.) But by far, *Rich Christians* is the most influential of these books. It was co-published by Inter-Varsity Press, the neo-evangelical Protestant publishing house which sells especially to Christian students, and the Paulist Press, a liberal Roman Catholic publishing house. The *ecumenical impulse* that was present in "Father" Groppi's inter-denominational rallies for masochistic caucasians is with us still. Today's radicalism is simply soft-core, more in tune with the "laid-back" *doormat psychology* of modern Protestant pietism.

("Verbally stomp me, whip me with guilt, make me feel that it's all America's fault! I'll even send you money, just as soon as Dad sends me my check for next semester." Sadly, Dad will indeed send him the money, as dads have been doing since the days of Aristophanes, the Greek playwright of the fourth century, B.C., who wrote a satire on the relationship between a father and his son, who was attending the "school" of Socrates, in his play, *Clouds*.) Rushdoony is correct; what we face is *the politics of guilt and pity*.[7]

**THE NORTH-SIDER DEBATE** No comprehensive criticism of *Rich Christians* appeared from 1977 until the publication of the first edition of this book. In fact, I am unaware of any published criticism of the book prior to 1981. *This indicates just how intellectually bankrupt the supposed defenders of Christian orthodoxy really are.* They were unable or unwilling to challenge either his theology or his economics. More than this: the students and faculties of Christian colleges and seminaries actively recruited Sider to speak. This even included the "bastions" of Calvinistic scholarship, Westminster Theological Seminary in Philadelphia (my old alma mater) and Reformed Theological Seminary, in Jackson, Mississippi. *These schools are rapidly abandoning their commitment to traditional Calvinism, and are becoming neo-evangelical in social and political perspective.* The "purging" of Dr. Greg Bahnsen at Reformed in 1979, and the attempted "purge" of Norman Shepherd at Westminster in 1980-82 (as of this writing, its outcome is problematical), are merely visible signs of the theological decay that has undermined the older tradition at both schools. The fact that the conservative financial supporters of both schools refuse to "pull the plug" in protest—the only kind of protest that seminary presidents respect or respond to—testifies to the applicability of Schumpeter's analysis to the bourgeois Christian world, and not merely to the bourgeois business world. (Interestingly enough, I studied theology under Shepherd during my first and only year of seminary at Westminster, and David

Chilton studied under Bahnsen during his first and only year of seminary at Reformed.)

In October of 1980, Scott Hahn, a student at the Gordon-Conwell School of Theology in South Hamilton, Massachusetts, phoned me. He had the responsibility, as a member of a student committee in charge of scheduling academic programs, to bring speakers to the campus. He asked me if I would come to speak. I declined. He offered an honorarium. I still declined. My time schedule was simply too jammed up. I was about to tell him that the only way he could get me to come to Massachusetts to speak to a group of students was to offer me an opportunity to debate Ron Sider, when he told me that he was inviting me to come to debate Ron Sider. At that point, I not only agreed, I said I would do it without any honorarium.

Now, my idea of the goal of this debate was to win. It was not to be a "friendly exercise." Ron Sider's theology and economics, if accepted by an educated elite of Christians (let alone a majority), will reinforce the forces of domestic and international socialism that are threatening the survival of the West—the conflict that Solzhenitsyn has said the West is rapidly losing. Thus, my debate with Ron Sider represented a clash between two incompatible theories of civilization: one based on personal responsibility, self-discipline, voluntary economic exchange, and biblical law, *vs.* another which is based on statism, political centralization, and "theft by majority vote." This would be no "sharing of ideas between Christians." This was—and is—*all-out intellectual and theological warfare*. It is the latest round in a war that has been going on since 1525, when Martin Luther attacked the savagery of the revolutionary Anabaptists.[8] I see myself as a neo-Puritan, and Sider is forthrightly an Anabaptist. I wrote my doctoral dissertation on the economic thought of the New England Puritans, and he wrote his on an aspect of Anabaptist history.

The Anabaptist ("baptize again") movement was an early offshoot of the Protestant Reformation. They did not baptize infants, and they required rebaptism to join their congregations.

There are two traditions in the history of the Anabaptist movement. The first is one of revolution, communism, and violence. The second is pacifist, communalist, and pietist. This second tradition is more familiar to us, since it is represented by the Mennonites and the Amish, who seem somehow quaint, posing no threat to society. But the earlier Anabaptists were anything but quaint. They were mass murderers. From 1520 to 1535, in what is now Germany, hordes of them challenged the civil order, and they began a revolution. John Bochhold (John of Leyden), a 26-year-old tailor, and John Matthias, a baker, led a proletarian revolution in the city of Münster, in Westphalia, which they captured in 1533. The intensity of the revolution grew: communal property was imposed, then a "New Zion" was announced by the "prophet," John of Leyden, who then became "king." He established polygamy, selecting several wives for himself. The churches were burned. Leyden established a reign of terror. He announced: "Impiety prevails everywhere. It is therefore necessary that a new family of holy persons should be founded, enjoying, without distinction of sex, the gift of prophecy, and skill to interpret revelation. Hence they need no learning; for the internal word is more than the outward expression. No Christian must be suffered to engage in a legal process, to hold civil office, to take an oath, or to hold any private property; but all things must be in common."[9] Apostles were sent out from Münster to deliver this message to all of Europe. The city fell to the regional civil authorities, after a bloody battle, in 1535.[10]

Is Sider a representative of the revolutionary tradition or the pacifist tradition of Anabaptism? It is possible to find elements of both in his books. He sometimes speaks as if he favors only voluntary political pressures to be brought against the present world's institutional structures. At other times, he sounds like a revolutionary. He certainly adopts revolutionary terms throughout his writings. There is no question that socialism must use State coercion to extract people's wealth from them—the kind of coercion the Internal Revenue Service has used on occasion against Amish farmers who refuse, on religious grounds, to pay their Social Security taxes (because they oppose all forms of insurance and rely on the charity of the brethren). Ultimately, he wants the State — possibly the United Nations — to extract wealth from "rich Christians" and anyone else who might make more than $1,800 per year, as you will read. He is not calling his followers to drop out of society and become communal farmers who use no electrical or gasoline-powered equipment. He is not calling them to join him in the Amish country of Pennsylvania for a life of hard labor in the fields. His listeners read books and pamphlets; they are not people who expect to get their hands dirty. The chosen topic for debate was not "Resolved: That Christians should let the world take care of itself, while we depart to our simple agricultural lifestyles in peace." The debate topic was: "Resolved: Christians have an obligation to the poor." The question really was: "Confiscatory taxes or the tithe?"

Having accepted the challenge, I then sat down to think about the best way to win, if not the evening's debate, then at least the long-term debate. I had discussed already with David Chilton the possibility of his producing a book refuting Sider, and he had been researching it for some time. Now I decided to go ahead with the project. I called him and told him that I needed a finished book for the first Monday in April, 1981, the night of the debate. I figured that Sider would not expect someone to have a book written to attack his position at the debate. Most people do not take debates this seriously. I do. Chilton was ready to write. We had to get it into print in six months.

We did it: from start to finish. Several hundred copies of the book were delivered to Scott Hahn at Gordon-Conwell during the week prior to the debate. I instructed him to set them out on a table outside the lecture hall on the night of the debate. I sold them for $1 each: nothing like price competition to get everyone to buy. As it turned out, we sold about 250 copies — one copy for every two people who attended the debate. Poor Ron: he was selling his *Rich Christians* for $3.75, and they weren't moving. (Of course, most of the students had probably already bought copies in the campus bokstore.)

I shall never forget Sider's response, as he stared at the book as it sat in front of me at the debate table. "How long has this been out?" he asked. "About 24 hours," I replied. Actually, it had been out—as far as the buying public was concerned—about 30 minutes.

I also handed out a 4-page summary of my position, which included a page of "compare and contrast" citations from Sider and the Bible, extracted from the introductory pages that begin each chapter of Chilton's book.

Furthermore, in the week before the debate, Dr. John Robbins of the Trinity Foundation had released a 4-page newsletter, "Ronald Sider *Contra Deum.*" He had sent copies to Hahn, unbeknownst to me, for distribution at the debate. They, too, were available free of charge to the students.[11]

The debate was rousing. The students of Gordon-Conwell were —and are—overwhelmingly favorable to Sider's position. This is not surprising; so are all but a handful—possibly only one—of Gordon-Conwell's faculty. One of them is regarded by some of his students as farther to the left than Sider is. This is not information the seminary's administration is anxious to have publicized to donors, although it really makes little difference. The school's financial supporters, like the donors to Harvard, Princeton, and Yale, will still pour in the funds that will be used to undermine everything they say they believe in. They are perfectly willing to finance their own destruction—and yours, and mine—just so long as their donations are tax-deductible. Unfortunately, Schumpeter's analysis holds up.

The school's Board of Trustees is well aware of the problem, since my going public with the story (and making available tapes of the debate) called it to their attention. Nothing, of course, was done about it, and nothing is likely to be done. Prof. Henry Manne [MANee], the controversial legal theorist and first-rate economist who heads Emory University's law and economics program, has explained why virtually all university Boards of Trustees are impotent. The same arguments hold true for most seminary Boards of Trustees, too. Manne writes:

*The most significant characteristic of the modern university trustee is his almost total lack of real interest in exercising any authority. He could hardly feel a real personal responsibility for the "values of western civilization" or whatever amorphous goal he might talk about at annual dinners. He does not have any feeling, certainly, for the question of who, generally, should be admitted to receive the school's subsidy in the form of lower-than-full-cost tuition. This right was given up long ago, as American society culturally forbade the older, restrictive standards, and as the faculty, the only group with a real interest in selecting students, took over the task.*

*Somewhat similarly, the trustees have no power whatever to determine what views will be taught in universities. There are still denominational schools where this is not completely true, but, save these, the modern notion of "academic freedom" has given the faculty effective power over subject matter in the university and its curriculum. Particularly in very technical fields, this was said to have represented merely the trustees' deferring to the expertise of the faculty. But what that indicates is that the trustees had nothing significant to gain by exercising this power; therefore, it was no great loss to give it up to teachers who have something to gain by it, as we shall see.*

*While it might be possible for one very wealthy individual to organize a university along certain lines, it would be extremely difficult for anyone to influence an existing institution by the use of donations. First of all, professional associations of teachers and accrediting agencies have removed some of the power to deal with that group. Secondly, laws now exist that forbid certain types of discrimination in the selection of students and faculty. Finally, even a very large donation to an existing institution does not give the donor any legal power of disposition over preexisting funds. . . .*

*Any prestige left to the position of university trustee no longer comes from the power the position carries. No longer are these favors that can be allocated to one's friends. Such prestige as there is today comes only from the traditional prestige of the office and certainly not from fighting for any particular ideology or standard. Although the trustees are still expected to assist in fundraising for the university, it is largely on the same basis as they would assist in fund-raising for the local art gallery, orchestra, or museum. It is just that the university is usually larger and still carries greater prestige than other community activities. But it is doubtful whether, in years to come, the relative status position of universities' trustees will be much higher than that of any other comparable-sized eleemosynary institutions' trustees.*

If the Trustees are unable to "clean house" on a drifting faculty, then what about the administration? Again, there is little hope. Faculties, in effect, "own" the institutions that hire them, if they are non-profit institutions. They have a vested interest in preserving their autonomy. No rival "owner" has a sufficiently high stake in challenging the faculty. The typical seminary president is a fund-raiser, a man whose job it is *to smooth over all institutional conflicts,* and this means *keeping donors in the dark about the ideological or theological opinions of the Darwinists who teach in the school.* Again, citing Manne:

*When we refer to the administration, we generally mean the top administrative executive, here called the president. Not surprisingly, the general style and character of a university president will reflect the real power interests within the institution. That is, he will be selected on the basis of characteristics that please those individuals actually exercising the selection power. . . . Whereas, in an earlier era, the trustees may have wanted simply a supply-and-personnel manager, the interest of faculties was a different kind of president. Perhaps first and foremost they were interested in a fund-raiser. He was not supposed to bring his personal influence to bear on issues of educational policy. He was simply supposed to keep the money flowing in from outside forces. . . . As we shall see, the traditional form in universities has been maintained, while the real power has shifted. In the case of presidential selection, it is largely a matter of trustees having no interests that they feel need to be protected or furthered by the selection of an individual dedicated to those interests. The faculty, on the other hand, address themselves to amorphous but generally accepted standards like "a man of high academic reputation" or "someone prominent in the university world" to guarantee that the man selected is, in fact, dedicated to the kind of university that faculties want.*

*University presidents today have almost no authorized discretionary power over academic matters like faculty selection and course content. They can, however, still wield some influence by tactical use of their power over budget matters. A strong president, with trustee support, can use the budget as a lever to gain some academic policy ends. But actually, in crucial areas like personnel selection and course content, few presidents really have any preferences contrary to those of the faculties.*

*A skilled president can still make matters uncomfortable for professors who are obnoxious to him, but even that power must be used sparingly, since faculties today understand the techniques necessary to force a president to resign. If enough trustees are made uncomfortable or embarrassed by complaints rightly or wrongly aired by the faculty about the president, most trustees will probably take the easy way out. Since trustees usually have no great interest in the doctrinal aspects of the dispute between the president and the faculty, their best strategy is generally to capitulate in a face-saving way to the faculty.*[12]

What does Manne's analysis reveal? That trustees have abandoned their sovereignty over academic matters, despite their legal authority over the academic institution. *The faculties have captured the institutions of higher learning in America.* They see to it that everyone works hard raising money to support the autonomy of each department to teach whatever it pleases, despite protests from students, parents, alumni, trustees, or any administration member who might be a bit conservative politically. Since no one "owns" the institutions, faculties have succeeded in getting their interests served by financial supporters. There is no group in power with vested interests stronger than the interests of faculty members, especially *tenured* faculty members who cannot be fired.

I wrote a letter to one of the trustees of Gordon-Conwell, sending a photocopy of my letter to another trustee (who is a friend of mine and a defender of free enterprise), and I included a copy of the first edition of this book, and a copy of Manne's article. A member of Gordon-Conwell's administration had written to me to protest my one-sentence reference, in a printed letter to Institute for Christian Economics supporters, to the somewhat ill-mannered performance of his school's students. His letter to me found more fault with my "indiscretion of going public" (not his phrase) with my mild one-sentence comment about the students (which some trustee had seen and inquired about) than with the students. I was explaining in my letter to this particular trustee just why I had made this one-sentence reference: my concern about the "liberation theology" that is being taught to Gordon-Conwell students. In that letter (dated June 4, 1981), I wrote:

*Why won't any of these so-called conservative schools hire Dr. Greg Bahnsen, the outspoken defender of biblical infallibility, with a Ph.D in philosophy from the University of Southern California and a Th.M from Westminster? I'll tell you: his book,* Theonomy in Christian Ethics, *is too controversial. But liberation theology, which is promoted in almost all the so-called Christian conservative seminaries, isn't that controversial. Bahnsen defends the free market; these tenured men don't. So who gets blackballed? Right: the defender of free enterprise. . . . I'm so convinced that the refusal to hire him is conspiratorial that I'll make you this offer: if you and the other members of the Board like his conservative stance, and are willing to personally donate funds to bring him to Gordon-Conwell as an untenured visiting professor, I'll personally match whatever you raise, dollar for dollar. But I warn you: even if 100% of his salary were raised in this way, the Administration, under pressure from the liberation theology people on the faculty, will almost certainly block his appointment. All the talk about too high a student-to-faculty ratio will disappear, once a really conservative, pro-free market, pro-infallibility man is proposed. If I'm wrong, call my bluff. I'll put my money where my mouth is.*

I knew my money was safe, although I would have followed up on my promise. The trustee never even bothered to reply to any of my letters, nor had I expected him to. I have known for a long time that Manne's analysis, like Schumpeter's, is correct. I was simply calling *his* bluff, as a trustee — to show him that all his supposed concern over the anti-business stance of the seminary was fluff, and that he and his capitalist colleagues were unwilling to press the issue, nor were they willing to resign in protest. *The forces of Darwinist statism have understood their enemies very well; they have known for decades that trustees will capitulate every time, in order to protect their "prestige position" as trustees.* As Lenin is reputed to have said (probably apocryphal): "If we announced today that we intend to hang all capitalists tomorrow, they would trip over each other trying to sell us the rope."

The results of the North-Sider debate, as far as the campus was concerned, were minimal. Not many people had their minds changed. This was predictable. The lines were drawn long before Sider and I arrived. I confronted them with the testimony of the Bible on State-financed welfare — there shouldn't be any — and the illegitimacy of liberation theology. What I was really after was a cassette tape of the confrontation. I wanted to flush Sider into the open, to get him to reveal what his theological position *really* represents. In this, I think I was successful. Readers can make up their own minds by ordering the tapes and listening to the whole debate. The two-cassette set sells for $10. The set is sold by

Dominion Tapes
P. O. Box 8175
Tyler, TX 75711

**MARXISM**   The issue is Marxism. When I wrote my now out-of-print book, *Marx's Religion of Revolution: The Doctrine of Creative Destruction* (Craig Press, 1968), I argued that the impulse behind Marxism has always been religious in nature. This has been confirmed by the extraordinary book by James Billington, *Fire in the Minds of Men: Origins of the Revolutionary Faith* (Basic Books, 1980). Billington, a former Harvard and Princeton historian, is the head of the Woodrow Wilson International Center for Scholars in Washington, D.C. His academic credentials are impeccable (for those who care about such matters), and the work is a masterpiece of historical scholarship. In it, he argues that the two main sources of revolutionary socialism in the nineteenth century were the occult underground (secret societies) and journalism. This was a true faith — a religion of revolution. (I was first informed of the existence of the book by David Chilton.)

Marxism possesses, for the moment, the three key features that are necessary for any world-transforming ideology: 1) an historical dynamic, 2) a doctrine of law, and 3) a doctrine of predestination. To some extent, this faith is dying inside the nations where Marxism has been politically triumphant, but in the Third World, this faith is the driving secular religion of our day. They believe in *historical progress* — a stage theory of social development, the so-called dialectic of history. They believe in a *unique law-order* which enables them to identify and promote "Marxist art," "Marxist social structures," "Marxist genetics" (e.g., the ill-fated Lysenko affair of the 1940's through the 1960's),[13] and so forth. Finally, they believe in the *inevitability of socialism,* with the impersonal forces of history guiding human institutions into the socialist stage of history. As an intellectual force, the Marxist movement has been almost irresistible.

Christianity offers an alternative. It does not offer a doctrine of historical progress based on class conflict, but a theory of history based on the *ethical* conflict between Satan and God, and between Satan's forces and God's. It offers a law-order based on the creative work of God, not on the work of impersonal, undirected "forces." It offers a doctrine of God's providence, not a doctrine of impersonal historical inevitability. *The warfare of this age is between Christianity and Marxism.* Christianity is Marxism's chief rival. When Christians affirm all three positions — historical (eschatological) optimism, a revelational law-order (law code), and the sovereignty of God (providence) — they can successfully challenge the Marxist religion of revolution.[14]

The problem is, certain intellectuals who hold essentially Marxist presuppositions about the nature of historical development have succeeded in becoming spokesmen for, and leaders of, the church. Liberation theology is only the latest of these Marxist "incursions" into the ranks of the church. These infiltrators have mastered the language of orthodoxy, just as the heretical followers of the Swiss theologian, Karl Barth, did from 1920 on.[15] The Barthians were successful in capturing most of the denominational seminaries in the 1950's (or earlier); the liberation theologians are simply following the strategy of the now-eclipsed Barthians. What is the secret of their success? Their secret is this: *use Christian terminology in order to promote Marxist and socialist goals.* These infiltrators assume that the faithful few who still send their money to the seminaries, church boards, and the mission fields will never know the difference. Sadly, *they have assumed correctly, so far.*

This is not to say that Ronald Sider is a Marxist. It is also not to say that he isn't. That is for him to say; or should he be somewhat reticent to say, then it is for the reader to determine after a careful examination of Sider's writings. The problem is, as Chilton's book demonstrates, Sider's language is suspiciously vague at key points. Sider avoids getting down to specifics — his recommended program. As Chilton has titled another article that deals with Sider's theology, it is "The Case of the Missing Blueprints."[16] Either Sider really doesn't know what ought to be done — in which case, he should stop calling for unspecified radical social change, which is luring naive Christians into a movement that can be (or may already have been) captured by Marxists — or else he is remaining deliberately vague, in order to confuse the orthodox Christians who support financially the institutions that he is steadily converting to his version of "liberation theology." Take your pick.

Sider uses what appears to be orthodox Christian terminology, but reaches socialistic (yet not openly Marxist) conclusions. He argues, for example, in the name of Christ, that a person who, as of 1977, earned over $1,800 a year, was earning too much,[17] and that some agency (possibly the United Nations) should redistribute the money above $1,800 per capita per year.[18] Yet all this is a bit vague. He does not say that the U.N. must do it; he only says that the U.S. government spends foreign aid money to undergird "repressive dictatorships" (meaning non-Marxist dictatorships), so presumably the U.S. government cannot be trusted to do it, since it has engaged in "the political misuse of food aid . . . ."[19] But neither can we rely heavily on private charitable agencies, since giving to them makes rich people feel less guilty. Chilton found this choice quotation in an obscure Sider essay — an essay whose incredible conclusions Sider was wise enough not to expose to the broad base of Christians who bought *Rich Christians:* "Personal charity and philanthropy still permit the rich donor to feel superior. And it makes the recipient feel inferior and dependent. Institutional changes, on the other hand, give the oppressed rights and power."[20]

What does all this mean? *It means that God's law for giving, the tithe, is not sufficient to create a godly social and economic order.* As you will understand after reading Sider's books, or after reading this book, or after listening to the tapes of the debate: *Ronald Sider does not have a lot of faith in biblical law.* Unfortunately, he shares this opinion with the overwhelming majority of those who call themselves Christians. Thus, *Christians in positions of leadership have been unsuccessful in refuting Sider's position.* How could they hope to refute him? *They share too many of his presuppositions.* Even the Chaplain of the United States Senate, Dr. Richard Halverson, has assigned *Rich Christians in an Age of Hunger* to his church's officers. Ron Sider is an influential man.

This is why I decided to have the Institute for Christian Economics finance the writing and publication of this book. The absurdities — from the point of view of both the Bible and economics — of *Rich Christians in an Age of Hunger* had to be exposed.

**CHILTON'S STYLE** If something is ridiculous, it deserves ridicule. This was the opinion of Augustine with respect to those who reject the idea of the recent creation of the earth. "For as it is not yet six thousand years since the first man, who is called Adam, are not those to be ridiculed rather than refuted who try to persuade us of anything regarding a space of time so different from, and contrary to, the ascertained truth?"[21] Today, it is those who proclaim the six-day creation position who receive ridicule, not infrequently from those within the church who have compromised with the Darwinian time scale.[22] But Augustine's point is well-taken: there comes a time for using ridicule—or even better, a bit of satirical humor.

The trouble is, the intellectuals who have adopted at least a working relationship with the cosmologies of humanism resent satire—not to mention ridicule—when it is used by orthodox Christians against those who proclaim the ridiculous in the name of Christ. *The intellectual allies of the compromising Christians, as far as the compromisers are concerned, are the humanists who proclaim socialism—New Deal, Marxist, Third World, or whichever variety is popular on campus—and not the orthodox Christians who proclaim biblical law.* These intellectual and theological compromisers review the books in the major journals of Christian intellectual opinion. This is the reason why Chilton's book has drawn so much fire from the compromising critics. He uses a rapier wit to good effect. But this is considered "unchristian." The critics forget that it was Christ who called the Pharisees sons of their father, the devil (John 8:44). They forget that Peter publicly condemned Simon the sorcerer, who had made a profession of faith and had been baptized (Acts 8:9-24). As he said to Simon, "thy heart is not right in the sight of God" (8:21b).

Christians who have agreed with many of the socialist recommendations that are found in Sider's works may be tempted to ignore the biblical critique Chilton offers because they think Chilton's style is unfair. *It does not matter what Chilton's style is, if his criticisms are accurate.* Those who have followed Sider in error are morally required to *repent*, whether or not Chilton's style is "fair." And if they do not repent, then they are hypocrites, because *it is not Chilton's style that offends them; it is his conclusions.* His style may serve as a convenient excuse; the real reason for not accepting his conclusions has to do with the *substance* of his critique.

I wrote a letter to Inter-Varsity Press, offering to co-publish Chilton's book with them, since they had co-published Sider's book with the Paulist Press. I received a reply on letterhead stationery from the editor, James W. Sire, dated August 26, 1981. His reply is indicative of the problem. His firm has made the book available to tens of thousands of students. Inter-Varsity has *corrupted*—no softer term will suffice—a generation of Christians. But he was not interested in offering these people the only book-length alternative presently available. Why not? The issue, he says, has nothing to do with economic theory. It has nothing to do with truth or falsehood of theology. No indeed; the issue is *style.* It is strictly a matter of good taste:

*While I have not finished reading the book* [Chilton's] *in its entirety, I have familiarized myself with it sufficiently to realize that it is not a book which we feel we should co-publish with you. In addition to the detailed analysis of* Rich Christians in an Age of Hunger, *which one could consider a tribute to the author and the publisher of the original work, I find the tone of the presentation rather more offensive than necessary. While Chilton occasionally says that he really isn't against Sider qua Ronald Sider, the tone belies him. . . . It is one thing to disagree with another Christian on economic theory or even theology, for that matter; it is quite another to turn the disagreement into personal attack.*

The editor thinks Chilton's response is a "tribute" to Sider and Inter-Varsity. Would he also regard Peter's condemnation of Simon the sorcerer as a "tribute" to Simon and the dark one who had supplied him with his occult power? Should we regard Solzhenitsyn's *Gulag Archipelago* as a "tribute" to Lenin, Stalin, and the terrorists who made the Gulag a reality? Does every book that ever draws a published criticism from an orthodox Christian automatically gain a tribute from its critic? Does the editor really believe this? If not, then he must be playing with words. He must be in basic agreement with Sider's conclusions. (When you finish this book, take another look at the editor's reply.)

I regard Chilton's book as a testimony, not a tribute, to the *suicidal intellectuals* who write socialist books in the name of Christianity, and who get a major campus evangelical organization to put its Protestant imprimatur on it. I also regard Chilton's book as a testimony to the *suicidal, naive donors*—in some cases, "professionally naive"—to Inter-Varsity and to the Christian colleges and seminaries that promote Sider's books in the classrooms. They will answer for much on the day of judgment.

**Conclusion**   We are at war. *War.* If Schumpeter was completely correct, then the socialists are going to win it. But he was not a Christian, and he did not understand the underlying nature of the struggle between capitalism and socialism. The underlying struggle is between *the kingdom of God* and *the society of Satan.* [23] Satan is going to lose, despite Soviet missiles, Cuban surrogate troops, liberation theology, Ronald Sider, and Inter-Varsity Press. Then we will have that most godly of economic arrangements: *rich Christians in an age of hungry socialists.* (To some extent, that is what we have today, which is why our domestic socialists in high positions continue to send them food that has been paid for with the tax dollars of Christians. Why, then, does Sider call for even more economic aid to the enemies of God? And why do so many of America's Christian intellectuals agree with him? There must be a reason, or perhaps several. Read Chilton's book to get a few reasonably good leads in your pursuit of the answers. And when you have those answers, or at least reasonably good guesses, you ought to rethink your present approach to charitable giving. *Who, precisely, have you been subsidizing?*)

You, as a reader, cannot escape your moral obligation of putting your knowledge into action. If you conclude, after reading Chilton's analysis, and after checking out the truth of his charges, that Sider's theology represents a threat to orthodox Christianity and the free market, what are you going to do about it? Which agencies that you support financially have opened their doors to Ron Sider, or *Sojourners* magazine, or *theOtherSide,* or The Jubilee Fund, or Evangelicals for Social Action, or any of the other outfits that are identified with Sider or a Sider-like theology of guilt-manipulation? Are you still going to support them, like a sheep going to the slaughter? Are you going to write a letter of protest, wait for the administration to do something (other than send you back a meaningless form letter), and then continue to send in your tax-deductible checks anyway?

Maybe you support one of the theological seminaries I mentioned earlier. Write to them. Ask to buy a copy of the audio tapes of Sider's campus presentations. See if I have exaggerated. Then write to the school to get the list of the names of the members of the Board of Trustees. Send them a letter of concern. And wait for them to do something. What will they do? Precisely what Henry Manne says they will do: nothing.

Then consider supporting the one seminary which takes a stand *against* Sider's theology: **Geneva Divinity School**. Here is the one school that offers an alternative to Sider. No form letters explaining away the visits by Sider: "We want to expose our students to *all* theological viewpoints" (except those of the pro-free market theologians, who are never invited by faculty-sponsored lecture series, and only rarely invited—despite faculty pressure—by student lecture programs). Since no one will "clean house" on any faculty today, *start sending your money only to those schools that are already clean.* If you finance the enemy, you are responsible.

Before sending another cent to any college or seminary, demand from the president or the dean of the faculty his assurance *in writing* that it is the policy of the school to oppose liberation theology in all forms. Make sure that you get a written statement that it is that school's policy to *dismiss* any faculty member who teaches Marxism, socialism, or liberation theology in the classroom. And I guarantee you: with the exception of Geneva Divinity School, and one or two fundamentalist colleges (such as Jerry Falwell's Liberty Baptist College, some Church of Christ colleges, and Christian Heritage College in California), *no administration official will sign such a letter.* How could he, in good conscience? He would have to fire half the economists, most of the political scientists, and all of the sociologists, not to mention his missions training program's staff. He could not do it if he wanted to, unless he is willing to face the wrath of the humanist-dominated accreditation committee that "licenses" the school. Only "troublemakers" like Bahnsen and Shepherd are fired; liberation theologians are untouchable.

The conservatives on any given faculty tend to be fairly quiet. They go about their business diligently, teaching their students the material related to the academic discipline they were trained to teach. The liberals, on the contrary, take every opportunity to proclaim the latest socialist fad, whether it relates to their course assignments or not, and whether or not they have any formal training or expertise in the area. This is as true on seminary campuses as on university campuses. Then why do the conservatives get in trouble? Why are they regarded as the troublemakers? Simple: *liberals are troubled deeply by any contact, no matter how slight, with the truth.* The truth divides the campus. This is the greatest sin in the eyes of the administrators, who are very often liberals themselves (since faculties are careful to screen out conservatives far in advance). The administration wants to avoid trouble. Also, the division may surface off campus, and administrators know that *donors are likely to be more conservative than faculty members, and they may side with the handful of conservatives on the faculty.* Result: the conservative faculty members get purged, unless they are so utterly innocuous that nothing that they say or do has any effect anywhere, on campus or off.

Conclusion: *stop financing the enemy with your tax-deductible donations.* Write letters of protest. Now.

For information on the home-study courses offered by Geneva Divinity School, write to

Geneva Divinity School
708 Hamvassy Road
Tyler, Texas 75701

# INTRODUCTION

**"DURING THE FIGHTING IN NICARAGUA, THE JUBILEE FUND—
A MINISTRY OF *THE OTHER SIDE*—GAVE MONEY FOR FOOD,
MEDICINE, AND CLOTHING. SOME WENT TO SANDINISTA
GUERRILLAS, AND THIS MAY HAVE HELPED THEIR FIGHTING."**
(*theOtherSide*, SEPTEMBER 1979, P. 41)

---

**RELIGION AND REVOLUTION**   Revolution is a religious faith.
All men, created in the image of God, are fundamentally religious: all cultural activity is essentially an outgrowth of man's
religious position; for our life and thought are exercised either in
obedience to, or rebellion against, God. All men, says St. Paul,
are conscious of their rebellion, self-conscious to a degree which
leaves them inexcusable (Romans 1:18-26); but the avowed
revolutionary is self-conscious to a greater degree—hence often
more obviously "religious"—than many of his fellow men.

Throughout history revolutionaries have demonstrated an
almost limitless facility for appropriating as their own the
religious terminology of the surrounding culture. Their works
abound with references to infallibility, regeneration, and faith.

Revolutionaries in France were offered a new version of Holy Communion, in which the priest would proclaim, "This is the body OF THE BREAD *which the rich owe to the poor!*"[1] Some spoke of "the holy Communist Church"[2] and of the "egalitarian church, outside of which there can be no salvation."[3] In Germany, revolutionaries published family devotional literature, responsive readings, and even a "Communist Lord's Prayer":

*So be it! In thy holy name*
*We'll overturn the old rubbish;*
*No masters and no servants! Amen!*
*Money and property shall be abolished!*[4]

This tendency to fuse Christian language with revolutionary concepts manifests itself again and again. The radical James Nayler rode into Bristol in 1656, seated on a donkey, with his disciples strewing palm branches before him. The terrorist John Brown claimed to be God's angel of death. Adolf Hitler represented himself as a defender of Christianity. One explanation for all this is the revolutionary's desire to be as God, to center all devotion in his own messianic program; but another reason may be just as important insofar as the cultural acceptance of the Revolution is concerned. James H. Billington writes: "Indeed, communism probably would not have attracted such instant attention without this initial admixture of Christian ideas."[5]

In the past, the evangelical wing of Christianity in the United States has been generally conservative in its political and economic views. There may have been more of instinct than of principle in some of this, but the usual assumption was that no one who claimed to believe in the authority of Scripture could seriously hold to socialistic or revolutionary ideas.

But there are new voices in evangelicalism today, claiming that a truly biblical Christianity demands centralized economic planning and the "liberation" of the downtrodden masses throughout the world. Faithfulness to Scripture is being equated with a redistribution of wealth. Notions of social reform once thought to be the province of aberrant liberals may now be heard down the street in the Baptist church.

Yet what they are preaching is the Revolution. It is not presented so baldly, of course; most Christians would not be so easily seduced if it were called by its true name. It is therefore altered into *revolution by installments*. The results are nevertheless the same. Expropriation of the wealthy is theft under any name. In every revolution of the past, words were revolutionized in meaning, and ordinary people were moved to extraordinary acts, without realizing that the impressive words had been redefined: justice meant injustice; freedom meant coercion; humanity meant savagery; non-violence meant war without end.

The mark of a Christian movement is its willingness to submit to the demands of Scripture. Not, mind you, merely to "principles" abstracted from their context and loaded with new content; but rather the actual, concrete, explicit statements of God's word. "You shall not steal," for instance: that must not be relativized on the mere excuse that the thief has no bread. It must not be violated just because someone has found a "principle" that God would like everyone to have bread. It must not be transgressed with the spurious rationale that the thief should have been given the bread in the first place. If you want principles, here's one: *theft is theft*. Easy to remember, uncomplicated and biblical. The "Christian" who advocates theft in the name of social justice is in truth calling for the Revolution, whether or not he fully realizes what he is doing. And we must not allow the lovely sounds of the words to disguise their meaning. The great Dutch Christian historian of revolution, Groen van Prinsterer, pointed out that "wherever the Revolution has been at work it has become apparent that it considers law to be mere convention, a product of the human will."[6] We shall see that this is the mark of the "Christian socialist" movement as well—that its only real principle is *the principle of unbelief*:

*The principle of unbelief—the sovereignty of reason and the sovereignty of the people—must end, while proclaiming Liberty, either in radicalism or in despotism: in the disintegration of society or in the tyranny of a state in which all things are levelled without any regard to true liberties and true rights.*[7]

A man or movement may claim to be Christian, and yet not be; a man or movement may *be* Christian, and yet have unbiblical ideas. The test is Scripture, and Scripture alone. Not wishes, not "rights," not wants or needs; try every word a man speaks at the bar of God's inerrant word. Those who advocate the lawless over-throw of society—even if it is technically "legal"—are opposing God's commands. The ultimate end of the Revolution is always unbelief.

*The defining feature of the Revolution is its hatred of the Gospel, its anti-Christian nature. This feature marks the Revolution, not when it "deviates from its course" and "lapses into excesses," but, on the contrary, precisely when it holds to its course and reaches the conclusion of its system, the true end of its logical development. This mark belongs to the Revolution. The Revolution can never shake it off. It is inherent in its very principle, and ex-presses and reflects its essence. It is the sign of its origin. It is the mark of hell.*[8]

The brutality of the French Revolution was not endemic to that particular situation alone: it is essential to the very nature of the Revolution itself. All revolutions have begun with sincere pleas for liberation; all have been carried on by ever-increasing justifications of infringements on liberty; all have ended in chaos and tyranny. Revolt against God's eternal standards can produce nothing else.[9]

One of the most prominent of the new voices in evangelicalism is Ronald J. Sider, professor of theology at Eastern Baptist Seminary in Philadelphia. He is the president of Evangelicals for Social Action, a national organization "committed to the preaching and practice of biblical justice and peace," as an ESA pamphlet puts it. The ESA sponsors a wide variety of activities: political action groups, pastors' conferences, economic work-shops, tracts, a newsletter, "church justice committees," and so on. Sider himself has convened conferences in this country and abroad to deal with social justice issues, particularly in the area of "simple living," the practice of living as closely as possible to a subsistence level in order to share excess income with others. He has written articles for several "standard" evangelical publications, such as *Christianity Today* and *His* magazine, as well as for more radical magazines such as *theOtherSide*. The latter is published by Jubilee Fellowship, an organization founded by Sider which shares ESA's Philadelphia address. Jubilee Fellowship sells "Third-World products" and administers the Jubilee Fund, a tax-exempt charity which sent money to the Sandinista (Marxist) guerillas during the revolution in Nicaragua. I have been unable to discover how the financing of terrorists serves the cause of "biblical justice and peace."

Sider is probably most well-known for his book *Rich Christians in an Age of Hunger,*[10] which presents in detail the ESA philosophy of Christian socialism—although he does not call it that in the book. He has also edited two other books: *Living More Simply*[11] (collected papers from his U.S. Consultation on Simple Lifestyle) and *Cry Justice*[12] (annotated Bible quotations on poverty).

The purpose of the present book is to examine and refute Sider's thesis from the viewpoint of biblical law.[13] My position is that the Bible calls for a free market in which the state does not intervene. This is not a "pure" laissez-faire economic system in an anarchic or antinomian sense: the laws of the Bible do prohibit certain activities from taking place. Consenting adults are not the highest authority. But in the normal transactions of the market, the government must not interfere. Prices and wages are to be set by consumers in the context of supply and demand. The state does not subsidize certain industries, nor does it prohibit men from making a profit. Charity is personal, though not purely "voluntary," since biblical law commands it—but on the other hand, those laws are not enforced by the state: the Bible mandates no civil penalties for failing to obey the charity laws. The Bible stands against all forms of socialism and statism.

Is Ronald Sider a Marxist? He claims that he is not[14], and in the technical sense there is no reason to doubt this, although he does hold to many Marxist economic fallacies. But Marxism is not the only form of socialism; after all, Hitler was a socialist also. (The common notion that Nazism and Communism are completely antithetical is wholly false: both are command systems in which the means of production are controlled by the state. Hans Sennholz once stated the difference in this way: "In Russia, all owners were shot; in Germany, all owners *who disobeyed* were shot." The hostility between Nazis and Communists arose because they were rivals, not opposites.) The issue is that Sider is a statist (state-ist). He holds that the state should control virtually every aspect of the economy. This belief is a complete denial of everything the Bible teaches on the responsibilities of government.

Is Ronald Sider a Christian? He claims that he is. He finds "the evidence for Jesus' resurrection . . . surprisingly strong" — so strong in fact, that Sider concludes: "Jesus was probably alive on the third day."[15] It's hard to imagine the Apostle Paul or St. Athanasius putting it quite like that — I think they were a little more convinced — but at least it is clear that Sider is *somewhere* in the Christian camp. Moreover, as an "evangelical" he opposes "theological liberalism" because "it is allowing our thinking and living to be shaped by the surrounding society's views and values rather than by biblical revelation."[16] Yet it is just that which Sider has done — he has allowed his economic views to be shaped by an increasingly vocal, socialistic element in our society, not by the word of God. The whole world is in the grip of the Idea of Revolution.[17] As John Chamberlain has said,

*"Thou shalt not covet" means that it is sinful even to contemplate the seizure of another man's goods — which is something which Socialists, whether Christian or otherwise, have never managed to explain away.*[18]

That is the issue: *Socialism is theft.* I am *not* speaking of the *voluntary* sharing of goods, but rather the state-enforced "redistribution" of wealth. If someone — even the government — takes your property against God's word, it is *theft.* And Sider advocates state socialism. As we shall see, he regards it as being morally superior to voluntary sharing. Which is to say: Legalized theft is better than personal charity and sharing. That is the main point of contention between us.

Another point has to do with his use of envy and guilt to manipulate "rich Christians" into accepting socialism. His arguments are only superficially biblical; in reality, they are psychological instruments to induce guilt. And the "guilt" is not objective, moral guilt but the psychological, sociological feeling of guilt because of transgressing some man-made law. God wants us to feel guilty only when we *are* guilty of breaking God's commands, and then we should repent and obey, and not have to feel guilty any longer, because God forgives those who turn to Him. But sociological guilt is used a a manipulative device to prepare us for socialism.[19] The Sider "guilt trip" is unbiblical.

The other aspects of my argument have to do with economics. Christians have generally left economics to the secularists, and that is why so many have fallen for Sider's socialistic fallacies. I have tried to explain the principles of biblical economics clearly and simply, without a lot of verbiage. But, just in case, I have included a glossary and a select bibliography of reliable books that are relatively easy. Of course, all books must be tested in the light of Scripture—which means you must acquire a familiarity with the Bible, particularly with regard to what it says on economics. The Book of Proverbs is important for this, as well as the books of Moses. Economics is not boring (in fact, these days it's a pretty scary subject). Most of what you do all day is an economic activity, and you need to know what God's word says about that big chunk of your life.

A few words about how to read this book would be in order. First, some may be offended at certain rather playful observations I make about Sider's position. On this point I stand firmly with the prophet Elijah: that which is ridiculous deserves ridicule. Besides, it helps you keep reading. But despite the occasional humor, I have taken Sider seriously as well; he is deadly earnest, and his policies are just plain deadly.

Second, the first two chapters form the basic argument for the rest of the book. They are longer chapters, but the reader is advised to start at the beginning. Most of what I say elsewhere will assume that you have absorbed the first two chapters.

**THE SIDER THESIS**  It may be helpful at this point to introduce some of Sider's ideas for those who are unfamiliar with them. A major theme is that of the "simple life," as I noted above. We shall see later that this official position of Sider's is actually a hoax (I won't tell you which chapter that's in; read the book!). But the fundamental principle behind this is the view that sin is built into the structure of reality; that sin is in *things,* and that things, in fact, actually cause us to sin. Consider the following lines:

*. . . possessions are highly dangerous . . . Jesus was so un-American that he considered riches dangerous . . . Riches are dangerous because their* seductive power *very frequently* persuades *us to reject Jesus and his kingdom . . . An abundance of possessions can easily* lead *us to forget that God is the source of all good . . . possessions* tempt *us to forsake God . . . riches often* harden *the hearts of the wealthy . . . possessions are positively dangerous because they often* encourage *unconcern for the poor, because they* lead *to strife and war, and because they* seduce *people into forsaking God . . . Possessions are highly dangerous. They* lead *to a multitude of sins . . . Possessions are dangerous . . . Possessions are dangerous . . .* [20]

It is probably safe to conclude that Sider thinks possessions are dangerous. In Sider's account, they seem downright malicious, willfully bent on evil. Possessions have seductive power. They harden our hearts. They persuade and encourage us. And although Sider inserts the disclaimer that possessions "are not innately evil,"[21] it is nevertheless clear from his discussion that possessions are up to no good. The true Christian will bravely do battle against these monsters, and Sider hopes to "win the war on affluence."[22] What seems most strange is that Sider goes on to request us to *share* these dangerous things with others.

Fun aside, is there any biblical evidence to indicate that possessions can really "tempt" us? Are they truly "dangerous"? Such pharisaical, environmentalist notions are completely condemned

by Scripture. It is an implication that God is really to blame, since
He created possessions in the first place.

*But each one is tempted when he is carried away and enticed by his own
lust. Then when lust has conceived, it gives birth to sin; and when sin is accomplished, it brings forth death. Do not be deceived, my beloved brethren.
Every good thing bestowed and every perfect gift is from above, coming down
from the Father of lights, with whom there is no variation, or shifting
shadow. (James 1:14-17)*

Out of the heart *come evil thoughts, murders, adulteries, fornications,
thefts, false witness, slanders. (Matthew 15:19)*

The problem is *sin,* not possessions. God owns everything, yet
He is not tempted by evil (James 1:13), for He is righteous. The
fact that a rich man forsakes God is not due to his riches "seduc-
ing" him, but to his own evil heart. You could as easily say that
the poor man's *lack* of possessions "seduces" him to steal (Proverbs 30:9b). But sin is in the heart of fallen man. I daresay
everyone reading these lines has heard the common misquotation
of I Timothy 6:10: "Money is the root of all evil." But Paul says it
is the *love* of money that produces the evil acts. The problem is not
with money but with *men.* Regardless of a wicked man's financial
condition, he will always seek an excuse to sin. If he is poor, he
will envy and steal; if he is rich, he will boast and oppress (Proverbs 30:8-9). But the godly man will say,

*I have learned to be content in whatever circumstances I am. I know how to
get along with humble means, and I also know how to live in prosperity; in
any and every circumstance I have learned the secret of being filled and going
hungry, both of having abundance and suffering need. I can do all things
through Him who strengthens me. (Philippians 4:11-13)*

But this the envious man cannot do. He frets and complains
over his wants, real or imagined; particularly, he is unwilling to
allow others to be content in their state. In another guilt-inducing
remark, Sider says that capitalists "worship Mammon by idoliz-
ing economic success as the highest good."[23] What *is* a capitalist?
Does he really *worship* money? Assuredly, many capitalists do
worship money — because they are *sinners,* not because they are

capitalists. But I must say after reading Sider's book, I find him much more preoccupied with money and possessions than any capitalist I ever met.

Sider's extreme generalization is without foundation. There are only two really valid definitions of *capitalist:* (1) a person who has invested capital in a business, and (2) a person who advocates the free enterprise/private property order known as capitalism. An offshoot from the first definition is (3) a person who is wealthy—but this is rather sloppy, since not all capitalists are wealthy. Sider's opposition to the wealthy has caused him to expand on that third definition (capitalist = wealthy) to come up with (4) a person who is *evil.* Thus, if you invest in business, if you believe in private property, if you are in any sense a capitalist, you are a Mammon-worshipper. Money is your god.

In terms of this, he urges us to cultivate a "carefree attitude toward possessions,"[24] using as his justification Christ's words about not being anxious about the future (Luke 12:22-31). The point of the biblical passage is to underscore the fact that all economic success comes from God, and that our concern about the future must not conflict with the demands of His kingdom. Jesus is saying, "Where is your heart? What is your motivation? Why are you alive? What are you seeking?" If we desire power, status or recognition above the demands of God's law, we are wrong. "Getting ahead" does not come by fretting, worrying and coveting, but by obeying God's word and trusting in His providence. This does not mean carelessness or lack of planning for the future. It means that we must not make wealth our god. It means realizing that if God so wonderfully and beautifully cares for the lower creatures, there is no reason to think that He will abandon His people. It means that we can go to sleep at the end of the business day in the secure knowledge that our Father in heaven never sleeps—that the Almighty Creator and Lord of the universe is watching over us. We *should* try to succeed in our business. The goal of success is a necessary aspect of all human action. But we must never try to be autonomous. In all that we do we must work

in the fear of God, desiring to glorify Him by our labors. Psalm 127:1-2 gives us both a stern warning and a great promise:
*Unless the LORD builds the house, they labor in vain who build it; unless the LORD guards the city, the watchman keeps awake in vain. It is vain for you to rise up early, to retire late, to eat the bread of painful labors; for He gives to His beloved even in his sleep.*

All our activity is vain apart from the blessing of God. Notice that God does not condemn the builder for constructing the house, or the watchman for guarding the city. These tasks require concern about possessions and their security. Builders and watchmen are needed. We are not to say, "Let the Lord provide," with no foresight on our part (and Jesus does tell us to plan ahead: Luke 14:28-30). But if we are under God's curse, no amount of planning will enable us to escape calamity. If the Lord does not build with us, if we do not seek Him as our highest good, we are lost — and our goods will eventually be inherited by those who *are* godly (Proverbs 13:22).

The man who obeys God has the deep assurance that God is always building, always watching. He can really *sleep* and *relax* under God's provision. The wicked businessmen of Amos' day were unable to rest during the Sabbath, anxious as they were to make the bucks in any way they could. But God was not building with them, and when the Assyrians invaded, the watchmen of Israel were unable to prevent destruction. The Bible encourages godly labor, thrift, diligence and planning; but the workaholic is condemned as well as the sluggard. Both live in defiance of the law of God. The lazy man will not work, and the man who is enslaved to his work cannot rest. Jesus rejects both. Obedience to Him requires careful stewardship *and* trust in His care. The acquiring of wealth must be done in accordance with God's law.

But God's law is not sufficient for Sider's unbiblical goals. He cheerfully goes beyond the law, demanding that "all income should be given to the poor after one satisfies bare necessities."[25] Why? Because no less an authority than John Wesley said so. He quotes Wesley's boast: "If I leave behind me 10 pounds, you and all mankind bear witness against me that I lived and died a thief and a robber"—and Sider gushes, "Wesley's practice reflects biblical principles."[26] *What* biblical principles? What Scriptural doctrine tells us to leave practically nothing behind us? Wesley was certainly no paradigm of biblical standards. Many of his actions were in flagrant contradiction to the actual laws of the Bible.[27] And when God's holy word informs us that "a good man leaves an inheritance to his children's children" (Proverbs 13:22), we are on dangerous ground if we depart from it on the mere basis of John Wesley's questionable authority.

Sider goes on to commend the communal way of life of such groups as Reba Place Fellowship, which practices "total economic sharing"[28] among its members. Just how biblical this practice is (as a *normal* lifestyle) will be indicated in Chapter 12. Scripture stands in terms of *community, not communes.* Complete economic equality is never stated as a Christian ideal. It may be a temporary necessity in an emergency; but it is not a "model" for the usual Christian lifestyle. God has called us to dominion, the developing of the earth by men with different gifts and abilities, increasing the earth's productivity for the glory of God. The communal ethic is not oriented toward dominion, but toward bare-minimum survival. Giving money away does not produce anything for the future: its whole function is to provide for *immediate* needs, for present consumption alone. This does not mean we shouldn't give our money away—we should. There are valid needs in the present. But God's law is structured so that, usually, a good portion of income can go toward production. This is the only way to bring lasting, long-term benefit to all.

That thesis will be developed in the chapters that follow. We must be sure that in all our thinking and acting, we are operating according to the clear mandates of Scripture. The Bible is law for all of life. To depart from it is *foolishness*—a word we should not use idly. Biblically, it describes the condition of the man who has departed from God's word, who constructs great programs on the powdery basis of autonomous reason, who self-consciously lives a lie; whose end is destruction. The words of Otto Scott[29] are especially relevant for our examination of Ronald Sider and his writings:

*The figure of the Fool is widely misunderstood. He is neither a jester nor a clown nor an idiot. He is, instead, the dark side of genius. For if a genius has the ability to see and make connections beyond the normal range of vision, the fool is one who can see — and disconnect.*

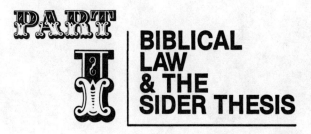

PART II

BIBLICAL LAW & THE SIDER THESIS

"I really believe I am not a legalist. But, somehow I'm coming across that way."

(Ronald Sider, *The Wittenburg Door,* Oct./Nov. 1979, p. 28)

---

"Beware of the false prophets, who come to you in sheep's clothing, but inwardly are ravening wolves. You will know them by their fruits."

(Matthew 7:15-16)

---

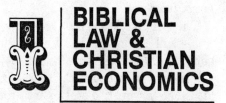

# BIBLICAL LAW & CHRISTIAN ECONOMICS

**"I DON'T WANT TO HAVE SECULAR PENALTIES EXERCISED BY THE STATE FOR PEOPLE WHO COMMIT ADULTERY OR HOMOSEXUAL SINS. PEOPLE NEED TO BE FREE TO MAKE CHOICES IN THAT AREA..." [RONALD SIDER, *THE WITTENBURG DOOR*, OCT./NOV. 1979, P. 16]**

---

**"IF THERE IS A MAN WHO COMMITS ADULTERY WITH ANOTHER MAN'S WIFE, ONE WHO COMMITS ADULTERY WITH HIS FRIEND'S WIFE, THE ADULTERER AND THE ADULTERESS SHALL SURELY BE PUT TO DEATH.... IF THERE IS A MAN WHO LIES WITH A MALE AS THOSE WHO LIE WITH A WOMAN, BOTH OF THEM HAVE COMMITTED A DETESTABLE ACT; THEY SHALL SURELY BE PUT TO DEATH." [LEVITICUS 20:10, 13]**

---

Does Ronald Sider believe the biblical standards of law and justice are normative today? A superficial reading of his books and articles would seem to indicate that this is the case. Sider often cites what he regards as biblical evidence for his thesis; his latest book, *Cry Justice,* is in fact almost entirely made up of Bible quotations. He refers to such biblical laws as the Jubilee, the Sabbath and the Sabbatical year, the tithe, gleaning, and restitution.

Moreover, he makes a grand statement of the Bible's relationship to economic concerns:

*According to biblical faith, Yahweh is Lord of all things. He is the sovereign Lord of history. Economics is not a neutral, secular sphere independent of his lordship. Economic activity, like every other area of life, should be subject to his will and revelation.* [1]

Thus, if God is Lord of economics, and if that field is "subject to his will and revelation," we might assume that God's laws regarding economics are binding, at least as far as Sider and his associates are concerned. This admirable declaration of God's lordship, however, dissolves into mere rhetoric when considered in the light of Sider's operating principle of antinomianism (anti-law-ism). After asking what kind of "structural change" Christians should work for, he says:

*The Bible does not directly answer these questions. We do not find a comprehensive blueprint for a new economic order in Scripture . . .* [2]

This, of course, means that Sider is free to devise his own blueprint, while using vague "biblical principles" to justify his thesis to the Christian community. Sider's blueprint calls for socialistic redistribution of wealth and government intervention — a blueprint not countenanced by Scripture, but which Sider claims to find in the fact that "biblical revelation tells us that God and his faithful people are always at work liberating the oppressed, and also provides some principles apropos of justice in society." [3]

In plain translation: where the Bible is *specific* on economic issues, it is not valid; where the Bible states a *general principle* that can be redefined in terms of "liberationist" specifics, it is valid. In Sider's hands, the Bible becomes no more than a ventriloquist's dummy. Or, to put it another way: "The hands are Esau's hands, but the voice is the voice of Jacob." Sider's thesis *feels* biblical, on the surface; but the voice is the voice of Ronald Sider.

Detailed documentation of this charge will appear in the following chapters. For the present, we will examine an outline of the biblical laws on economics and government. There *is* "a comprehensive blueprint" for economics in Scripture, but it is not the kind Sider wishes to implement. Therefore, he has to deny that such a blueprint exists.

**GOD'S BLUEPRINT: BIBLICAL LAW** Christian economics begins with God the Creator, "who created heaven and the things in it, and the earth and the things in it, and the sea and the things in it" (Revelation 10:6). As Creator, God is supreme Lord of His workmanship. No aspect of reality is autonomous or neutral: everything is completely subject to His commands. What we call physical laws (such as gravity, photosynthesis and the principles of thermodynamics) are simply the outworking of God's eternal decree and continual providence. And the same is true of economic laws. You may (as one man did) write to Congress and request that our legislators repeal the law of supply and demand, but it is God's law, not subject to human control. The world runs according to God's principles. Man—whether individual anarchist or totalitarian state—cannot transgress God's laws without suffering the pre-ordained consequences, in this life and the next. If you defy God's law of gravity, you will go *splat*; if the state defies God's law of honest money, the economy will go *splat*.

The Bible tells us that God's law is the foundation of *wisdom*, and that we will be *wise* to the precise extent that we submit to Him and His law (Deuteronomy 4:6; Psalm 19:7; 119:98; Proverbs 9:10; 21:30; 28:7). Wisdom is the ability to apply the principles of God's law to the specific issues in life—such things as, for instance, "justice and equity" (Proverbs 1:3; 2:9). The Book of Proverbs is preeminently the book of *Wisdom*: it consists of practical applications of biblical law to precise cases in life. The first third of this legal commentary is one lengthy exhortation to "get wisdom." From various perspectives, Solomon urges the importance of understanding the law as it relates to the concrete problems we face in the world. Yet, on two occasions, Solomon interrupts this discourse with what might seem to be an irrelevant digression: he suddenly starts talking about God's creation of the universe (3:19-20; 8:22-31). Of course, Solomon never really changed the subject at all. His point in both digressions is that "the LORD by *wisdom* hath founded the earth"; that the same God who is Lord of the physical universe has established laws in justice and economics that are as absolute and irrevocable as the laws of physics; and that, to "get along" in His world, you may engage in economic fraud with the same assurance of success you would have in jumping from a plane without a parachute. Success, in any area of life, comes from *wisdom*: conformity to the Creator's law (Joshua 1:8).

Man's ethical rebellion against God, therefore, inflicted disaster upon his every activity and relationship. The essence of the sin in the Garden — and ever since — was man's attempt to be his own god, to set up his own standard in place of God's command. "You will be like God," the Tempter promised, "knowing good and evil." And how does God know good and evil? Not by referring to some external standard of justice; for God, there *is* no external standard — *He* is the standard. He "knows" the difference between good and evil by simply determining it. His law alone is the yardstick of right and wrong. And that was the privilege coveted by Adam and Eve. They wanted to know good and evil, not by submitting to the external standard of justice provided by God's commands, but by usurping the prerogatives of Deity, determining for themselves the difference between right and wrong. As the Apostle John succinctly stated it: "Sin is *lawlessness*" (1 John 3:4).

"Wait a minute," you say. "Isn't that legalism? Didn't Jesus and the apostles declare that we are free from all those Old Testament regulations?" It wouldn't really be fair to reply that the strictest adherence to Old Testament law allows for much more freedom than do the more "enlightened" stipulations of our benevolent despots in the federal bureaucracy. That issue will be temporarily shelved, and I'll answer your questions directly: *NO.*

Let's begin with a working definition of legalism. Legalism cannot be defined simply as rigorous obedience to the law: after all, Jesus Christ obeyed the law fully, in its most exacting details — and He, certainly, was no legalist. The true legalist is the person who subscribes to one or more of the following heresies—ideas which are roundly condemned in Scripture:

1) *Justification by works.* This is the most critical aspect of the legalistic faith. It was abhorred and refuted by the writers of both Old and New Testaments. We must note here that *no one*—not even in the days of Moses—was ever justified by his works. The only basis of salvation is the finished work of Jesus Christ, in fully satisfying the demands of God's law, and suffering its penalties, in the place of all His people. The view that God accepts us as His children because of our works is completely at odds with the teachings of Scripture. One who is a legalist in this sense is not a Christian.

2) *The requirement of obedience to Old Testament ceremonial laws.* Before Christ came, God's people were required to observe certain ceremonies—sacrifices, feasts, and so forth—which symbolically portrayed the way of restoration to God's favor. These received their completion in Jesus Christ, and are no longer literally binding upon us. There is a very real sense, of course, in which we still keep these laws: Jesus Christ is our priest, He is our sacrificial atonement, and we cannot approach God apart from Him. Thus, in their real *meaning*, all these laws are observed by all Christians. But consider what a literal observance of these laws would mean, now that Christ has fulfilled these shadows: if you were to sacrifice a lamb today, you would be saying, in effect, that Christ's atonement on the cross was insufficient—that you need an additional sacrifice to be accepted with God. That is heresy. Before the coming of Christ, observance of the ceremonial law was *obedience*; after His death and resurrection, it is *disobedience*. The false teachers opposed by Paul in Galatians held to both of these two aspects of legalism—*salvation by works* and *the requirement of Old Testament ceremonies*.

3) A third form of legalism is addressed in Romans 14 and Colossians 2: *The requirement of obedience to man-made regulations.* The Galatian legalists at least may be commended for their insistence upon *biblical* regulations. They were very wrong, but their stand-

ards were derived from Scripture. But Paul also had to contend with a host of regulations which originated from mere human prejudice, and which some Christians attempted to impose upon others. "Touch not; taste not; handle not," they demanded — when God had said nothing of the kind. There are many matters of individual conscience, taste, and idiosyncrasy which should remain so. But we are all dictators at heart, and we often like nothing better than to force others to submit to our eccentricities. It is in this sense that Ronald Sider is a legalist. He comes very close — without going over the brink in many of his actual statements — to making requirements out of all sorts of non-biblical standards. According to him, Christians should "live simply," eat less meat and no bananas, oppose production of liquor, and give away all income above what is required for bare necessities. Does the Bible say one word about any of this? No — which is not to suggest that we *must* be heavy meat and banana eaters (since that isn't commanded either). The point is that we must never uphold as "more Christian" a standard that is not based on clear Scriptural grounds. Still less should we urge Christians (as Sider does) to support governmental taxation and redistribution programs which are in specific violation of God's commands.

4) Another form of legalism — of which Sider is also guilty — is *confusion of sins with civil crimes*. There are many things the Bible condemns as sins, for which there is no civil penalty attached. For example, God certainly regards unjust hatred as a form of murder. Yet while He commanded that the murderer be executed, He made no such stipulation for the sin of unjust hatred. In the same way, God's word condemns the slave mentality of gluttonous consumption as a sin — yet it mentions no civil penalties (or "tax incentives") against it. But Ronald Sider wants the structure of public policy altered to make gluttony a crime, or at least a much more costly practice than a free market would provide. Again, it is a sin to ignore the legitimate needs of immigrants, and God threatens to destroy a nation that neglects strangers. But the Bible mandates no civil penalties for commit-

ting such a sin. In other words, some things are reserved for God's providential judgments in history, and for the final judgment, when the very thoughts and intents of the heart will come under severe scrutiny, to be dealt with according to strict justice. It is surely wrong for a nation to mandate any unbiblical legal structures which discriminate against certain races. But, it is also wrong for a nation to legislate *against* discrimination, even if that discrimination is sinful—unless it is a violation of biblical laws in the area of civil justice. For instance, the government must not force blacks to ride in the back of a bus. But, biblically, it is just as wrong to force a bus company to integrate its passengers. Neither option is allowable in terms of Scripture. Where God has not provided examples of legislation, we may not legislate. To do so is legalism. And it is interesting to note that, while Sider is quite anxious to legislate where God has not spoken, he is also anxious to do away with biblical penalties for such crimes as adultery and homosexuality[4]—revealing the basic motive of legalism: *antinomianism*. The antinomian is opposed to the authority of God in human affairs. While he may cloak his humanism in a garb of extreme religiosity (as did the Pharisees) or "radical Christianity," his primary goal is to abolish God's law and replace it with his own laws. He wants to be "like God, knowing good and evil." On the surface, antinomianism and legalism appear to be diametrically opposed; in reality, they are both rooted in the sinful attempt to dethrone God.

**LAW AND THE NEW TESTAMENT** What does the New Testament say about the validity of the Old Testament law? It is often assumed that Christ's death and resurrection have freed us from any obligation to keep the law—and, in the sense of *justification*, that is certainly true. Because of Christ's finished work, no believer is under the law's condemnation: our obligations have been fully met by our Lord. But that was true of Old Testament believers as well. Abraham and David, for instance, were justified by God's grace through faith, just as we are (Romans 4:1-8).

Therefore, justification by faith cannot be claimed as a basis for rejecting the law's demands, since the Old Testament believers, who were told to keep the law, were justified by faith as much as we are.

**THE TEACHING OF CHRIST**   Any examination of the New Testament teaching on law must begin with Jesus Christ's declaration of His relationship to the law, and the law's continuing requirements of His disciples:

*Do not think that I came to abolish the Law or the Prophets; I did not come to abolish, but to fulfill. For truly I say to you, until heaven and earth pass away, not the smallest letter or stroke shall pass away from the Law, until all is accomplished. Whoever then annuls one of the least of these commandments, and so teaches others, shall be called least in the kingdom of heaven; but whoever keeps and teaches them, he shall be called great in the kingdom of heaven. For I say to you, that unless your righteousness surpasses that of the scribes and pharisees, you shall not enter the kingdom of heaven (Matthew 5:17-20).*[5]

First, Jesus says He came to "fulfill" the law. What does "fulfill" mean? Perhaps the grossest misunderstanding of this is the idea that He meant to replace or put an end to the law. That is specifically denied here: "Do not think that I came to abolish the Law." In no way was it Christ's intention to invalidate or repeal the law. Nor did He intend to add to or "perfect" the law, for it was already *perfect* (Psalm 19:7; Romans 7:12). Some have thought that our Lord added a more spiritual or inward dimension to the external demands of the law, but that cannot be the case either: the Old Testament already commanded internal obedience (Deuteronomy 6:5-6; Psalm 51:10). Now, it is true that the Pharisees had perverted the law by focusing on external obedience (as we shall see, they weren't even consistent in *that*); and Jesus plainly condemned them for distorting the law in this way. But this was merely to restore a proper understanding of the true nature of the law; it does not explain how Jesus planned to *fulfill* the law. Another interpretation has held that Jesus was speaking of His own "fulfilling" of the law, by obeying it Himself. While it is true that Jesus *did* obey the law's demands fully, that is not what He is saying here. The context shows that He was using this statement as a basis for teaching *others* to obey the law. Not one word regarding His own obedience is mentioned in this entire passage. Rather, He enforces upon His hearers their duty to obey the law. The only possible meaning of "fulfill" here, supported by the passage itself, is that *Jesus came to fully confirm and establish the continuing validity of the Old Testament law for His people.*

Christ's confirmation of the law, moreover, includes the law's most minute details: "Not the smallest letter or stroke shall pass away from the Law." Even the smallest points of the law are valid "until heaven and earth pass away." Jesus did not want the law altered by so much as a tiny stroke. Let us remember: this is our Lord speaking, and we, as His followers, must obey Him. "If you love Me," he said, "you will keep My commandments. . . . He who has My commandments, and keeps them, he it is who loves Me" (John 14:15, 21). Christians must be concerned to obey even the smallest details of the law—not to earn acceptance with God (Christ earned that for us), but because our Saviour commands us to obey. Every single stroke of the law is applicable to this age, until the end of the world.

Jesus goes on to underscore the importance of obedience. He tells us that God is displeased when we break even "the least of these commandments"; and teaching others to break them makes God angry as well. The law of God is our standard for godly living. "Holiness" and "righteousness" are constantly defined by Scripture in terms of the law; in fact, "justice, mercy, and faithfulness" are impossible apart from God's law (Matthew 23:23).

If we are faithful to the details of the law, Jesus says that our righteousness will exceed the righteousness of the scribes and Pharisees. Contrary to popular myth, the Pharisees did *not* observe the law. While they claimed to be teachers of the law, in reality they were hypocrites. They taught (1) *legalism* (upholding justification by works) and (2) *antinomianism* (replacing God's law with the legalistic traditions of men). At every point in His conflicts with the Pharisees, Jesus stood for the law against their perversions of it (see, e.g., Matthew 12:1-14; 15:1-20; 19:1-9; 23:1-39). By perverting the law, the scribes and Pharisees demonstrated their rebellion against God's authority; therefore they were not members of the kingdom.

In His Sermon on the Mount, Jesus never criticized the law as such, but the Pharisaic perversion of the law instead. Not once did he oppose what was *written* ("the smallest letter or stroke" of the law itself); rather, he contradicted what was *said* in the "traditions of the elders" which were contrary to God's genuine law (see Matthew 5:21, 27, 33, 38, 43; cf. 15:3, 6, 9). In all these statements, Jesus did not add to or detract from the law, but established its full meaning—that the way of righteousness lies in determined obedience to the most minute details of God's law. Emphasizing the awesome seriousness of this fact, Jesus closed the Sermon by pointing out why many professing Christians will be damned at the Last Day: "I will declare to them, 'I never knew you; depart from Me, you who practice *lawlessness*' " (Matthew 7:23). Christ clearly saw faith and obedience as united: a man's true *faith* is revealed by his *practice*, his observance of Christ's sayings (7:24)—including, of course, His sayings about observing the minutest details of the law. Throughout His ministry, Jesus Christ presented Himself as both *Saviour* and *Lord*; and just as we must not attempt to be our own *saviours* by a legalistic faith in our own works, so we must not attempt to be our own *lords* by an antinomian practice of "Christian living" that is separated from the requirements of God's holy law.

**THE TEACHING OF THE APOSTLES** The most systematic analysis of the Christian's relationship to the law is found in the Apostle Paul's letter to the Romans. The first several chapters deal with our guilt before God's law, and the provision of complete justification for the believer through the finished work of

Christ. All that the law demands for acceptance with God has been perfectly satisfied by our Substitute: we are identified with Him in His full payment for sin, so that—as far as the law's penalty is concerned—we *legally* "died with Christ" (6:8). In Christ, we have received the full penalty of the law, because He endured its curse in our place. No longer are we "under law" and its condemnation; rather, we have been placed "under grace" as our means of justification. For this reason, sin cannot have dominion over us (6:14). The believer has been freed from his slavery to *sin*, and is now enslaved to *righteousness* (6:17). But since righteousness is defined in terms of God's law, this means that the believer now fulfills the righteous requirements of the law (8:4). He does not live according to sinful principles, but according to the Spirit. And how do we know what the Spirit wants us to do? Simply by referring to the law which He authored. "The law is *Spiritual*" (7:14)—which doesn't mean that the law is other-worldly or non-physical, but that it is *from the Spirit*. The law is "holy, just and good" (7:12): it is our continuing standard of right living in every area.

Some hold that the Christian is not motivated by considerations of *law*, but by *love* instead. This is to place an unbiblical distinction between law and love, a distinction opposed by the Apostles. "Love," said Paul, "is the fulfillment of the *law*" (Romans 13:10). "This is the love of God, that we keep His commandments," John wrote (I John 5:3). The standard of love is nothing other than the law of God. If we are disobedient to the law of God, we do not love; conversely, if we do not love, we are breaking the law, which commands love. If, in the name of "love for the poor," I transgress God's law by supporting legal plunder of my rich neighbor to fund a poverty program, I am not really loving, regardless of my profession; for love is always concerned to fulfill the law of God. Where that concern is absent, love does not exist.

In fact, *obedience to God's law is the mark of genuine Christianity*. Disobedience to the law of God is the sign that we do not have a relationship to God at all:

*By this we know that we have come to know Him, if we keep His command-ments. The one who says, "I have come to know Him," and does not keep His commandments, is a liar and the truth is not in Him (I John 2:3-4).*

It might be argued at this point that the Apostles do oppose the Old Testament law in certain sections of their writings. A super-ficial reading of Galatians, for instance, would seem to substan-tiate such an idea. But this interpretation overlooks Paul's thesis in writing the book. First, he was denying the legalistic heresy that our obedience to law is the condition of our justification: "A man is not justified by the works of the Law but through faith in Jesus Christ" (2:16). In withstanding legalism, *Paul was not objec-ting to the law itself, but to a perversion of the law* — a perversion that is not countenanced in either Testament. Second, Paul wrote in op-position to *ceremonialism* — the teaching that the observance of Old Testament ceremonies was still binding on believers, and in fact necessary for salvation. He chided the Galatians for observing ceremonial "days and months and seasons and years" (4:10), and for being circumcised in the attempt "to be justified by law" (5:2-4). It is most significant that when the Apostles speak of our freedom from certain Old Testament regulations, *they cite only ceremonial laws* — such as sacrifices, the priesthood, circumcision and feasts — which pictorially represented the mediatorial work of Christ until He came. For example, no New Testament text con-demns the practice of restitution (and, in fact, Jesus pronounced Zaccheus to be saved after he had demonstrated his willingness to obey this detail of the law); no New Testament text can be used to support unlawful practices of homosexuality, usury, or debase-ment of currency. These are all aspects of God's abiding moral law, and not one word of Scripture alters their force.

Both Testaments distinguish between laws that were ceremonial (and thus merely temporary) and those laws which were moral. The moral law is the abiding definition of sin and righteousness (Romans 3:20; 7:7; 1 John 3:4). The ceremonial regulations, on the other hand, symbolically represented the means of restoration to God's favor through the Mediator who was to come (Hebrews 7:10).The moral law answers the question, "How should I live?"; the ceremonial law symbolically answers the question, "How can I be restored to God's favor after breaking His moral law?" Thus the Old Testament writers were aware of the crucial difference between *obedience* on the one hand (observance of God's requirement of justice, mercy and faithfulness in every area of life), and *sacrifice* on the other hand (observance of the ceremonies which symbolized restoration). This distinction was much more clearly revealed in the New Testament, of course, since it was written after the symbols had met their fulfillment in Christ (see e.g., Romans 2:28-29; Philippians 3:2-3; Colossians 2:11-14). But the distinction was also understood in the Old Testament (Isaiah 1:11-23; Hosea 6:6; Amos 5:21-26; Micah 6:6-8). The ceremonial law was never intended to be a permanent feature of the duty of believers. But the moral law has lasting validity. God has not surrendered His authority in any area of life. In the family, education, government, economics, science, the arts, and everything else, He is always Lord. His commandments for righteous living—by the individual, the community, social institutions and departments of government—have not been altered. Their relevance and authority will remain until heaven and earth pass away.

**GOD'S LAW AND THE STATE**   In some ways, this section is the most important part of the book: a great deal of what I will say in later chapters will simply expand on the doctrines presented here. This is because Ronald Sider's assumptions about the role of the state underlie much of his argument. If Mr. Sider had agreed with the biblical view of the responsibilities and limits of civil government, his book would be the size of a small pamphlet: he would have had very little to say.

The basic outline of the duties of civil government is found in Romans 13:4. Paul tells us that the civil authority "is a minister of God to you for good. But if you do what is evil, be afraid; for it does not bear the sword for nothing; for it is a minister of God, an avenger who brings wrath upon the one who practices evil."

Every civil ruler, Paul says, has an obligation to be "God's *minister*." In other words, he must *administer* the word of God in his sphere of authority. To the extent that he fails to do this, he is an unfaithful minister—just as I would be an unfaithful minister of the gospel if I failed to apply God's word to my congregation. Jesus Christ is Lord of all rulers, in heaven and in earth (Ephesians 1:20-22), and all rulers are commanded to submit to His Lordship or be destroyed:

*Now therefore, O Kings, show discernment;*
*Take warning, O judges of the earth.*
*Worship the* LORD *with reverence,*
*And rejoice with trembling.*
*Do homage to the Son, lest He become angry,*
 *and you perish in the way,*
*For His wrath may soon be kindled.*
*How blessed are all who take refuge in Him!*
*(Psalm 2:10-12)*

As God's minister, the ruler has two responsibilities, both of which are mentioned in Romans 13.

1. *He must do good.* What is "good"? Is God's minister of justice free to decide that for himself? If so, we cannot condemn anything that rulers have done in the past. Hitler regarded the extermination of Jews as good; Nero thought it was a good idea to tax his citizens in order to fund his private orgies and public slaughters; obviously, we could go on and on. Public health care, minimum wage laws, and state-financed education may all seem "good" to us; but how can we be sure? There is only one way: we must go, as Isaiah said, "to the law and to the testimony." God's law is "holy, righteous and good" (Romans 7:12; Matthew 23:23). If God's ministers in the state are faithful, they will go to God's Old Testament laws to find out what they should do. Any standard of goodness which is not based on the law of God is not good; it is mere humanism. A state that departs from God's standard is engaged in a vain and cursed attempt to deify itself.

2. *He must punish evildoers.* What is an "evildoer"? Again we must ask: Is the ruler free to decide the answer for himself? To answer *Yes* is to give a despot a blank check for statist absolutism: he may decide that all babies in Bethlehem are "evildoers," for instance. King Herod was only doing his job, therefore, when he ordered the murder of the infants (Matthew 2:16). Clearly, God has given civil rulers the power of the sword: obviously, they are supposed to execute *somebody.* But whom? If your answer is based on anything but God's law, I repeat: you've just handed the state a blank check—and God's civil minister just might add *you* to his hit list.

But that's not the end of the problem. Once you have decided who is to be punished, another question arises: What is the appropriate penalty for a particular crime? (Should a petty thief be hanged? Should a rapist be forced to stand in a corner? Should the entire Federal Reserve Board be flogged?) Again, the answers to these questions must be sought from God's law. The ruler must study God's standard of justice for the exercise of his ministry (Deuteronomy 17:18-20). And, as Jesus pointed out, *justice is defined by Old Testament law.* If we discard the law, we are left to wander aimlessly, with no basis for justice, no means of recognizing it, and no principles with which to apply it. Without God's law, we have nothing but the "justice" of autonomous, rebellious humanism—which is to say, *injustice.* Conservatives and libertarians are fond of talking about "the rule of law"; but if it is not the rule of *God's* law, it is nothing but anarchy, the rule of lawlessness.

God's commandments state precisely the responsibilities and limits of the state. And built into the law is a "strict constructionist" interpretation: the ruler "may not turn aside from the commandment, to the right or to the left" (Deuteronomy 17:20). The ruler is a *minister* of God, not an advisor or legislator. His responsibility is to do *all* that God commands, and *only* what God commands. To do more or less, to turn to the right or to the left, is to deny the crown rights of King Jesus. The ruler is a man under authority, and his rule must reflect the revealed justice of God. He must steadfastly resist the perennial suggestions of the Tempter: "Has God said? . . . You surely shall not die. . . . You will be like God!"

**GOD'S LAW AND ECONOMICS** Although Sider is fond of repeating his notion that the Bible does not contain a blueprint for economics, the fact is that the Bible tells us a great deal about the subject. Much of the biblical teaching on economics will be seen in later chapters, but a summary of basic principles will be helpful at this point.

**PROPERTY** As I have already noted, we must begin with God as Creator and Owner of all things. "The earth is the LORD's, and all it contains, the world, and those who dwell in it" (Psalm 24:1). Sider strongly hints that this verse involves a repudiation of private property and laissez-faire economics, giving governments the right to redistribute wealth and enforce sharing.[6] But the point of the biblical emphasis on *God's* ownership is that all property must be held in strict accordance with His commands. His commands do not allow for government redistribution of wealth. Property will always be owned; if we take it away from individuals and families, it will be owned by the government's redistributive agency. It is true that I do not have an absolute right to my property. Nor do I have an absolute right to dispose of my wife and children as I see fit. *Everything I have must be owned in terms of God's requirements.* But to acknowledge the limits on my use of my property is very different from asserting that the government or the poor are free to transgress God's laws regarding the same property. Sider seems very concerned to make sure *property owners* stay within their biblical limits (actually, he goes much further than that, but let's give him the benefit of the doubt for a moment); it is striking that he does not manifest a similar concern that *civil government* not transgress its divinely-ordained limits. God's ownership of the land is a limitation on absolute ownership by anyone. The biggest single offender against God's ownership of property in this century is the very civil government to which Sider wishes to give more power. Civil government in the United States, in direct violation of biblical law, owns *all* the land in the country, and rents some of it out to its citizens. If you don't pay the property tax (*rent*), you will be evicted. This is theft: the government has no right whatsoever to tax property, and the practice of eminent domain is a claim to deity. It is specifically forbidden in Scripture (I Samuel 8:14; I Kings 21; Ezekiel 46:18).

God's total ownership is the basis for our limited ownership, as His stewards. Thus, half of the Ten Commandments are prohibitions against theft: I must not rob my neighbor of his life, his wife, his property, or his reputation; nor may I covet anything that belongs to him. This has direct relevance to the Sider Thesis. For, while he pays lip service to the rights of property, Sider actually encourages coveting and theft. "Private property is legitimate. But since God is the only absolute owner, our right to acquire and use property is definitely limited. The human right to the resources necessary to earn a just living overrides any notion of absolute private ownership."[7] In terms of this, Sider calls for a national (state) food policy,[8] (state to state) foreign aid,[9] a guaranteed national income,[10] international taxation,[11] "land reform" (i.e., expropriation of lands from the rich),[12] bureaucratically determined "just prices,"[13] national health care,[14] population control,[15] and the right of developing nations to nationalize foreign holdings[16]—all of which involve theft of one sort or another. In Sider's Robin Hood Theology, loving my poor neighbor means robbing my rich neighbor.

This is not to suggest that the rich have no responsibility to help the poor. But it does mean that the poor have a responsibility not to steal from the rich. "You shall do no injustice in judgment; *you shall not be partial to the poor nor defer to the great*, but you are to judge your neighbor *fairly*" (Leviticus 19:15)—which does not mean Karl Marx's definition of a "fair" distribution of wealth, but rather according to the standard of God's law. Any judgment of a man on the basis of his property (or his lack of it) is *theft*. In attempting to justify coveteousness and theft in the name of God's ownership, Ronald Sider has committed blasphemy. "Woe to those who call evil good, and good evil!" (Isaiah 5:20).

**WORK AND DOMINION**    The biblical method of attaining dominion is through diligent labor. When Adam rebelled, he chose instead to have dominion by playing god, rejecting God's leadership over him. He wanted power over the creation, not legitimately, through God-ordained work, but by becoming his own god. The world doesn't work that way, of course; and man was driven into slavery, losing dominion. But sinful men still seek power outside of the pattern God has commanded. The envious do not want to take the time and energy to get wealth by godly diligence; rather, they want to plunder and destroy those above them. George Reisman correctly observes:

*The essential fact to grasp about socialism . . . is that it is simply an act of destruction . . . it destroys private ownership and the profit motive, and that is essentially all it does. It has nothing to put in their place. Socialism, in other words, is not actually an alternative economic system to private ownership of the means of production. It is merely a negation of the system based on private ownership.* [17]

Scripture is insistent in its demand for *diligent, hard work* in our tasks. Constantly we are told that this is *the means of dominion*. A few samples from the Book of Proverbs:

*Ill-gotten gains do not profit, but righteousness delivers from death The Lord will not allow the righteous to hunger, but He will thrust aside the craving of the wicked. Poor is he who works with a negligent hand, but the hand of the diligent makes rich (10:2-4).*

*He who tills his land will have plenty of bread. . . . The hand of the diligent will rule, but the slack hand will be put to forced labor (12:1, 24). The soul of the sluggard craves and gets nothing, but the soul of the diligent is made fat. Wealth obtained by fraud dwindles, but the one who gathers by labor increases it (13:4, 11).*

It might be objected that this is simply another means of "Let them eat cake," that it does nothing to wrest power from the ungodly; but this is not the case. The Bible teaches the paradoxical truth that power flows to those who work and serve: the industrious meek shall inherit the earth. We are not to fret nor be anxious toward evildoers, but to "trust in the LORD, and *do good*" (see all of Psalm 37). God gives the power to get wealth (Deuteronomy 8:18), and He gives it to the diligent workers in His kingdom.

*And calling them to Himself, Jesus said unto them, "You know that those who are recognized rulers of the Gentiles lord it over them; and their great men exercise authority over them. But it is not so among you, but whoever wishes to become great among you shall be your servant; and whoever wishes to be first among you shall be slave of all. For even the Son of man did not come to be served, but to serve, and to give His life a ransom for many (Mark 10:42-45).*

Even powerful statist oppression will be overcome, not by revolution, but by godly dominion in the sphere of work, as God showed the prophet Zechariah during a period of ungodly statist domination:

*Then I lifted up my eyes and looked, and behold, there were four horns. So I said to the angel who was speaking with me, "What are these?" And he answered me, "These are the horns which have scattered Judah, Israel and Jerusalem." Then the Lord showed me four craftsmen. And I said, "What are these coming to do?" And he said, "These are the horns which have scattered Judah so that no man lifts up his head; but these craftsmen have come to terrify them, to throw down the horns of the nations who have lifted up their horns against the land of Judah in order to scatter it" (Zechariah 1:18-21).*

The earthly victory of God's people will come about through diligent work. Ungodly powers must and shall fall through the daily work and prayer of the godly. Like the spider in Proverbs 30:28, if we take hold with our hands, we will someday find ourselves in the palaces of kings. But Scripture never countenances the idea that we are to attain dominion by demanding our "fair share" of resources owned by others, or by using governmental coercion to redistribute wealth. We must encourage ourselves and each other to labor diligently in obedience to God's commands, in the confident expectation that God will honor His promises—that we and our seed will inherit God's good blessings in this life and the next.

The reason for Western prosperity is not accidental. It is the direct outgrowth of the "Puritan ethic," which involved diligent labor, saving, investment, and the philosophy of free enterprise and initiative. God's law clearly promises external blessings in response to external obedience. This is the function of profits: they are the sign of success in serving the wants of consumers. Profits are possible because of the biblical principle of "dominion through service": the efficient (least wasteful) producer receives the greatest return. The moment he turns from serving the public, his profit will disappear, because the consumers will take their business elsewhere. The consumers always decide which producer will get the profits. Now it is true that some of the "bigness" of big business has been made possible by unbiblical government subsidy and protectionism. But apart from such ungodly activity, the characteristic feature of big business is efficient mass production for the needs of the public. And the more efficient a producer is, the more profit he earns, and consequently he is able to exert even more influence upon business, which is as it should be: the control of production is in the hands of those who are the best in serving consumers. Thus, as Ludwig von Mises observed:

*The standard of living of the common man is highest in those countries which have the greatest number of wealthy entrepreneurs. It is to the foremost material interest of everybody that control of the factors of production should be concentrated in the hands of those who know how to utilize them in the most efficient way.*[18]

**EXCHANGE**    The nature of biblical free enterprise and exchange can perhaps be best understood by examining it in contrast with the popular con game that resurfaces occasionally, known as the "pyramid plan." The idea here is to recruit a number of people under you in successive levels, each of whom pays $1000 for the privilege of joining the "game." The money is divided between you and the person at the next level above you, so that by the time you have recruited 62 suckers, you have "won" $16,000. In the summer of 1980, the craze swept Southern California into a mad frenzy of pyramid-playing. Virtually every non-Christian I knew was involved in it, greedily swallowing the ridiculous promise of the promoters: "We've worked out a way for *everyone* to win!"—a plain mathematical impossibility, unless it can be proven that dollar bills can mate and reproduce as long as they are properly introduced (presumably, it helps if this is done in a house full of people with IQs set firmly at room temperature). Astonishingly, this experiment in collective greed was touted as a "business," as "free enterprise," and as an "investment." Nothing could be further from the truth. Biblical free enterprise increases the wealth of society as a whole: both the producer and the consumer are enriched by any exchange. "Investment" means *putting capital to work*. It aims at increased productivity, and thereby benefits *all*, not just the investor. *A true investment, meaning a non-fraudulent investment, in fact, cannot benefit the investor without benefitting others.* A pyramid game cannot increase wealth. It can only transfer wealth, by fraud. It is gambling, not production.

Our purpose in life is not to become wealthy, but to serve God and our neighbor. God gives us the power to get wealth, but not exclusively for our own sakes. Wealth is given for the purpose of dominion: under biblical law, wealth ultimately passes to those who are exercising dominion under God, and who are thereby increasing the earth's productivity for His glory. God's law demands that we work and produce, and promises that God will bless us for it. But, again, our gain is not for ourselves alone, but for the glory of God. Thus, we are to work for the good of others as well as for ourselves. A basic rule in economics was stated by Jesus in His Sermon on the Mount: "Therefore whatever you want others to do for you, you do for them; for this is the Law and the Prophets" (Matthew 7:12). As the Puritans observed in the Westminster Catechism, this is also the meaning of the commandment against stealing: "The eighth commandment requireth the lawful procuring and furthering of the wealth and outward estate of *ourselves and others.*"

In other words: Biblical exchange prohibits fraud and coercion in the marketplace. The Bible does not set up a so-called "just price"; rather, *the Bible establishes the conditions for a free market.* In biblical capitalism, the seller does not "rip off" the buyer. Instead, he produces something for the other's benefit, and society as a whole is enriched. (I am not speaking of innately immoral transactions, such as heroin sales.) It is often felt that the only way to make a profit is at someone else's expense. That is the principle behind pyramid games in which the "entrepreneur" gets his investors to give up their wealth for his benefit, giving nothing in return, producing nothing but poverty. It was also the basis for eighteenth-century mercantilism, as it is now the basis for modern policies of inflation, collective bargaining, and protectionism. But the amazing fact of a truly biblical free-market economy is that *everyone makes a profit!*

How can this be? The answer is in the nature of the exchange. Where a true marketplace exists—where there is no fraud or coercion—this is what happens: each party to a transaction exchanges something that is less desirable to him for something that is more desirable to him. He values the seller's goods more highly than he values his own. When you exchange money for, say, a pair of shoes, it is because you would rather have the shoes than the money. The shoes are more valuable to you than the money you give in exchange. On the other hand, the shoe salesman would rather have your money than the shoes. Thus, the result of any free exchange is that *both* parties make a profit. Neither one makes a profit at the other's expense. Both parties come away from the transaction wealthier than when they entered it, because each one now has something more valuable—to him—than he had before. The "Golden Rule," which expresses the teaching of the Old Testament Law and Prophets, sets the conditions for a free exchange of goods, by prohibiting fraud and coercion; and the consequence of free exchange is the increased wealth of society as a whole.

**MONEY** Throughout the Bible, money is spoken of as weight. The law specifically commands that financial transactions be made in terms of honest measurements of weight:
*You shall do no wrong in judgment, in measurement of weight, or capacity. You shall have just balances, just weights, a just ephah, and a just hin: I am the LORD your God, who brought you out from the land of Egypt. You shall thus observe all My statutes, and all My ordinances, and do them: I am the LORD (Leviticus 19:35-37).*

Historically and biblically, gold and silver in particular have served as money. The important thing to remember is that money is a *commodity in itself.* Gold and silver emerged as media of exchange precisely because they have always been *the most marketable goods* — in other words, they can easily be exchanged, again and again, for other commodities. Money is not a measurement of value (there can be no measure of value) or of wealth. Money does not "represent" wealth. Money is a commodity, a good, a form of wealth.

Dishonest governments have always hated this fact, because it prevents them from controlling money and society. "Hard money" is a strict limitation on a government's ability to grow beyond biblical boundaries. For this reason, governments have sought to have a monopoly as the sole suppliers and regulators of currency. This enables government to go into the counterfeiting business, whereby it can debase the currency (by mixing the honest gold or silver weight with dross) and create as much "money" as it needs. This has happened again and again in history. It is forbidden by the law (as in the passage cited above; see also Proverbs 11:1; 20:10, 23) and the prophets (Isaiah 1:22: Amos 8:5, 6; Micah 6:10-12). This is an absolute biblical prohibition against inflation, which is a dishonest increase in the supply of money. Counterfeiting is condemned by Scripture, no matter whether it is done by individuals or governments. Inflating the currency is theft, for it reduces the wealth of everyone who does not have access to the "new money."[19] Prices rise in response to the addition of new currency, and those who are last in getting the newly-created money inevitably lose.

With the rise of paper money and, later, of computers, governmental creation of money became much more sophisticated. By means of printing presses and electronic blips, inflation can speed right along, with little to impede its progress. The government spends money (stolen from taxpayers and inflation victims) on projects which are biblically forbidden; and the beneficiaries of inflation (debtors and those who receive government checks), while they complain about the effects of inflation in higher prices, nevertheless greedily consume "the leeks, and the onions, and the garlic" dispensed by the lawless largesse of an omnipotent, enslaving state. Perhaps more than any other single factor, it is the willful government policy of inflation, aided and abetted by the citizens' coveteousness, that causes poverty and unemployment.[20] In light of this, it is striking that much of Ron Sider's proposed "remedy" for poverty can only be funded by theft (through unjust taxation and/or inflation). Citizens of affluent nations, he says, should "demand that their governments pay the price" for all these marvelous programs.[21] But how do governments pay for anything? There are only two ways: taxation and inflation. Thus, Sider is really demanding that *his neighbors* "pay the price"—not voluntarily, but by being plundered. This is Robin Hood Theology with a dangerous twist: King John and the Sheriff of Nottingham backing the thieves with legal force. The state robs from the rich and gives to the poor (minus 30%, for administration).

The Bible does, of course, allow for some government taxation, but not much. Specifically, there was a "head tax" upon every male citizen over twenty years old (Exodus 30:11-16). The tax was not graduated in terms of ability to pay: everyone, rich or poor, paid 1/2 shekel of silver (that's about 1/5 ounce).

As an absolute, outside limit, any tax of ten percent or more is specifically regarded by Scripture as *tyranny*—an attempt by rulers to be like God, extracting a "tithe" (I Samuel 8:15, 17). See what I mean about limited government? There's no way such a tax could possibly support a massive power-state; and certainly the kind of omnipotent paternalism envisioned by Sider would be out of the question.

In summary: Ronald Sider, with varying degrees of accuracy, has pinpointed certain problems regarding poverty in our age. But almost without exception, his proposals for solving these problems are unbiblical to the core. It is not difficult to find Scriptural proof for the assertion that we should "do something" about the poor. But that alone does not guarantee that our solutions will be biblical in the slightest. We must follow through with the Bible's answers, in *concrete applications of biblical law.* And that is exactly what Mr. Sider consistently refuses to do. Talk about "justice" is cheap: the Pharisees did it all the time. They chattered around the periphery of biblical law, taking the smorgasbord approach of picking and choosing laws they liked; but the Lord Jesus condemned them for abandoning "the weightier provisions of the law: justice and mercy and faithfulness" (Matthew 23:23). Ronald Sider has made the same deadly error. He has forsaken the only standard of justice and mercy, the sole blueprint for a just social order. He has substituted his own outline of social justice—an outline which more closely resembles Marx's *Communist Manifesto* than it does the book of Deuteronomy. He has called for dozens of interventionist and socialist programs which Scripture specifically forbids; he seems to assume that envy is a virtue; he writes of social problems, not in terms of sin, but of class war and hatred; he opposes biblical ethical standards; he specifically teaches others to break God's commandments with regard to personal and social moral issues.

And he has done all this in the name of God.

# GOD'S LAW & THE POOR

> "SLAVERY IS AN EXAMPLE OF AN INSTITUTIONALIZED EVIL." [RONALD SIDER, *JOURNAL OF THEOLOGY FOR SOUTHERN AFRICA*, DECEMBER 1979, P. 38.]

> "YOU MAY ACQUIRE MALE AND FEMALE SLAVES FROM THE PAGAN NATIONS THAT ARE AROUND YOU." [LEVITICUS 25:44]

God's genuine concern for the poor is manifested throughout the Bible. *Cry Justice,* Ronald Sider's anthology of the Bible quotations on the subject, certainly bears out this point well (although I can't say much for Sider's annotations). Indeed, God's word has quite a lot to say about specific remedies for poverty, and much of the Old Testament law deals with the problem. As we shall see, however, Sider glosses over these clear biblical commands in favor of his own solutions — solutions which are usually opposed to biblical law. In this chapter, we will first take a look at who the poor are, and then we will examine the specific biblical laws which seek to alleviate poverty. It should be kept in mind, however, that *none* of the biblical Poor Laws is intended to be of long-term benefit to the poor: all are stop-gap measures, designed to allow some breathing-space in order to provide time for the real, long-term solutions to poverty. The Poor Laws alone will not suffice; what is needed is a *total reconstruction of our lives and society in terms of biblical law*. As we shall see in a later chapter, it is my firm contention that poverty can—and will—be almost entirely eliminated in this earth. But that will come about only as men are converted and nations discipled to the obedience of the Christian faith. The Poor Laws are crucial, and if we ignore them we will incur national judgment. But we cannot regard them as the ultimate solution. They are intended to serve only as emergency measures. The final solution will come about through strict cultural adherence to the whole of God's law.

One further fact must be noted. In general, the laws which specifically provide for the poor are not enforced by the state. This is not to suggest that these laws are unimportant. They are very important. Too often we assume that a crime is inconsequential if the state cannot punish its offenders. This is a form of state-worship. The Bible prohibits us from turning every sin into a civil crime under state jurisdiction. The civil government cannot punish criminals unless given the right to do so by Scripture. But that is not the end of the story, of course: God is Judge, in history and at the Last Day, and He brings punishment against those who violate His law. In particular, He has declared Himself to be the Defender of the poor, and He judges men and nations in terms of their obedience to the Poor Laws (see e.g., Exodus 22:21-27; Psalm 12:5; Proverbs 22:22-23).

The Bible distinguishes two groups of people in particular who may be defenseless against oppression, and who are to be especially regarded as objects of our concern.

1. *Strangers.* Biblical law assumes that a nation which is materially blessed will attract immigrants. There is no biblical justification—and hence no economic justification—for prohibiting immigration. According to popular mythology, immigrants take jobs away from American citizens. It is ironic that this belief is held by many who are often in violent opposition to

one another. In Southern California, Ku Klux Klansmen often patrol the Mexican border to aid Immigration and Naturalization Service agents in rounding up illegal aliens (occasionally, immigrants caught by our loyal defenders have been raped, beaten, and shot in the back); on the other hand, consider this report on the United Farm Workers from the *New York Times:*

*During the union's 1974-75 strike near Yuma, Arizona, which was led by Manuel Chavez (Cesar's cousin and long time top aide—D.C.), hundreds of Mexican aliens were brutally beaten by UFW representatives to keep them from crossing the border and taking the jobs of striking melon workers.* [1]

So much for solidarity.

God is firmly opposed to this activity. Not that our borders shouldn't be protected against military invaders and criminals—but mere immigration is not a crime. Virtually all the activity of the Immigration and Naturalization Service is thus in flagrant violation of the law of God. God tells us that He loves the stranger, and commands us to love him also:

*He . . . shows His love for the alien by giving him food and clothing. So show your love for the alien . . . (Deuteronomy 10:18-19).*

Note: in the Bible, *love* is always *action*. It is defined here as providing strangers with what they need in order to live. Obviously, then, it angers God if we abuse them, trouble them, or make life hard for them. They are to receive the same justice in court as native citizens: "There shall be one standard for you; it shall be for the strangers as well as the native, for I am the LORD your God" (Leviticus 24:22); "You shall have one statute, both for the alien and for the native of the land" (Numbers 9:14). Specifically, any oppression of strangers is strictly forbidden, and brings on divine judgment (Exodus 22:21-24).

This does not mean the abolition of all distinctions, however. It does not constitute a legal mandate for integration. Indeed, Israelites were permitted to sell diseased meat to strangers, since pagan cultures generally have no objection to eating it (Deuteronomy 14:21). In addition, full citizenship in Israel was denied to certain ethnic groups for three and sometimes ten generations (Deuteronomy 23:3, 7-8). But while the Bible maintains a realistic appraisal of the often heathen backgrounds of immigrants, it nevertheless commands justice, fair treatment, and positive concern for their welfare. (For the advantages of population growth, including immigration, see Chapter 7.)

God blesses nations for obedience. If we practice kindness and justice towards strangers, we are promised national blessing (Jeremiah 7:3-7); on the other hand, if we disregard this law, we are warned that we will become immigrants ourselves (Jeremiah 22:3-5). The land of Judah refused to heed Jeremiah's warnings about this, and the curses of the law were fulfilled in their national captivity. After their return, Zechariah reminded them of this fact, and exhorted them again: "Dispense true justice, and practice kindness and compassion each to his brother; and do not oppress . . . the stranger . . ." (Zechariah 7:9-14).

The prophet Ezekiel, as he looked forward to the flowering of Christian culture through universal obedience to biblical law, spoke of the complete assimilation of strangers into the covenant — an assimilation which would come about, not through positive legal enforcement of external integration, but through a common adherence to the true faith. The evangelical witness to strangers by observing God's justice toward them will result in their conversion and discipleship. While it is couched in the symbolism of prophetic language, it is no less clear that the inclusion of strangers in the covenant will result from obedience to God's word:

*So you shall divide this land among yourselves according to the tribes of Israel. And it will come about that you shall divide it by lot for an inheritance among yourselves* and among the aliens who stay in your midst, *who bring forth sons in your midst. And* they shall be to you as the native-born *among the sons of Israel;* they shall be alotted an inheritance with you *among the tribes of Israel. (Ezekiel 47:21-22)*

2. *Widows and Orphans.* These are often mentioned in connection with strangers, as those who must be especially protected against oppression.

*You shall not afflict any widow or orphan. If you afflict him at all, and if he does cry out to Me, I will surely hear his cry; and My anger will be kindled, and I will kill you with the sword; and your wives shall become widows, and your children fatherless. (Exodus 22:22-24)*

*Cursed is he who distorts the justice due an alien, orphan, and widow. And all the people shall say, "Amen." (Deuteronomy 27:19)*

More than this, *we are commanded to be positively involved in the lives of these people:* "Seek justice, reprove the ruthless, defend the orphan, plead for the widow" (Isaiah 1:17). This is, in fact, the essence of Christian living: "This is pure and undefiled religion in the sight of our God and Father, to visit orphans and widows in their distress, and to keep oneself unstained by the world" (James 1:27). The church has a special responsibility in this regard. Paul exhorted Timothy to "honor widows" (I Timothy 5:3). The Greek word translated "honor" is often used in Scripture to indicate *payment,* and it obviously has that meaning here in I Timothy 5 (in fact, Jesus clearly used the term in this way when he commanded that children should provide their aged parents with financial support: Matthew 15:4-6). There is, however, a limitation on the church's responsibility to aid widows: regular support must be given only to those widows "who are widows indeed," who are without a family, too old to remarry, and thus unable to receive support from relatives (I Timothy 5:3-16). The *family* bears the major responsibility for financial (and other) aid, and no other institution or group must usurp this responsibility. "If anyone does not provide for his own, and especially for those of his own household, *he has denied the faith,* and is worse than an unbeliever" (I Timothy 5:8). These are strong words, and we must take them with utmost seriousness. When we are too quick to call for aid to the unfortunate from some non-family agency, we undercut the responsibility of families to care for their own. We all have a tendency to abandon our responsibilities if some agency is there to assume them for us. The basic social institution is the family. Family members are best equipped to deal with needy relatives, in terms of personal care and attention. They are more aware of the real wants of the person, and, because they are close to the situation, are most able to detect abuses of charity. God wants to build responsible relationships within families, and the church's responsibility in caring for needy members grows out of the fact that it is our larger family, "the household of God." But any appeal to the larger family must be only as a last resort.

Even then, *charity is restricted.* A widow is to be placed on the list for aid only if she herself is engaged in charitable service, "having a reputation for good works; and if she has brought up children, if she has shown hospitality to strangers, if she has washed the saints' feet, if she has assisted those in distress, and if she has devoted herself to every good work" (I Timothy 5:10). Biblical charity, as we shall see again and again, *never subsidizes irresponsibility.* A crucial principle of biblical law is that "if anyone will not work, neither let him eat" (II Thessalonians 3:10). The further away we get from familial charity, the more likely it is that this principle will be abused. State welfare fraud is so universal as to be practically axiomatic; but it is virtually impossible to engage in long-term deception of one's family.

Biblical law is geared toward responsible action on the part of individuals and families. National greatness does not come about through legislation or governmental coercion. Ronald Sider's call for a "guaranteed national income"[2] is geared only toward national irresponsibility. It is based on the ethic that I have a right to as much money as I can vote out of my neighbor's pocket. In short, "thou shalt not steal, except by majority vote." Moreover, it will only enslave us to the state, as Auberon Herbert pointed out a century ago:

*So long as great government departments . . . supply our wants, so long shall we remain in our present condition, the difficulties of life unconquered, and ourselves unfitted to conquer them. No amount of state education will make a really intelligent nation; no amount of Poor Laws will place a nation above want; no amount of Factory Acts will make us better parents. These great wants which we are now vainly trying to deal with by acts of Parliament, by prohibitions and penalties, are in truth the great occasions of progress, if only we surmount them by developing in ourselves more active desires, by putting forth greater efforts, by calling new moral forces into existence, and by perfecting our natural ability for acting together in voluntary associations. To have our wants supplied from without by a huge state machinery, to be regulated and inspected by great armies of officials, who are themselves slaves of the system which they administer, will in the long run teach us nothing, will profit us nothing.*[3]

*It is a mistake to suppose that government effort and individual effort can live side by side. The habits of mind which belong to each one are so different that one must destroy the other. . . . Men will not do things for themselves or for others if they once believe that such things can come without exertion on their own part. There is not sufficient motive. As long as the hope endures that the shoulders of some second person are available, who will offer his own shoulders for the burden? It must also be remembered that unless men are left to their own resources they do not know what is or is not possible for them. If government half a century ago had provided us all with dinners and breakfasts, it would be the practice of our orators today to assume the impossibility of our providing for ourselves.*[4]

Thus, as we examine the biblical Poor Laws, we must constantly remind ourselves of this central fact: *The Bible commands responsibility.* Apart from individual and familial responsibility, these laws indeed will not work. Basic to social change and reconstruction must be regeneration by the Holy Spirit through the propagation of the gospel, in order that men and women newly created in God's image will begin to assume their responsibilities under God. With this in mind, we may turn our attention to the Poor Laws of the Bible.

**TITHES** We must begin our analysis of the biblical Poor Laws with a consideration of tithing, since this is a basic duty of the Covenant. It is commonly held that we are no longer under any obligation to tithe in this "dispensation." There is not a shred of evidence to support such a position: the law of the tithe has never been revoked. And, it should be noted, while the modern abandonment of tithing has a superficial appearance of freedom, it has actually been replaced with a tyrannical legalism. Listen to any radio or television preacher—or perhaps your own pastor—appealing for funds. If he rejects the tithe, what is the basis for his plea? *LOVE.* He does not, of course, define love as the Bible defines it—keeping God's commandments (Romans 13:10; I John 5:3)—but rather according to the perceived "needs" of his own ministry. God's simple requirement is that we give ten percent of our income; once we have paid His tax, we know that no more is demanded. The modern preacher, on the other hand, defines your love for God in terms of how much you give. ("How much do you love God? Only ten percent? Only twenty? Only thirty? Shame on you! You should love God lots more than that! If you really, completely love Him, you'll sign over your next paycheck to me and drop it in the plate. And don't worry about taking care of your family. How selfish of you. God will take care of them. After all, He's taking care of *me*, isn't He?")

Ronald Sider's approach is not really much different. His scheme for a "graduated tithe" (which he claims is only a "modest beginning" for whatever it is he really has in mind) is based, *not* on Scripture, but on the Club of Rome's fallacy-ridden publication entitled *Limits to Growth.* Where God requires ten percent of our income, Sider demands that *all* income above $14,850 (figured for a family of five) be given away.[5] Now, Sider may object to this charge, claiming that he isn't *demanding* anything. But it's difficult to read it any other way. Perhaps he is, after all, only hinting. But it's a pretty strong hint, spiked heavily with guilt-manipulation. The relationship of antinomianism and legalism is very close indeed. Those who discard God's law wind up replacing it with commands that are truly despotic.

But while God's laws are not burdensome (I John 5:3), they are *laws* nevertheless. Tithing is an inescapable requirement, and churches should strictly enforce it. We do not need to engage in a lengthy exposition of the tithing laws here, but three important aspects should be outlined.

First, the biblical tithe was brought to a central location for a yearly national festival (Deuteronomy 12:10-28; 14:22-27), to be spent on "oxen, or sheep, or wine, or strong drink, or whatever your heart desires; and there you shall eat in the presence of the LORD your God, and rejoice, you and your household" (Deuteronomy 14:26). God wants His people to rejoice, to glorify Him by enjoying the good gifts of life which He provides. Nowhere is there the implication that the exuberance of the people was to be lessened by the ravings of guilt-manipulators pointing out that heathen cultures were suffering from malnutrition. *God showers economic blessings on His people, and they are to receive them with gratitude and jubilation.* Moreover, they were encouraged to purchase wine and strong drink (Scripture forbids drunkenness, but not drinking). Ronald Sider, in sharp contrast, tells us that the production of alcoholic beverages is a "flagrant abuse of grain."[6] God did not regard it as abuse, and neither should His people. One of the specific purposes for which God created vegetation was the production of "wine which makes man's heart glad" (Psalms 104:14-15). In this law, God very definitely commanded that a portion of our tithe be given for the purpose of delighting and revelling in the gifts He provides us. Other cultures in the days of ancient Israel suffered famine and starvation, as they do today. But that had no bearing on the fact that God commanded Israel to celebrate its own bounty.

How can this aspect of the tithe be applied today? Since the resurrection of Christ, there is no longer any national or centralized feast in which we are to participate; in the New Covenant, the gospel has been dispersed throught the whole world. There is, however, a *local feast* that is required: the love-feast, a weekly celebration in which food is to be shared at the Lord's Table (I Corinthians 11:20-34; Jude 12). It is completely within the scope of the law to use the first part of our weekly tithe to finance our participation in the love-feast, remembering also to provide food for the poor in the congregation, that all may feast together (Deuteronomy 14:29; I Corinthians 11:21-22, 33).[7]

A second aspect of the biblical tithe was that the portion left over after the feast (the bulk of the tithe) was to be given to the national Levites, the special officers of the Old Covenant congregation, who functioned as theologians, advisors to the state in legal matters, professional musicians for the worship services, and instructors in God's law (Numbers 18:24). The tithe thus financed Christian reconstruction of the whole society by providing for the social centrality of God's word, proclaimed as the basis for every area of life. The job of the Levites was to bring God's word to bear upon all the issues facing the culture, making sure that the people were always conscious of their covenantal duties. They led the people in worship through teaching, administering the sacraments, and instructing the people in singing and dancing to the Lord. The faithful proclamation of Scripture and the right worship of God are foundational elements of Christian culture: everything else flows from them. The tithe (after the love-feast) is thus to be used in financing the work of professional theologians, experts in biblical law, teachers of God's word, and skilled leaders in worship.

A third and very important aspect of the tithe law was the third-year tithe. The people of the Bible lived in seven-year cycles, and in the third year of each cycle the remainder of the tithe (after the feast) was to be brought back home (i.e., not left with the national Levites) and deposited in the "gates" of the individual's local town (Deuteronomy 14:28-29). This meant that the tithe went to *the elders of the gate*, since the gate was the place where the elders sat in judgment (cf. Deuteronomy 22:15; 25:7). The local elders of the covenant community supervised the administration of the third-year tithe, dispensing it among the local Levites and the needy aliens, orphans and widows residing in the town. In the New Covenant there is no longer a central sanctuary; thus *the third-year tithe is to be the regular pattern of our tithing today*. Normally, the tithe should be paid to the elders of our local church (I Corinthians 16:2), and the elders are responsible for administering it in the direction of Levitical activities and for charitable purposes. If, however, a church is not fulfilling its mandate to proclaim God's

GOD'S LAW AND THE POOR

word as law for society, the tithe should be withheld from it and given instead to institutions which more fully conform to Levitical standards. We must not rob God by tithing to apostates. Thus, for example, a man brought his offerings to the prophet Elisha during a time of national apostasy, when the prophets formed a remnant church (II Kings 4:42-44). As faithful Christians, we are responsible for the godly disposition of our tithes.

The local administration of charity is crucial. It ensures that funds go to those who are truly needy, rather than to professional paupers. The charitable aspects of the tithe did not mean simply a handout to everyone who lined up. Charity is to be dispensed by responsible leaders of the covenant community who are in daily contact with the needs of the people. The general principle still holds: those who won't work don't eat. Those who attempt to live by a welfare ethic are quickly exposed in a locally-administered program, and will be unable to get away with "mooching." Even in charity, God's law teaches responsibility. This is in stark contrast to the governmentally-financed "charity" promoted by Ronald Sider. Murray Rothbard observes:

*State poor relief is clearly a subsidization of poverty, for men are now automatically entitled to money from the state because of their poverty. Hence, the marginal disutility of income foregone from leisure diminishes, and idleness and poverty tend to increase further, which in turn increases the amount of subsidy that must be extracted from the taxpayers. Thus, a system of legally subsidized poverty tends to call forth more of the very poverty that is supposedly being alleviated.* [8]

Rothbard notes further: "Private charity to the poor, on the other hand, would not have the same vicious-circle effect, since the poor would not have a continuing compulsory claim on the rich. This is particularly true where private charity is given only to the 'deserving' poor."[9] And that is exactly the case with the biblical Poor Laws. They are not enforced by the state, nor does the state collect or dispense the tithes. The individual is expected to obey God's word, and he is responsible to administer the tithes in a conscientious, faithful manner. Biblical law aids the poor, yet makes it economically desirable for them to work their way out of poverty. This fact is even more obvious in the following section.

**GLEANING**   The primary source of regular charity to the poor was the practice of gleaning, in which farmers were required to let the poor gather the fruit that remained after the harvest (Leviticus 19:9-10; 23:22; Deuteronomy 24:19-21). The farmer was prohibited from completely harvesting his crops: he had to leave the corners of his field untouched, and the fruit which was left on the trees after they were beaten or shaken had to remain there. The poor were then allowed to pick the fields clean. Related to this was the law of the sabbatical year, when the land received its rest; no real harvesting was allowed, but the poor were allowed to glean whatever fruit was there (Exodus 23:10-11). A similar law, not dealing with poverty as such, allowed anyone entering a neighbor's field to pick grapes or grain and eat his fill, as long as he did not carry any food away from the premises (Deuteronomy 23:24-25; see Matthew 12:1).

Two points are of special importance here. First, *gleaning was not indiscriminate.* Landowners apparently had the right to specify which of the "deserving poor" could glean on their land, and special favors would be granted by the owner (Ruth 2:4-16). Gleaning was not simply a "right" which could be claimed by any poor person against the field of any landowner. In no sense was property held in common. God required landowners to allow the poor to glean, but the owner nevertheless had the right to dispose of his property as he saw fit, within the boundaries of the law. The gleaning law cannot be used as a basis for social redistribution of wealth.

Second, *gleaning was hard work*—much harder than normal harvesting. Gleaners had to labor arduously in order to gather sufficient food. Only a little would be left after the reapers were finished: a small cluster of grapes here, a sheaf of grain there. Israel was no Welfare State. Recipients of charity had to be diligent workers. The lazy and improvident could expect no saving intervention by a benevolent bureaucrat. God's law commands us to "bear one another's burdens" (Galatians 6:2), but not in such a way as to produce dependence on charity. The result of charitable activity should be responsibility, so that eventually "each one shall bear his own load" (Galatians 6:5).

**LENDING** A third remedy for poverty was that the poor man could take out a loan. While there is no biblical evidence that it was forbidden to charge interest on a *business* loan to a fellow believer (Matthew 25:27), loans to a believer for *charitable* purposes had to be interest-free (Exodus 22:25; Leviticus 25:35-37). Moreover, any loan to a believer had to be wiped out in the seventh year.

*At the end of every seven years you shall grant a remission of debts. And this is the manner of remission: every creditor shall release what he has loaned to his neighbor; he shall not exact it of his neighbor and his brother, because the LORD'S remission has been proclaimed (Deuteronomy 15:1-2).*

Thus, no believer could be charged with debt for longer than six years. Wealthy Israelites were strictly commanded not to withhold charity loans to believers on the grounds that the sabbatical year was close at hand:

*You shall not harden your heart, nor close your hand from your poor brothers; but you shall freely open your hand to him, and shall generously lend him sufficient for his need in whatever he lacks. . . . You shall generously give to him, and your heart shall not be grieved when you give to him, because for this thing the LORD your God will bless you in all your work and in all your undertakings (Deuteronomy 15:7-10).*

If the poor man was unable to repay the loan within the specified time, the creditor was to cross the debt off his books altogether, accepting the loss, strong in the faith that, since all events move in terms of God's law, he would receive God's blessings—not merely the warm feeling that "virtue is its own reward," but material, economic blessings.

A zero-interest loan which would automatically be dropped without charge at the end of six years (at most) looks tempting, and might appear to be rather one-sided, costing the poor man nothing. Such was not the case. While this was truly a charitable law, it did not breed irresponsibility. That, in the long run, would not be "charity" at all. To qualify for a charity loan, the recipient had to be genuinely poor, with only a cloak (Exodus 22:26-27). I cannot qualify for a charity loan if I have resources of my own to fall back on. The wealthy were not required to give interest-free loans to those who were not really destitute. The Poor Laws of the Bible did not subsidize irresponsible greed. My brother has no obligation to lend freely to me if I "need" a new stereo, television, or even a refrigerator. These loans were geared to help those who were actually in want, with nowhere else to turn. Needless to say, there are many living even below the "poverty level" who would not be eligible for this loan.

The cloak of the poor man was to be used as collateral. It was taken from him every morning, but returned to him at night so he could be warm (Exodus 22:26-27). This was to prevent him from using the same collateral for more than one loan, while recognizing his need for a covering during the cold nights. Multiple indebtedness was forbidden. And even though the poor man was able to have his cloak returned each evening, he would be without its comfort during the daytime. This gave him incentive to repay the loan as soon as possible. The law, while helpful to those in desperate straits, still militated against irresponsibility. It was not easy to get a charity loan; and it wasn't easy to live with it, either.

The case of the unbeliever (many strangers would fit into this category) was even more difficult. For him, there was no release in the sabbatical year, or the year of Jubilee (Deuteronomy 15:3; Leviticus 25:44-46). He could be charged interest as well, regardless of his poverty—and there was *no limit* on the interest rate (Deuteronomy 23:20). Because unbelievers are by nature irresponsible, they need the incentive of increasing debt to get them to repay loans. Again, the laws are not indiscriminate. They do, in fact, discriminate against the irresponsible poor, and press home the fact that poverty is a liability. Poverty is never allowed to be used as a lever against those who are better off. The only ones who benefit from the poor laws are those who are willing to work diligently for the future. Eventually, those who merely desire to plunder or sponge off the rich will bite the dust. God's laws are intended to further His kingdom. They cannot be used successfully in oppositon to Him.

**SLAVERY** The Bible permits slavery. This statement will come as a shock to most people. The laws in the Bible concerning slavery have very seldom been studied, much less preached upon. But the biblical laws concerning slavery are among the most beneficent in all the Bible. The biblical institution of slavery has as its basic purpose the elimination of poverty and its foremost cause, the *slave mentality*. Ron Sider constantly connects slavery with oppression, and seems to think the two are identical. "Slavery is an example of an institutionalized evil," he tells us;[10] and he speaks of "the sin of participating in slavery."[11] Many people, when they think of "slavery," think of the pre-Civil War South, where certain aspects of slavery were in violation of biblical law. Thus many know only of an abused, unbiblical form of slavery. But since the Bible allows for slavery, it is clearly unbiblical to speak of slavery as being wrong or sinful. (Even Southern slavery was not as unbiblical as many have charged. The common conception of the slavery of that age is quite distorted; the Abolitionists were often as guilty of transgressing God's laws as were slave-holders, as we shall see in our next chapter.) If slavery were a sin, God would not have provided for it. Indeed, since *God* is the Standard of right and wrong, the fact that He gives rules for the proper management of slavery shows that to *disregard* the laws of slavery is a sin. For example, since fornication is a sin, God does not give directions for the right management of a brothel. Nor does he offer instructions about successful methods of murder or theft. Slavery is not a sin, but the violation of God's slavery laws is.

To understand God's slavery laws, we must understand a basic biblical fact: *slavery is inescapable*—no culture is without it. Apart from God's grace, all men are enslaved to sin. Salvation liberates us from slavery to sin and makes us slaves of righteousness, obedient to God's word rather than to Satan's (Romans 6:16-22). I am not playing with words here, for this point is central to social and cultural issues. If men are not slaves of God, they are already enslaved to sin. As sinners, they abandon their duty of dominion over the creation, with the result that they become slaves of other men, worshipping and serving the creature rather than the Creator (Romans 1:25). The issues of life flow from the heart (Proverbs 4:23), and a man's relationship to God, or lack thereof, has immediate and long-lasting consequences in every area. Every culture that has not served the true God has eventually become enslaved to the state.[12] Ron Sider's thesis will not "liberate" anyone in this regard: his solution to the problem of poverty is merely a plea for increased slavery to the state through radical government intervention in all of life.

Since slavery will always exist, the biblical answer is not to try to abolish it, but to follow God's laws for slavery.[13] While many of these laws may seem harsh, we must recognize that, first, these laws are remedies for irresponsibility, and seek to drive men out of slavery; and second, the laws of God are not nearly so harsh as the laws of men. While God's law produces a responsible, stable social order, man's slavery laws are chaotic, oppressive and tyrannical. The biblical worldview is not a fairy-tale, or romantic perfectionism, but a realistic appraisal of men with their sins and shortcomings. God's word meets us where we are in our slavery, and shows us the way toward responsible dominion under God.

1. *Obtaining slaves.* Kidnapping is forbidden as a method of acquiring slaves, and deserves capital punishment (Exodus 21:16). Basically, there are only four legal ways to get slaves. They may be purchased (Leviticus 25:44-46), captured in war (Numbers 31:32-35; Deuteronomy 21:10-14), enslaved as punishment for theft (Exodus 22:1-3), or enslaved to pay off debts (Leviticus

25:39; Exodus 21:7). We should especially note God's merciful justice here. Heathen slaves who were purchased or captured in war were actually favored by this law, since it placed them in contact with believers. They received the relatively lenient treatment of the biblical slavery regulations, and they were also able to hear the liberating message of the gospel. Slaves making restitution for theft or debt were also benefitted by this law. The Bible does not allow imprisonment (except for a man held for trial or execution). The thief was not caged up at taxpayers' expense and treated like an animal; he labored productively, in an evangelical family context, and made proper restitution to the victim for his crime. He earned back his self-respect, and restored what he owed to his victim. (If those who so fervently desire "social justice" wouldn't mind a suggestion, here's one: Work to implement "structural change" in our criminal and penal codes, and bring back restitution. Whoops—that would mean slavery! Oh, well. Better to keep the status quo, and let the victims of theft live with their losses while supporting their attackers in tax-financed penitentiaries. Better to pen up the criminal with murderers and homosexuals in an "impersonal" environment than to have him work in a godly home.)

2. *The care of slaves.* Slaves have no economic incentive to work, since they cannot improve their situation regardless of how hard they labor. Therefore the master is allowed to provide that incentive by beating them (Exodus 21:20-27). Obviously, the slave is not regarded as having equal rights as a free man. But this very fact would keep a man from entering slavery too hastily. Slavery has certain benefits (job security, etc.), but it has serious drawbacks as well. Slavery was not allowed to become irresponsible welfare or paternalism. The law limited the master, however. If he murdered his slave, he was executed (Exodus 21:20). On the other hand, if the slave survived a beating and died a day or two later, there was no punishment (Exodus 21:21); there was no evidence that the master had actually intended to murder him. Again, this risk was a serious incentive against enslaving oneself.

God did not want men to heedlessly abandon their freedom, and this law would tend to keep men working hard and living responsibly in order to avoid the threat of losing their liberty and civil rights. Relatively minor but permanent injuries (such as the loss of an eye or a tooth) resulted in the slave's freedom (Exodus 21:26-27). This was also an economic incentive to keep the master from hitting the slave in the face, since a heavy blow could mean the loss of his "investment." Naturally, this law protected slaves from severe mutilation.

3. *Freedom for slaves*. Free Hebrews who had been reduced to slavery were freed in the seventh year (Deuteronomy 15:1-2), or at the latest in the Jubilee year (Leviticus 25:40-41), depending on the severity of the situation. (Slaves who escaped from ungodly cultures were not returned to their masters, but were set free instead; Deuteronomy 23:15-16). A slave also had the right to save up enough money to purchase his own freedom (Leviticus 25:49) —a fact which indicates two things: first, the slavery laws, in common with the other Poor Laws, provided for "upward mobility"; and second, private property rights were protected at all levels of society, so that even slaves were able to acquire and dispose of property. Freed slaves were liberally furnished with gifts: from the master's flock, threshing floor, and wine cellar (Deuteronomy 15:14). The freed slave was thus enabled to make a living for himself, be fed, and rejoice in his freedom. God's law is strict, but merciful. A freed slave can get back on his feet and resume a productive place in society. To repeat the basic lesson: *God's law encourages responsibility*. It provides many incentives against men enslaving themselves, and when men do become slaves, they are protected but not coddled. When the period of slavery is over, they are able to hold their heads up with other men, possessing the tools with which to start over without debt.

For the heathen slave, however, the situation was different. Although he was protected by the same slavery laws, he was *never* freed (unless he redeemed himself)—not even in the Jubilee, which freed only Hebrew slaves (Leviticus 25:40-46). Unbelievers are slaves by nature, and there is no reason to free them as long as they remain in their spiritual bondage. The enslaved foreigner who was converted would, of course, demonstrate his spiritual freedom by responsibly saving and purchasing his own freedom. Does this appear harsh? It is, certainly, a very different view of slavery than that held by Ronald Sider. But let us be sure that our standards in ethics really come from the Bible. If the slavery laws seem unjust to us, it is because *we* are wrong. God's law is the perfect transcript of His justice. Any protest against God's laws is a moral indictment of God, in the same class with the original sin in the Garden. By substituting our laws for God's, we produce only injustice and increasing slavery. James B. Jordan comments:

*The problem in the Old South came about because converted slaves were not freed, and thus no mechanism was instituted whereby men might rise to freedom. As we have seen, the purpose of the enslavement of unbelievers is evangelism, and the purpose of the enslavement of believers is to train them to be responsible free citizens. Thus, there is an upward thrust to the Biblical laws concerning slavery. It is the goal of slavery to eliminate itself by producing responsible free men. Where that upward rise is cut off by Statist legislation, as it was in the Old South under both slavery and paternalism, God is offended.* [14]

Now contrast the biblical form of slavery with some of Ronald Sider's proposals. He declares himself to be against slavery (since it's a "sin"), but life in his statist paradise is a form of slavery that is truly oppressive, and outlawed by God's word. The Bible warns us against slavery to the state, and biblical law works to prevent it (see, e.g., I Samuel 8). State-provided welfare causes dependence on the state, and is surely slavery. It is used by greedy politicians to buy votes and to create a class that is beholden to the rulers. Where we become used to benefits, we lose our reliance upon God, neighbors, family, and self, and we increasingly are unable to act responsibly. Already, it is common to find people (even Christians!) who simply cannot conceive of certain tasks being performed without state aid. It is a marvel to them that people have ever had housing, education, health care, jobs, transportation, postal service, food, and money apart from state monopolization. And *this is slavery*, as Auberon Herbert argued:

*Treat the people as unworthy of trust, and they will justify your expectation. Tell them that you do not expect them to possess a sense of responsibility, to think or act for themselves, withhold from them the most natural and the most important opportunities for such things, and in due time they will passively accept the mental and moral condition you have made for them. . . . Each man unconsciously reasons, "Why should I do that which the state will do for me?"*[15]

Sider believes that the wealthy have unjust power, that they usually become wealthy by oppressing the poor.[16] (The validity of this notion will be examined later.) He thus seeks to break this economic power through granting more power to the state. Are those greedy, laissez-faire capitalists charging "too much" for their products? Are those "bourgeois running dogs" paying the noble worker an "unfair" wage? Let's bring in some heavy-handed government clout to take care of the problem. What we need is an omnipotent state that will enforce price and wage controls on corrupt businessmen. (Never mind that such controls inevitably result in shortages and unemployment. Why, that's a doctrine of the deist, Adam Smith. His law of supply and demand has been repealed. Lord Keynes has revolutionized us, ridding us once and for all of Enlightenment philosophies and secular economic theories.[17]) Of course, various societies for at least the last 4000 years have attempted such measures before. Some men who implemented price and wage controls are, in fact, quite justly famous for their actions. One government leader of a generation ago will be long remembered. For a time, he was able to stabilize prices, wages and employment at a level that modern bureaucrats can only dream of. He was so successful that even if you aren't a history student you may recall his name: Adolf Hitler.

The point is that economic controls require an omnipotent, enslaving state to enforce them. If you aren't willing to have totalitarianism, the controls won't work. Price and wage management is impossible without complete oversight of every sector of society. Halfway measures will not suffice. Herman Goering, Hitler's economic planner, admitted this to an American correspondent in 1946, when he was a prisoner of war. Speaking of American economic programs which were similar to some of his own past endeavors, he offered this revealing comment: "You are trying to control people's wages and prices—people's work. If you do that *you must control people's lives. And no country can do that part way.*"[18] That was the thrust of Hilaire Belloc's mocking advice to those who desired "gradual socialism." It cannot be done, he said; it cannot come about without violent expropriation. The basic rule is this: "*If you desire to confiscate, you must confiscate.*"[19]

Ronald Sider claims to be working for liberation and equality for the oppressed. He declares that slavery is wrong, and appears to damn it with every breath. Yet his concrete proposals for reform look quite the opposite under the searchlight of biblical law. I am willing to grant him some measure of sincerity—*some*; but whether or not he is aware of what he is really doing, the effect of his proposals would be a totalitarian, oppressive regime the likes of which Hitler was never able to achieve. It would make the state nothing less than God. And when man plays god, the result is always bondage. During the Second World War, F. A. Hayek published a stirring warning to the people of England, who were blindly pursuing the policies which had brought the Nazis to power in Germany. He wrote:

*The "substitution of political for economic power" now so often demanded means necessarily the substitution of power from which there is no escape for a power which is always limited. What is called economic power, while it can be an instrument of coercion, is, in the hands of private individuals, never exclusive or complete power, never power over the whole life of a person. But centralized as an instrument of political power it creates a degree of dependence scarcely distinguishable from slavery.*[20]

**THE JUBILEE**  With everything Ronald Sider has said about the "Jubilee Principle," it might be expected that an extended discussion of the subject would naturally fall under the heading of the biblical Poor Laws. However, it will not be examined in this chapter, for two reasons.

First, Sider refers to the Jubilee so often, and draws so many fallacious conclusions from it, that it really requires separate treatment in another chapter.

But there is a much more important reason for excluding it from the present chapter. Shocking as it may seem, *the law of the Jubilee was not a Poor Law.* That is, its primary intent and function had nothing to do with the alleviation of poverty as such. Certainly, it did affect the status of certain poor people. But that was only incidental to its true purpose. In fact—in contrast to the Poor Tithe and the laws on gleaning, lending, and slavery—most of the poor may not have been affected by the observance of the Jubilee at all. Honesty to the biblical evidence prohibits us from dealing with it as a Poor Law.

In concluding this chapter, a brief anecdote may illustrate a fundamental principle for which I am contending. I once heard a well-known college professor debate Dr. Gary North on the subject of "Care for the Poor." He took a position similar to Sider's, and, since he was speaking to a seminary audience, his lecture appropriately had three points. *First*, he said, *the individual* has a duty to the poor. With an open Bible before him, he admirably defended this from Scripture. *Second*, he observed, *the church* has a duty to the poor; again he quoted copiously from Holy Writ. *Third*, he declared, *the state* has a duty to the poor. He then picked up the Bible, closed it, and put it aside.

# 3 THE EXODUS AS A LIBERATION MOVEMENT

**"GOD DISPLAYED HIS POWER AT THE EXODUS ... TO FREE A POOR OPPRESSED PEOPLE." [RONALD SIDER, *THE CHRISTIAN CENTURY*, MARCH 19, 1980, P. 315]**

**"HE BROUGHT FORTH *HIS* PEOPLE WITH JOY, *HIS* CHOSEN ONES WITH A JOYFUL SHOUT." [PSALM 105:43]**

As we have seen, Ronald Sider regards slavery as always a sin. In terms of this, he naturally feels that all slaves should always be liberated. A recurring theme in his writings is that the biblical account of the Exodus of Israel provides a divinely inspired precedent for liberating the oppressed peoples of the world through political action. In other words, at "pivotal points of revelation history," God worked to free slaves. Since this indicates God's concern for the oppressed of the world, we too should work for their liberation from unjust economic and social structures, etc., etc.

It is crucial to examine carefully Sider's principle of interpretation here. Summing up the Exodus account, he says that God "acted to free a poor, oppressed people . . . he acted to end economic oppression and bring freedom to slaves. . . . The liberation of a poor, oppressed people was right at the heart of God's design."[1]

But this is a serious misreading of the biblical record. Consider how God described what He was doing:

*And the LORD said, "I have surely seen the affliction of My people who are in Egypt, and have given heed to their cry because of their taskmasters, for I am aware of their sufferings. So I have come down to deliver them from the power of the Egyptians, and to bring them up from that land to a good and spacious land, to a land flowing with milk and honey . . ." (Exodus 3:7-8).*

What's the difference? Isn't God saying the same thing Sider says? Not at all. God saw the affliction of *His* people, not just "*a* people," as Sider rephrases it. God was not liberating slaves in the abstract; He was not simply bringing freedom to slaves in general. He was taking His people to the land which He had promised their fathers. As Moses pointed out to the Israelites, the Exodus occurred "because the LORD loved you and kept the oath which he swore to your forefathers." Israel was "a holy [i.e., *separate, distinct*] people to the LORD . . . a people for His own possession out of all the peoples who are on the face of the earth"; and for this reason they were redeemed (Deuteronomy 7:6-8). Israel was unique. God's redemption of them cannot be classified with liberation movements in general. They were His people, who cried out to *Him*. The Exodus was not a freeing of slaves in the abstract, but a special, redemptive, covenantal event in fulfillment of God's oath to Abraham, Isaac, and Jacob. It cannot be generalized. It is not an umbrella which we can place over every revolutionary "liberation movement" which may exist anywhere in the world. Of course, there is the principle here that God will bring socioeconomic freedom to His people who call upon His name: as we have seen, spiritual liberty in Christ flows out into every area of life. But we cannot use the Exodus as a precedent for supporting so-called liberation movements in general.

To illustrate, let us apply Sider's principle of abstract,

generalized interpretation to other aspects of the Exodus. "When God freed Israel, He struck dead the firstborn sons of all the Egyptians (Exodus 12:29-30). Thus, we can say that, at this pivotal point in revelation history, God showed that He was working to slay firstborn children. Let us work to implement this principle in our modern, ungodly society which idolizes its offspring."

Or: "When God liberated His people, bringing them into a land occupied by various heathen cultures, He commanded them to kill every man, woman, and child in the cities (Deuteronomy 20:16-18). Surely, this reflects a central, fervent concern of our Lord. The annihilation of unbelievers is right at the heart of His design in history. We should organize a society—Evangelicals for Genocidal Action—which would begin immediately to study, pray, and gather munitions. Start in your own community: simply surround an unbelieving neighbor's property, blast him and his children into eternity, and occupy his house as a concrete act of biblical commitment."

Obviously, these examples are absurd. The destruction of Egyptian firstborn and the slaughter of Canaanites were unique events which cannot be generalized. And the same is true of the Exodus. It was not simply "the liberation of oppressed slaves." It was the liberation of God's people who were in covenant with Him. Abstraction here is distortion. Ronald Sider is not exegeting Scripture, but manipulating it. The fact that he gets away with this sort of thing in "evangelical," "Bible-believing" circles indicates that we ourselves are in need of liberation—theological liberation.

An important distinction should be made here, between two words which are similar in form but radically different in content: *liberty* and *liberation*. "Liberty" has historically signified self-government and freedom from undue state control (although it has also been used by socialists and anarchists, as in the French Revolution). It speaks of a free, mature, self-reliant people, able to govern themselves under God, without intervention from government beyond its God-ordained boundaries. "Liberation," in the sense of socialist revolution, means the destruction of liberty. Sider's social reforms necessitate stern, coercive measures by an omnipotent state, controlling the lives of people at every level. Of course, this is done in the name of liberating the poor from economic injustice. But what it really means is *power*. The intellectual who agitates for statist liberation always assumes that in the Workers' Paradise *he* will be at the top of the pyramid. Provided that *he* is the dictator—that *his* property will not be "liberated" when the Revolution comes, and that *his* notions of justice will be enforced on the unjust rich—he has no reason to regard tyranny as anything but freedom. Ronald Sider, with bureaucratic omniscience, *knows* what kind of products we really "need," and generously pronounces that "it's okay to make a lot of money on that needed product."[2] But, to their everlasting shame, businessmen don't seem to listen to his suggestions. They foolishly are intent on producing what people say they *want* rather than what experts say they *need*. What is required, therefore, is Liberation. Liberation will apply Sider's good intentions by force, at the point of a policeman's gun. Just as in the Vietnam War it became "necessary to destroy the village in order to save it," society will achieve liberation through totalitarianism.

Committed as he is to liberation from slavery, Ronald Sider is not ignorant of past attempts. One movement particularly revered by him is the Abolitionist activity of the nineteenth century. He especially applauds the radicalism of the preacher Charles Finney, who founded Oberlin College as a haven for abolitionism and feminism. Jonathan Blanchard, an early student at Oberlin, went on to become Wheaton College's first president, and Sider mourns that Wheaton eventually declined from its original position as a hotbed of social activism.[3]

However, it is Sider's statements on Finney and Abolitionism which are of special interest. Writing in the *Christian Century*, he claims that "Charles Finney's evangelical abolitionists stood solidly in the biblical tradition in their search for justice for the poor and oppressed of their time."[4] Expanding on this theme, he writes elsewhere:

*Finney was the Billy Graham of the nineteenth century. He led evangelistic crusades throughout the country. The filling of the Holy Spirit was central in his life and preaching. He was also one of the leading abolitionists working to end the unjust system of slavery. Church discipline was used at his church at Oberlin College which he founded against anyone holding slaves. Finney and his students practiced civil disobedience to protest unjust laws. Over Christmas holidays, Finney's students went out by the scores to hold evangelistic meetings. And they preached against the sin of participating in slavery as well as personal sins. Recent study has shown that the abolitionist movement in many states of the mid-West U.S. grew directly out of these revival campaigns by Finney and his students.*

*I dream of that kind of movement in the church today. . . .*[5]

The abolitionist movement was, it is true, a *religious* movement. But its religion was antichristian humanism. Otto Scott, in his masterful study of the conspirators who financed John Brown's murderous exploits, shows the development of the abolitionist campaign — a description which may contain a prophecy of Sider's evangelical liberationism as well:

*The new religion had started with arguments against such relatively harmless sins as smoking and drinking, had then grown to crusades denouncing and forbidding even commerce with persons whose morals were held to be invidious; it had expanded into antislavery as the answer to every ill of humanity; and it had finally come to full flower in the belief that killing anyone — innocent or guilty — was an act of righteousness for a new morality.*[6]

American abolitionism took a very different route from that of the British, who were able to eliminate colonial slavery in a lawful, peaceful manner, without the shedding of blood. The British process was gradual, and over a period of years the slaves were apprenticed and enabled to earn their own keep, while slaveholders were compensated for their financial loss. But the abolitionists in the United States refused to acknowledge any law but their own. Although they knew that most Southerners were not slaveholders, they agitated for chaos and revolution. As John

Brown put it: "If any obstacle stands in your way, you may properly break all the Decalogue in order to get rid of it."[7]

Men have always had to choose between two methods of social change: regeneration and revolution. The Christian seeks first to discipline *himself* to God's standard. He then publishes the gospel and attempts to peacefully implement the laws of God into the life of his culture, trusting in the Spirit of God for the success of his efforts. He knows that there is not, and never will be, a perfect society in this life. He knows that the Kingdom of God spreads like leaven in bread—not by massive, disrupting explosions, but by gradual permeation. He knows that justice, righteousness and peace result from the outpouring of the Spirit in the hearts of men (Isaiah 33:15-18); a nation's legal structure is, therefore, an indicator, not a cause, of national character. Law does not save.

But the revolutionary believes that a perfect society is possible,[8] and that it must be coercively imposed on men. He seeks to overthrow everything which threatens to obstruct the coming of his made-to-order millennium. God's providence is too slow, His law too confining. Society must be perfect—tomorrow—or be blasted to rubble. As the slogan of the French Revolution put it: "Liberty, Equality, Fraternity—or Death."[9] The abolitionists, rising out of the early nineteenth-century religious turmoil, yearned for such a perfect society, and were willing to slaughter innocent people in order to achieve it. The atmosphere in which abolitionism thrived was produced by such men as the creedless Unitarian crusader, William Ellery Channing, who called for "guerrilla war . . . at every chance."[10] Channing was a major influence on young Ralph Waldo Emerson, the chief exponent of New England pantheism and transcendentalism—and a considerable warmonger as well. To many, his pacifistic nature-worship seems harmless: the very mention of *Emerson* conjures up serene visions of gurgling brooks, sparkling dew on new-fallen leaves, and Henry David Thoreau behind bars. The soporific calm is shattered as we read such lines as these, uttered by the venerable Sage of Concord: "If it costs ten years, and ten to recover the general prosperity, the destruction of the South is worth so much."[11] The benign mask dropped altogether when Emerson and Thoreau compared the terrorist John Brown, murderer of innocents, to Jesus Christ. The gallows on which he was hanged became "as glorious as the Cross."[12]

And Charles Grandison Finney, "the Billy Graham of the nineteenth century," was at the heart of the movement. Theologically, he was a Pelagian, a heretic. Bennet Tyler observed, in 1854, that "no orthodox body of Christians could receive him into their pulpit. No doubt he published works that contained rousing and startling truths; but even truth was given forth alongside of much error which counteracted all. And now he seems to be drifting no one can tell whither. . . . He adjusts whatever he finds in the Bible to his own preconceived metaphysical determinations, instead of submitting his metaphysical musings to the test of unerring wisdom."[13]

Finney, in his dedication to the cause of peace, became a member of the "National Kansas Aid Committee," and pledged his support in raising *two million dollars* to provide arms for gangs of abolitionist thugs invading Kansas.[14] The Committee financed John Brown, who claimed to have been appointed by God as His "special angel of death."[15] These radical abolitionists often claimed to be pacifists, but eventually came to applaud bloodshed as the only means of purging away the "sin" of slavery. As we have seen, there were sins associated with much of the slavery of the era. But salvation is not political, nor is Christianity revolutionary. The abolitionists were not content with the gradual, legal abolition for which many in the South longed. Their concern was not with justice, but with revolution—and to say they were unruffled by the disruption it would cause is an understatement: they hoped for destruction. They rejected the biblical position on slavery, which mandated that both slaves and slaveowners abide by God's law, and which encouraged slaves to gain freedom legally and responsibly.

Sider claims to be a pacifist, and calls for a "nonviolent revolution."[16] But so did the abolitionists. Somehow, revolutionaries find a way to sidestep this restriction, once they discover that bloodshed is quicker. In one of the "tough, weighty" questions at the back of *Cry Justice*, he asks: "Is God at work in history today pulling down unjust rulers and unjust societies? If so, how?"[17] Every time some Third World terrorist blows away a banker or a few schoolchildren? And we must not forget that Sider has already called for violence. Price controls and expropriation of lands and businesses all require guns and men who are prepared to use them. Apart from the threat of violent, coercive enforcement of the regulations, no landowner or businessman will relinquish his property. That is the dilemma of all "peaceful" revolutionaries; eventually, they pick up their bazookas and solve the problem. Sider's stated goals, his deliberate and repeated identification of himself with violent revolutionaries of the past, and the fact that his Jubilee Fund has financed modern terrorists,[18] should be enough to warn us of what lies ahead. He may personally eschew the use of arms to bring about the revolution. But bloodshed, or the threat of it, is a necessary component of statism. Wherever Sider's principles are effected, he might as well be pulling the trigger himself. In the name of "liberation" he is calling for class war. The Exodus provided the Israelites with both *liberty* and *law*. Sider's liberationist "exodus" is merely lawlessness, and leads back to slavery.

# IS GOD ON THE SIDE OF THE POOR?

**"I WANT TO ARGUE THAT ONE OF THE CENTRAL BIBLICAL DOCTRINES IS THAT GOD *IS* ON THE SIDE OF THE POOR...." [RONALD SIDER, *THE CHRISTIAN CENTURY*, MARCH 19, 1980, P. 314]**

**"GOD IS NOT ONE TO SHOW PARTIALITY, BUT IN EVERY NATION THE MAN WHO FEARS HIM AND DOES WHAT IS RIGHT, IS WELCOME TO HIM." [ACTS 10:34-35]**

Ronald Sider's answer to the question posed in this chapter is an unequivocal *Yes*. Well—not quite unequivocal. In a recent article published by *The Christian Century*, he did back away from certain extreme implications of such a stand. In fairness to Sider, we will allow him to speak for himself on what he does *not* mean by this statement.

*I do not mean that material poverty is a biblical ideal. . . . Second, I do not mean that the poor and oppressed are, because they are poor and oppressed, to be idealized or automatically included in the church. . . . Third, . . . I do not mean that God cares more about the salvation of the poor than the salvation of the rich or that the poor have a special claim to the gospel. . . . Fourth, to say that God is on the side of the poor is not to say that knowing*

*God is nothing more than seeking justice for the poor and oppressed. . . .*
*Finally, . . . I do not mean that hermeneutically we must side with some*
*ideologically interpreted context of oppression (for instance, a Marxist*
*definition of the poor and their oppressed situation) and then reinterpret*
*Scripture from that ideological perspective.* [1]

While some of Sider's disclaimers are debatable—particularly
the last point—let us accept them for now. There remain several
serious objections to what he *does* clearly mean by claiming that
God is on the side of the poor. His defense of this central thesis, in
most of his writings, is structured around three basic points. *First*,
he claims that, at "pivotal points of revelation history" (i.e. the
Exodus, the destruction of Israel and Judah, and the
Incarnation), God intervened to liberate the poor. *Second*, he says,
God is always at work in history, casting down the rich and ex-
alting the poor. *Third*, he states that God's people are on the side
of the poor. [2]

A basic objection to all this is that Sider has committed the
same fallacy of equivocation that we examined in the previous
chapter. Who are "the poor"? Who are "the rich"? Is God *always*
for the one and against the other? If we desire to be biblical, we
can no more make "the poor" an abstraction than we can make
"slaves" an abstraction. *God's law is not abstract, but specific.*

The Bible declares that God is actually *against* certain poor
people. The sluggard, who is lazy and thoughtless about the
future, has no claim on God's mercy (Proverbs 6:6-11; 13:4, 18;
19:15; 20:13; 21:25, 26; 24:30-34; 28:19). God certainly is not
"on the side" of any lawbreakers who happen to be poor. Just as
the rich often are tempted to be proud, denying God's goodness, so
the poor are tempted to covet the possessions of others and to take
God's name in vain (Proverbs 30:7-9). In fact, this is a prominent
theme in the biblical definition of God's relationship to the poor
man: God promises, "When he cries out to Me, I will hear him,
for I am gracious (Exodus 22:27). But immediately, God offers
this warning: "You shall not curse God, nor curse a ruler of your
people" (Exodus 22:28). If we are unjust to the poor, and they cry

out to God, He will hear and avenge them, and provide for their needs. But a poor man must not curse God, as if He has been unfair in His providential dealings with him; also, he must not revile those in authority over him. These are special temptations to which the poor can easily fall prey, and the poor are sternly cautioned against succumbing to them. Whenever we feel oppressed, we want to lash out at God for dealing us a bad hand. The ungodly poor will blame God for their misfortune, and they are promised nothing but judgment. Any man who blasphemes God, be he rich or poor, is to be put to death (Leviticus 24:13-16). Moreover, the ungodly poor, with their slave mentality, are apt to regard the state as their rightful savior; if the ruler does not step in to bail them out, they will curse him as well. God will not hear the prayers of those who thus defy Him and His constituted authority. Emphatically, He is *not* on their side.

Covetousness and theft are strong temptations to one who is in want. If a starving man steals food, we can understand his reasons; nevertheless, Scripture says he must make a "seven-fold" (i.e., complete) restitution (Proverbs 6:30-31). Until he does, he is still a thief—and God is not on his side, either, regardless of "mitigating circumstances." The disobedient have no claim on God's mercy or protection. "He who turns away his ear from listening to the law, even his prayer is an abomination" (Proverbs 28:9). "Better is the poor who walks in his integrity, than he who is crooked though he be rich" (Proverbs 28:6).

The message of Scripture is that God is a refuge to those who call upon Him. But if the poor man curses the Lord, and breaks His law, not trusting in Him, God has only condemnation. Socioeconomic status is no guarantee against His wrath:

> Therefore the LORD does not take pleasure in their young men,
> Nor does He have pity on their orphans or their widows;
> For every one of them is godless and an evildoer,
> And every mouth is speaking foolishness. (Isaiah 9:17)

Sider loves to quote from Luke 4:18-19, where Jesus declares:

> The Spirit of the Lord is upon Me,

*Because He anointed Me to preach the gospel to the poor.*
*He has sent Me to proclaim release to the captives,*
*And recovery of sight to the blind,*
*To set free those who are downtrodden,*
*To proclaim the favorable year of the Lord.*

Thus, Sider claims, Christ's mission "was to free the oppressed and heal the blind. . . . The poor are the only group specifically singled out as recipients of Jesus' gospel. . . . At the supreme moment of history when God took on human flesh, the God of Israel was still liberating the poor and oppressed and summoning his people to do the same."[3]　There he goes again: "the oppressed," "the blind," "the poor," as if Christ makes no distinction. Yet what Jesus says a few verses later is very important with regard to God's care for the poor. Jesus was preaching in Nazareth, His home town, where He was faced with rejection and unbelief—even, apparently, by "the poor and oppressed." Our Lord responded by leaving town, permanently: the poor of Nazareth were henceforth excluded from His ministry. Before He left, Jesus explained His actions by reminding them of Elijah and Elisha's ministry to the poor and afflicted. Although there were those in their day who had not bowed to Baal, still it was a time of rampant, vicious ungodliness. "The poor" of Israel received no help from God's prophets; instead, the prophets aided *foreigners* who had called on the name of the Lord and were obedient to His word. Our Lord's comment stung, and the people of Nazareth felt it:

*"But I say to you in truth, there were many widows in Israel in the days of Elijah, when the sky was shut up for three years and six months, when a great famine came over the land [note: God afflicted both the rich and the poor by withholding rain]; and yet Elijah was sent to none of them, but only to Zarephath, in the land of Sidon, to a woman who was a widow. And there were many lepers in Israel in the time of Elisha the prophet; and none was cleansed, but only Naaman the Syrian." And all in the synagogue were filled with rage as they heard these things; and they rose up and cast Him out of the city, and led Him to the brow of the hill on which their city*

*had been built, in order to throw Him down the cliff. (Luke 4:25-29)*

In this important statement, Jesus declares that God's concern for the poor is discriminatory. It is not just "the poor" in some abstract, general, universal sense who are the objects of God's care. Here they are on the same level with the rich: if they reject Christ, they are themselves rejected by Him. They wanted benefits, but were ready to murder Him when they discovered that He practiced discrimination in His welfare plan. There is no getting around this text. It stands in the same passage with the previous one about Christ's ministry to the poor, to guard against the false impression (perpetrated by Sider *et al.*) that He came to relieve the sufferings of "the poor," without distinction. God's mercy is neither promiscuous nor partial, in terms of economic status; but He hears those who call upon Him in truth (Psalm 145:18), and He hates all those who do iniquity (Psalm 5:4-5), regardless of the size of their paycheck. It is for this reason that the Psalmist can exult:

*The LORD also will be a stronghold for the oppressed,*
*A stronghold in times of trouble,*
*And those who know Thy name will put their trust in Thee;*
*For Thou, O LORD, hast not forsaken those who seek Thee.*
*(Psalm 9:9-10)*

God does not merely relieve the oppressed or troubled in general. He graciously relieves the sufferings of those who seek Him. The poor man who is treated unjustly and has no legal recourse in an ungodly society need not despair. If he seeks the Lord with his whole heart, he will find Him. God will arise in deliverance, breaking in pieces the oppressor, avenging injustice, and satisfying the needs of His people (Psalm 12:5; 34:6; 68:10; 72:2-14; 113:7-8; 140:12; 146:7). If the poor man commits himself to the Lord (Psalm 10:14), he will be delivered. God "will deliver the needy *when he cries for help*" (Psalm 72:12). But not before. And if the needy opts for revolution instead, God will crush him to powder.

By appealing to class-consciousness, by inciting resentment

against a state which does not dispense enough benefits, by encouraging covetousness, envy, and theft against the rich, Ronald Sider has chosen the way of revolution. This is underscored by his belief in chaos as a key to history. Implying that the rich are, *ipso facto,* oppressors, he turns revolution into an almost metaphysical principle: "God *regularly* reverses the good fortunes of the rich."[4] God is on the side of the poor; as a matter of principle, He constantly, *"over and over again"*[5] overthrows the rich and exalts the poor; and we must side with Him in the revolution. As Karl Marx phrased it, the battle cry of the revolutionaries must be: "permanent revolution!"[6] Anarchist Leo Tolstoy agreed: "The only revolution is the one that never stops."[7]

(Actually, this notion of permanent revolution brings up an intriguing point: the "see-saw philosophy of history" is apparently required here. When God overthrows the rich, they become poor, and the oppressed become rich. Since God always sides with the poor, and regularly overthrows the rich, He must side with the formerly wealthy against the *nouveaux riches.* In Sider's social theory, everyone is miserable: if you're poor, the rich oppress you; and if you're rich, God overthrows you. Sort of like Cosmic Hot-Potato—up, down, up, down, up, down; the last one with the money goes to hell.)

But this is not an accurate statement of biblical social justice. Siding with the poor is not automatic with God, nor should it be with His people. As we have seen already, the law demands *justice:*

*You shall not follow a multitude in doing evil, nor shall you testify in a dispute so as to turn aside after a multitude in order to pervert justice; nor shall you be partial to a poor man in his dispute. . . . You shall not pervert the justice due to your needy brother in his dispute (Exodus 23:3,6).*

*You shall do no injustice in judgment; you shall not be partial to the poor nor defer to the great, but you shall judge your neighbor fairly (Leviticus 19:15).*

We may not mechanically assume that the poor man's cause is right. "The first to plead his case seems just, until another comes and examines him" (Proverbs 18:17). The issue in justice is not

*Which one is the underdog?* but *Which one is right?* And the standard of justice is not relative wealth or poverty, but the abiding law of God.

When God does "reverse the good fortune of the rich," in judgment, it is because of sin. And since the rich can be tempted to forget God, and to trust in their own might, there is always the danger of sneering at and oppressing those below them. God hates this. It is He who gives the power to get wealth; oppression of others is a denial of the divine origin of riches. But oppression of the poor is wrong, not because God "sides" with them any more than with others. It is wrong to oppress *anyone*. You are commanded to return even your enemy's lost possessions to him (Exodus 23:4-5). Let's suppose, for example, that you have an enemy who has truly wronged you. Still, you may not pervert the justice due him. You may not like him; but you must observe *the rights God has established.*

For a more extreme example, let us suppose that a really worthless, lazy bum has committed a rape. Biblical law commands that he be executed; but it also commands us to give him a fair trial, with proper evidence, regardless of how much we may (rightfully) despise him. And if the evidence is insufficient to convict him biblically, he must go free. In a word: *justice.* We won't have perfect justice in this fallen world, not ever. Some criminals will undoubtedly go unpunished for lack of evidence. But we can have swift, substantial justice, and we should work diligently to that end. The biblical standards for treatment of the poor acknowledge the fact that we men are sinners, and that we tend to look down at those who are less well-off, or a bit *more* well-off, than we are. So the Bible reminds us repeatedly to abide by God's strict canons of justice. Fairness to our fellow men — even if they have done wrong — is the biblical mandate. God is not "on the side" of the poor. He demands that we treat them according to His law. If we oppress them, He will punish us; and if they call upon Him, He will hear and deliver them.

Whose side is God on? Not the rich; not the poor; not any social

or economic class; not any race. The answer to the question can
be easily determined when we answer a much more important
question, posed by Moses in Exodus 32:26 (KJV):

*Who is on the LORD'S side?*

# 5 | THE THIRD WORLD

**"... THE RIGHT TO NATIONALIZE FOREIGN HOLDINGS."
[RONALD SIDER, *RICH CHRISTIANS IN AN AGE OF
HUNGER*, P. 145]**

**"YOU SHALL NOT STEAL." [EXODUS 20:15]**

About 25 years ago the term "Third World" came into prominence. It is a concept of primary importance for socialists, a fraud which can be used for many purposes. Clarence B. Carson observes: "For a brief period it looked as if the Third World might become a definite entity, but it did not. It has remained largely a concept with whatever content one wished to ascribe to it . . ."[1] Where the world *had* been "divided" into capitalist and communist factions, the Third World concept is supposed to refer to nonaligned, less-developed countries—although exactly *which* countries are included depends entirely on who is currently using the term, and what ax he is grinding.

"Nonalignment" in Third World nations serves the purposes of revolutionary socialism as well. *Now* the world is divided between the industrialized, Western exploiters and the non-industrialized, exploited nations of the Third World. Western businessmen who invest in less-developed countries are, it is said, neo-colonial powers, obscenely profiting from their economic control over the poor nations. Of course, now that some of the Third World countries are making money, a new division is required, and a "Fourth World" has emerged.[2] The culprits absconding with "the best of both Worlds" are, naturally, the industrial concerns of the West.

There is a great political advantage brought about by making use of this concept, particularly for the leaders of Third and Fourth World nations. All their woes have been visited upon them by outsiders. As Carson describes it:

*Not only did communists subscribe to the notion that Western imperialism had been a system of exploitation of subject peoples but so did most Western intellectuals. This gave Third World politicans ready-made enemies— "Western imperialists"—something most useful to politicians, especially when the enemies are not constituents. They could appeal for the unity of their peoples against these outsiders. It also provided an explanation and an excuse for their economic backwardness. They were not to blame for their conditions; they had been overcome by superior technology and exploited by Westerners. . . .*

*Indeed, the Third World concept was, and is, an irresponsible concept. The Third World countries are not, according to the concept, responsible for the conditions which prevail there, and they accept little or no responsibility for what goes on in the world. If, or better still, when, since it is only a matter of time, they confiscate the private property of foreign investors, or foreigners in general, the concept justified that too. After all, the foreigners had only been there to exploit them.[3]*

One example of such "exploitation" given by Sider is that of the infamous Banana Caper, in which three large Western fruit companies used economic leverage in order to keep from paying a new dollar-per-case tax on the bananas they exported from countries in Central America. Sider explains how the tax was reduced in one country: "In order to increase profits for a U.S. company and to lower banana prices for you and me, the Honduran government agreed, for a bribe, to cut drastically the export tax, even though the money was desperately needed in Honduras."[4]

Sider gives the impression that somehow this tax would have helped relieve poverty; it was "desperately needed." Yet, a page later, Sider (trying to increase our guilt) charges: "Dictators representing a tiny, wealthy elite that works closely with American business interests rule Honduras"; thus the poor are helpless.[5] If the dictators do nothing for the poor, and if they represent a "tiny, wealthy elite," just what was the money *desperately needed* for?

The truth is this. This "tax" was set by the Central American dictators in order to raise reserves for themselves. In other words, it was a *bribe*. The fruit companies made a very logical decision, in terms of a complex economic theory that goes something like this: A Higher Price Costs More Money Than A Lower Price Does. The "bribe" they paid was simply the result of economic bargaining with unjust dictators who were seeking to line their own pockets—and who, by the way, were charging a tax which they had no biblical right to charge. The fruit companies saw an opportunity to *reduce the ransom* for their products. The guilt lies not with them but with the dictators who demanded the bribe in the first place. Sider's attempt to make you feel guilty for eating bananas is a hoax. In his twisted system, it is perfectly all right for a poor, oppressed (wealthy, elitist) dictator to force you to pay a bribe—but it is a sin for you to try to lower the price. Get it? His logic is as solid as a banana.

The Third World concept implies (and often states) that the economics of underdeveloped countries is somehow different from traditional economics—that the Third World operates by different economic laws. It presents the less-developed countries "as a substantially homogeneous and stagnant mass, sharply distinct from the developed world."[6] The most succinct statement of this position was made by Ragnar Nurkse: "a country is poor because it is poor."[7] A vicious cycle of poverty exists, and there is no way for a poor nation to advance. The Gap between the rich and poor nations is enormous, and (in Sider's words) "the chasm widens every year."[8] What to do? The only answer that occurs to

Gapologists is that of foreign aid from industrial nations. Sider's whole book, in fact, is premised on the idea that there is just no other way out. P. T. Bauer comments:

*Much of the literature suggests that the world was somehow created in two parts; one part with a ready-made infrastructure of railways, roads, ports, pipe lines and public utilities, which has therefore been able to develop, and the other which the Creator unfortunately forgot to endow with social overhead capital. This is not the way things have happened.*[9]

Economic laws do not change from country to country, or from age to age. "Underdeveloped" countries can progress only in the same ways that developed countries have grown—through capital investment (which should be distinguished from foreign aid, as we shall see later on). But many in the leadership of the Third World are blind to this fact. Rothbard mentions a central problem: "Underdeveloped countries are especially prone to the wasteful, dramatic, prestigious government 'investment' in such projects as steel mills or dams, as contrasted with economic but undramatic, private investment in agricultural tools."[10] It must be acknowledged that Ronald Sider wants to concentrate on agricultural production.[11] But (1) he wants to accomplish it through unbiblical means—foreign aid, government intervention and redistribution programs, etc.; and, therefore (2) it won't work. He admits that the poor in these nations are oppressed by their dictatorial leaders, yet he plans to alleviate their problems by increasing the wealth and power of the very states which are oppressing them! P. T. Bauer explains how it works:

*Unlike manna from heaven, official aid does not descend indiscriminately on the population of the recipient country; it accrues to specific groups of people in positions of power and sets up repercussions often damaging to development, notably by contributing to the politicisation of economic life.*[12]

Sider's proposals will not result in *more* agricultural production, but *less:*

*The flow of aid and the preferential treatment of governments engaged in comprehensive planning or experiencing balance of payments difficulties have reinforced the tendency of governments of underdeveloped coun-*

tries to neglect agriculture. *They assume that aid givers will come to their rescue in the event of a serious food shortage, and consequently feel freer to divert their resources to industrial and to prestige projects.* [13]

One of the fallacies of much of the Gap rhetoric is the idea that per capita income statistics are at all meaningful. Sider notes that 750 million people live on less than $75 per year,[14] though he admits that "exact figures are not available."[15] That's putting it mildly. The margin of error in international estimates of incomes and living standards is really quite large.[16] The bases of such statistics — population estimates — are very unreliable, often with discrepancies in the tens of millions. This fact is compounded by the conceptual errors of income figures themselves. *Purchasing power in underdeveloped countries is radically underestimated and camouflaged by such measurements.* For example, that $75 per year figure above — could you possibly live on that sum? Sider's implication is that 750 million people subsist on nothing more than the goods and services which you could purchase in the United States for $75. If this were true, they would not live out even a year. Yet Sider tells us they are having a population explosion which threatens to engulf the world![17] Naturally a rise in population means a corresponding fall in the death rate, and *"income" is more than money alone* — regardless of Sider's materialistic (!) assumptions. There is also "psychic income," the pleasure derived from having children. And, contrary to Sider's patronizing attitude, these people are not stupid. They could, if they chose, refrain from having so many children. To assume that they are unable, rather than unwilling, to do so betrays a condescending air which is certainly unwarranted, and neglects to treat them as men. In addition, most people do derive satisfaction from living longer, and this too is "psychic income." The statistics also disregard bartering, an oversight which can throw off the figures widely. For all these reasons, monetary income figures are virtually meaningless in comparing international living standards. But, skillfully manipulated, they can produce guilt, and guilt sells books.

There is no doubt, however, that hunger and starvation exist in many "Third World" countries, and we need to have a biblical understanding of this. Before man fell in the Garden, his labor was not spent in scrounging for food; it was abundant and cheap. Instead, labor was expended in scientific, aesthetic, and productive activity (Genesis 1:26-29; 2:15, 19-20). Man was able to turn his energy toward investigating, beautifying, and developing his environment. But when man rebelled and attempted to steal God's throne, he was expelled from the Garden, and forced to spend much more of his time and energy obtaining food—and food became much harder to get (Genesis 3:18-19). This is God's curse on men whenever they rebel: the land itself spews them out (Leviticus 18:24-28; Isaiah 24). The curse devours productivity in every area, and the ungodly culture perishes (Deuteronomy 28:15-26). They suffer terrible disease (Deuteronomy 28:27), and are politically oppressed (Deuteronomy 28:28-34). This is how God controls heathen cultures: they must spend so much time *surviving* that they are unable to exercise ungodly dominion over the earth. In the long run, this is the history of *every* culture that departs from God's word. While a culture may seem, in the short run, to prosper, it is headed for annihilation if it is unfaithful to the standards of biblical law. A heroin addict who has just gotten a fix undoubtedly feels better than you and I do at this moment; but misery and suffering will eventually catch up with him. In terms of biblical law, a culture that engages in long-term rebellion against God's law will sink to the level of abject poverty and deprivation. The law promises that. Conversely, if a culture has suffered long-term misery, we can make a judgment about its history—which is not to say that we may automatically assume anything about its *present* inhabitants. They may indeed be very godly. If so—if a cultural transformation has taken place spiritually—they are already on their way toward godly dominion, although the process may take a generation or more to become materially evident. But if God is on His throne, His people will be blessed. He controls the environmental conditions, and

**117**

He can cause the desert to blossom (Isaiah 35; 43:19-21). But He will not do it without the Spirit being poured forth in regeneration and sanctification; physical, material, economic blessings flow from cultural obedience (Isaiah 32:15-16).

As the gospel progresses throughout a society, food becomes easier to obtain, and attention turns again to the original tasks of godly dominion which were mandated in the Garden. No Protestant culture has—yet—been plagued by famine (but we should expect famine and more if our national apostasy remains unchecked). Godly cultures have the "Puritan work ethic" deeply ingrained into their natures, and this has notable effects in economics: rising productivity, rising real wage rates, and accelerating dominion over every area of life.

But ungodly men, as we have seen, are slaves by nature. Their sin drives them to lord it over others in ways that are forbidden and economically unproductive, and they are driven to relinquish their proper responsibilities (which *are* productive), to seek present benefits rather than to sacrifice in the present for future rewards, and to be enslaved by others. The unbelieving culture thus gravitates toward statism and socialism. We can see this in the story of how the Egyptian people became enslaved to Pharaoh (Genesis 47). Pharaoh was their god, and they desired that he should save them; they therefore lost their cattle and land, and finally sold themselves and their families into permanent bondage to him. The principle here is that your Savior will be your Lord as well, and that when you are *saved* you are also *enslaved.* Ungodly cultures invariably become enslaved to the state. The economic problem is that a socialist society has no means of economic calculation, as Ludwig von Mises constantly pointed out: "Where there is no market there is no price system, and where there is no price system there can be no economic calculation."[18]

Thus, without the market mechanism of profit and loss, the socialist Planner has no way to tell where energy and capital should be directed. Surpluses and shortages become the norm, and unanticipated (and thus unplanned-for) events—unusual weather, for instance—produce catastrophes as a matter of course. Famine is a commonplace of socialist states. The "controlled" economy is in fact controlled not by the planners, but by vicissitude. It is at the mercy of its environment—which is to say *God,* our ultimate Environment, at whose hands a self-deified state may expect little mercy.

In a truly Christian culture, the market is free from state control, and the result is that scarcity does not produce shortages. The free market adjusts immediately to continually changing conditions, and a shortage does not occur. Shortages have one real cause: *price controls.*[19] Moreover, God physically blesses the nation that obeys Him, and natural disasters are considerably lessened—making it even more certain that goods and services will be available in abundance.

An important principle is at work in history. It is this: *God is continually at work to destroy unbelieving cultures and to give the world over to the dominion of His people.* (That, by the way, is what is meant by those verses about God uprooting the rich; see Leviticus 20:22; Deuteronomy 28; Proverbs 2:21-22; 10:30). God works to overthrow the ungodly, and increasingly the world will come under the dominion of Christians—not by military aggression, but by godly labor, saving, investment, and orientation toward the future. For a time, ungodly men may have possessions; but they are disobedient, and become dispossessed:

> *Though he piles up silver like dust,*
> *And prepares garments as plentiful as the clay;*
> *He may prepare it, but the just shall wear it,*
> *And the innocent will divide the silver. ( Job 27:16-17)*

This is where history is going. The future belongs to the people of God, who obey His laws. "The wealth of the sinner is stored up for the righteous" (Proverbs 13:22), and "to the sinner He has given the task of gathering and collecting so that He may give to one who is good in God's sight" (Ecclesiastes 2:26). This is what God did with Israel. They inherited already settled lands, while God smashed the heathen, having allowed them to build up capital

while incurring increasing judgment because of their sins
(Genesis 15:13-16; Joshua 11:19-20). The seventeenth-century
Puritan Thomas Watson understood this well:

*The meek Christian is said to inherit the earth, because he inherits the bless-
ing of the earth. The wicked man has the earth, but not as a fruit of God's
favour. He has it as a dog has poisoned bread. It does him more hurt than
good. A wicked man lives in the earth as one that lives in an infectious air.
He is infected by his mercies. The fat of the earth will but make him fry and
blaze the more in hell.* [20]

The "Third and Fourth Worlds" are suffering under the judgment
of God. This does not mean we should disregard the real misery of
these people, or sneer at their plight. But it does mean we must approach them with a biblical, theologically-informed mind. Our
actions toward them must be concerned with *transforming their culture
by the word of God.* They will not be economically blessed unless they
obey Him, and *we* will be cursed if we seek to help them in ways that
are forbidden. Poor people need the gospel. The truly liberating
message of the salvation provided in Christ must sink down into
their innermost beings, changing their perspectives completely.
They must become disciplined, obedient to God's law. They must
renounce their state-worship and their envy of those who are better
off. They must seek to become free, responsible men under God,
building for the future, working and investing in every area of life for
the glory of God. And they must keep the state in its place, not
allowing it to take God's place in controlling the economy. Under
God's blessing they will then prosper. And they need have no fear of
a "tiny, wealthy elite" of dictators, for the ungodly will have fallen—
not by a revolution, but by the providential judgment of God.

*He brought forth His people with joy,*
*His chosen ones with a joyful shout.*
*He gave them also the lands of the nations,*
*That they might take possession of the fruit of the people's labor,*
*So that they might keep His statutes,*
*And observe His laws.*
*Praise the LORD! (Psalm 105:43-45)*

# FOREIGN AID

"INCREASED FOREIGN AID IS IMPERATIVE. THE DEVELOPING COUNTRIES SIMPLY DO NOT HAVE THE RESOURCES ... OUTSIDE HELP IS ESSENTIAL." [RONALD SIDER, *RICH CHRISTIANS IN AN AGE OF HUNGER*, PP. 218F.]

AND THE LORD WILL MAKE YOU ABOUND IN PROSPERITY, IN THE OFFSPRING OF YOUR BODY AND IN THE OFF-SPRING OF YOUR BEAST AND IN THE PRODUCE OF YOUR GROUND, IN THE LAND WHICH THE LORD SWORE TO YOUR FATHERS TO GIVE YOU. THE LORD WILL OPEN FOR YOU HIS GOOD STOREHOUSE, THE HEAVENS, TO GIVE RAIN TO YOUR LAND IN ITS SEASON AND TO BLESS ALL THE WORK OF YOUR HAND; AND YOU SHALL *LEND* TO MANY NATIONS, BUT YOU SHALL NOT BORROW. [DEUTERONOMY 28:11-12]

The biblical form of government is extremely limited. The state may not tax oppressively (i.e., beyond the biblical allowance); nor may it engage in the theft of inflation by debasing the currency or expanding credit. It follows that the state cannot deal in foreign aid, since it has no lawful means to do so. Nevertheless, Ronald Sider demands "a foreign policy that unequivocally sides with the poor."[1] In the face of the Bible's clear limits on government, how can he take such a position? After all, he says: "Following biblical principles on justice in society is the only way to lasting peace and social harmony for all human societies."[2] One would think such an endorsement of the Bible's program might lead Sider to actually take it seriously. But he has a way out. He claims that "the Bible does not directly answer these questions."[3] Oh, yes it does. The trouble is that Sider doesn't like the Bible's answers.

In discussing foreign aid, Sider sets up an interesting dichotomy: Should the U.S. provide other countries with "bombs or bread?"[4] That's clever, but false. Those aren't the only choices. The right answer is: Don't give either one. There is no biblical law for either one. No government willing to abide by biblical limits will be able to afford to give anything away. Again, biblical law is not enough for Sider.

Sider attempts to frighten us into joining his campaign for unjust aid. The opening pages of his book contain some chilling futuristic speculations in which the Indian Prime Minister threatens to blow up Boston and New York with nuclear explosives, in retaliation for not receiving U.S. aid.[5] "Responsible people consider even this horrifying prospect a genuine possibility . . . in times of severe famine, countries like India will be sorely tempted to try nuclear blackmail."[6] Perhaps. But Sider is stacking the deck considerably. He implies that the United States is evil and heartless, preoccupied with other concerns, unwilling to comply with "just trade patterns." Meanwhile, the Prime Minister is stricken with compassion for the hungry, pleads to deaf ears, and becomes deperate. She really doesn't like the idea, but "the momentum of events could *force* her to explode one of the bombs. Terrible retaliation might follow. But she is desperate."[7] In sum, we are the guilty ones for not dispensing government aid, while this potential mass murderer deserves our pity. She was "forced" to give the order, because our program was insufficient: "A little was given, but it was never enough."[8] Nor will any amount of aid ever be enough for those whose envy of the rich is so vicious that they can contemplate the slaughter of millions. God commands the poor to call upon Him for deliverance. When, instead, they are ready to destroy those who fail to "share" sufficiently, they are not to be pitied. Envy cannot be appeased.[9]

**MODEST PROPOSALS?**   In addition to the usual methods of foreign aid, Ronald Sider proposes two measures which should receive particular attention in this discussion: *tariffs* and *commodity agreements*. I don't wish to sound repetitious, but it must be stated again: these policies are immoral. The state has no biblical right to intervene in the market system or to interfere with trade. (Again, I am not speaking of the sale of innately, biblically defined, immoral goods or services). Sider's proposals are in absolute defiance of God's word. And *because* these practices are forbidden by God, *they don't work*. Note: I am not saying they are wrong because they inevitably fail. I am saying they fail because they violate biblical principles. This is God's world, and it moves according to His laws.

**TARIFFS**   These are protective barriers to trade which a country erects in order to guard its own industries from external competition. The idea is that, for example, our television manufacturers will lose their jobs if cheaper and better sets from Japan are available to the American consumers. The American people will stop buying the more expensive American-made TVs in favor of the imported ones. This will mean fewer jobs in the TV industry, and hence rising unemployment and poverty in our country. Thus, to protect our people, we force importers to pay a tax on their manufactures, which will raise the price of their goods to a level at which our industries can successfully compete. And, of course, we Americans firmly believe in competition. We need protection from free trade.

This is merely a bundle of fallacies. *First,* a tariff is *theft,* since it confiscates the property of others ("strangers," among others) in the name of protection for ourselves. Breaking God's law will lead to national judgment, not higher employment. *Second,* it steals from the consumers, who are forced to pay higher prices for goods, and must therefore reduce their spending on other products if they wish to buy a "protected" item. *Third,* it turns trade into warfare, regarding foreign producers as enemies against whom we must defend ourselves — thus creating, not free competition, but a dangerous conflict (which has historically led to actual war again and again). *Fourth,* it does not keep Americans employed. The tariff adds to consumer cost, and many will forgo the purchase of *any* TV, which will bring about unemployment in the industry anyway. *Fifth,* it subsidizes inefficiency by prohibiting competition. Free trade means that a producer must strive constantly to make his product better or cheaper than those of his competitors. Free trade presents consumers with goods that are continually improving. *Sixth,* free trade does not ultimately produce unemployment at all. The less efficient producers *will* be forced out of a market in which they are doing poorly; but they will then turn their energies toward manufactures which they can produce well — and the consumer, having saved money from the lower cost of the Japanese TV, will be able to spend whatever is left over on another item. Also, Japanese buyers can now use American dollars to buy American products — soybeans, for example, or lumber. The same amount of money is spent — but now with more efficiency, greater diversity, higher productivity, no theft, and no warlike activity on the part of the state.[10]

Since governments presently control over 46% of international trade,[11] Sider is correct:

*"Tariffs and other import restrictions are still an essential part of today's unjust international economic order . . . The United States charges the highest tariffs on processed and manufactured goods from poor countries . . . The result, unfortunately, is to deprive poor countries of millions of extra jobs and billions of extra dollars from increased exports."*[12]

If Sider had been concerned with biblical justice, he might have stopped there. But he is not interested in biblical justice. He is interested in the plunder of the rich. Thus, after calling for developed nations to end trade restrictions, he announces the following as "necessary" further steps: "Developed nations will need to grant trade preferences to developing nations and also permit them to *protect their infant industries with tariffs* for a time."[13] We'd never have guessed it, but Sider actually regards injustice as desirable, so long as it is the poor nations who are committing it. As we have seen (Proverbs 6:30-31), the fact that a thief is starving does not change the fact that he *stole,* and he must make restitution for his theft. In contrast, Sider says that *wrong* is *right,* when the "oppressed" do the oppressing. We can abolish "the secular laissez-faire economics of the deist Adam Smith," who so effectively exploded the mercantilist fallacies of our predecessors. We can construct a new economics, an economics of "compassion for the poor," an economics of the Tender-Hearted Elimination of Free Trade (THEFT).

The argument that "infant industries" need tariff protection is false. If the new industries are productive, they won't need to steal to survive. If they are unproductive, they are unnecessary, and capital should be invested elsewhere. Without state aid, the new industry may not become a superpower overnight, but if it is really needed — if it is supplying consumers with demanded goods — it will grow as other businesses have. But protected industries have a way of *never* growing up, always dependent upon legal plunder. Tariffs bring nothing but subsidized irresponsibility and more poverty — poverty caused by outright theft, and by teaching the ethic of remaining an unproductive, irresponsible "infant."

**COMMODITY AGREEMENTS** The warfare mentality is exhibited in commodity agreements as well. These, like tariffs, are legally-enforced price supports for certain goods — with the difference that these price levels are agreed-upon on an international basis. The purpose of commodity agreements is to "stabilize" prices of "primary products" (raw materials and foodstuffs) exported by less-developed countries, to prevent "devastating" price fluctuations. Sider approves of such controls, because they mandate prices that are "just."[14] (We should note, by the way, that the radical price fluctuations of 1974-75 mentioned in support of his thesis[15] would never have happened without government tinkering with the money supply in the first place, particularly from 1970-74.[16] Price fluctuations are *always* an adjustment of the market to reality.)

As with other interventions into the market, commodity agreements are immoral. Instead of allowing prices to conform to the realities of the marketplace—and rather than tackling the main problem, which is government-produced inflation—state coercion is applied to enforce a "just price." But "just" is supposed to mean "justice," and justice is defined by God's law. The Bible does not set a just price for commodities. It prohibits fraud and coercion, and it sets the conditions in which the free market can operate. With statist economic regulations, men are not free to act. They become enslaved to the government, their whole futures tied to the decisions of planners and bureaucrats (who act in their own self-interests as much as anyone else), rather than to their own responsible choices under God's law. Commodity agreements are theft.

Let's consider an example, using those bananas Sider is so concerned about. Suppose an international agreement is reached to double the price of bananas exported from Central America. What would happen? Since the price cannot be legally lowered, there is an immediate incentive for producers to produce bananas. Other countries—the Philippines, for instance—would begin competing more heavily to obtain the new, higher price for bananas. Competition would accelerate between growers in Central America as well, forcing the various governments to establish limits on acreage for each grower. On these smaller plots, agriculture intensifies, with the use of more productive methods of cultivation—better irrigation and pest control, more fertilizer, etc.—in order to obtain the largest possible yield. More is being produced than ever before, but the price cannot fall to conform to the surplus. The governments must now set marketing quotas for each grower, and must purchase and store the surplus output.

Bananas begin rotting by the ton in warehouses, yet the price remains inflexible. If the government does not buy (or confiscate) the surplus, black markets in bananas will arise around the world—as indeed they will anyway, requiring stern, police-state measures: spies, informers, fines, imprisonment, and perhaps executions. Meanwhile, banana consumers around the world have reduced their consumption (somehow, the governments have been unable to repeal that bothersome law of supply and demand that Adam Smith invented). The lower demand means an even greater surplus, which means the government must reduce the growers' marketing quotas. Banana producers are basking in the glow of higher prices, but they are making less money than they did before. They scramble to intensify farming methods to the maximum, and the surplus swells to gigantic proportions. The governments must build more warehouses, destroy more bananas, and hire more police to stamp out the black markets. Rents and leases of agricultural land have surged, increasing the cost of production. This causes riots. Fights break out between rival growers, some complaining that bananas of lower quality receive the same price of those of the highest quality. More and more growers are impoverished, except for those willing to take the risks of selling at an illegal but profitable price. Finally, to add to the misery of the Third World, Ronald Sider publishes a new book demanding foreign aid to poor banana farmers in Central America.

**DIRECT FOREIGN AID**   Because government foreign aid is prohibited by Scripture, many serious problems are inseparably linked to it. We will consider here the implications and results of such aid, and then list the biblical alternatives.

**IMPLICATIONS**   The most significant implication of foreign aid is *externalism,* the idea that economic progress can only be imposed on a culture from the outside. The poor are regarded as helpless in the face of their surroundings. Says Bauer:

*This suggestion reinforces the attitude widely prevalent in the underdeveloped world . . . that the* opportunities and the resources for the economic advance of oneself or one's family have to be provided by someone else—*by the state, by one's superior, by richer people, or from abroad. This attitude is in turn one aspect of the belief of the efficacy of external forces over one's destiny. In parts of the underdeveloped world this attitude goes back for millennia and . . . has been reinforced by the authoritarian tradition of the society.* It is an attitude plainly unfavourable to material progress.[17]

Sider believes that "outside help is essential."[18] This externalist thesis is plainly untenable in view of the fact that all developed countries began as poor nations, with the same basic economic conditions as the underdeveloped countries. Most societies benefited from foreign private investment, but that profit-seeking private investment came because foreigners saw the potential in the underdeveloped society. The society was not helpless. Again, we should note that the most important factor in development has been Christianity. Where the people have established the godly basis for progress, in personal lives, social mores, and political freedoms, development will occur without government programs. If the people are not morally capable of progress, no amount of aid will produce it. Economic development requires a great deal more than money—a fact which is ignored by materialistic socialists. The Puritans progressed because of ethics, not grants. A stagnant culture needs the conditions which favor development, and money is the least of its worries. As Bauer says, "If all conditions for development other than capital are present, capital will soon be generated locally," or will be available on loan from the outside.[19]

A further implication of foreign aid is that a nation can benefit only at the expense of another. In this framework, the rich much be decapitalized and impoverished in order to enrich the poor. Thus, instead of the idea that *both* parties profit from a free exchange of goods—a concept which aids progress and friendly relations—the notion is fostered that profit is possible only through rip-offs. Inescapably, this produces a warfare mentality.

A world immersed in the idea that material advance is to be made by plundering others will be a world at war.

**RESULTS** Although as we have seen, government-to-government (bureaucracy-to-bureaucracy) foreign aid cannot change the real factors of productivity, I do not mean to give the impression that it has no results at all. It has three very important results.

First, *foreign aid produces irresponsibility and dependence.* Capital is turned over to be spent by people who do not bear the cost. This creates waste. If you are spending your own money, you have an incentive to be careful, and to make sure that it is invested in productive, profitable enterprises. The executive with an unlimited expense account will be tempted to eat lavish dinners with the company money. He will use his own funds to save toward a new set of tires, reducing his personal spending in less important areas. Foreign aid beneficiaries are spending other people's money, and thus much of it goes to prestigious and wasteful government projects, such as universities that are not really needed. They produce professionals who are trained in nonexistent technological fields, and an increasing problem in underdeveloped countries is the high number of unemployed university graduates. Socialism, being inherently rebellious, morally, wants the social rewards without the underlying base of gradual economic growth. The result is that socialist bureaucracies get everything backwards, imposing the fruit of generations of progress upon a society that is culturally unprepared for it—sort of like giving light bulbs to a tribe 1,000 miles away from a generator. Where biblical aid seeks to train men in responsible, future-oriented action, ungodly aid makes its recipients more helpless than ever. India is a case in point. Its large-scale trade deficits began *after* substantial foreign aid programs started (1956), and have continued ever since.

*India has depended on foreign aid for so long that this dependence has come to be taken for granted. Indeed the economic history of that country since about the mid-1950s has been one of progression from poverty to pauperism. Yet it was an explicit objective of Indian planning to reduce or eliminate economic dependence.*[20]

Second, *foreign aid helps those who are better off, rather than the poor.* This astonishing fact must be thoroughly comprehended. Remember that "tiny, wealthy elite" Sider speaks of? *They,* and not "the poor," are the recipients of aid. Simply stated by Bauer, "Foreign aid is paid by governments to governments."[21] Most of it never reaches the poor, and is used by governments for projects that have nothing to do with getting food, such as expensive airlines or universities or government buildings.

*The situation . . . is plainly not that there is not enough food for the subsistence of the existing population or populations. If this were the position there could be no growth in numbers, much less a huge increase. If there is starvation in some underdeveloped countries this must mean that part of the population cannot fend for itself, either because it lacks the ability to do so or because it is prevented from doing so by institutional factors, such as organized barriers to entry into wage employment or restrictions on access to land. Apart from occasional ad hoc emergency measures foreign aid is irrelevant to the relief of starvation. As we have argued, it benefits primarily the better-off sections of the populations in the recipient countries, and these sections are certainly not threatened by starvation. And it leaves very largely unaffected the poorest and most backward groups — both the poorest sections of the urban and rural proletariat and also the primitive tribal and aboriginal societies — who are most exposed to famine.*[22]

As UCLA's black economist (and former Marxist) Thomas Sowell points out, similar problems afflict welfare programs in the United States:

*Despite the public image of a typical welfare recipient as a Negro mother with a large brood, most welfare recipients are neither Negro, Puerto Rican, nor Mexican-American. It is also worth noting that while government figures show that $11.4 billion would raise all the poor above the officially defined poverty level, in fact more than $30 billion are spent on programs to get people out of poverty, and there are still more than 5 million families below the poverty level. Clearly most of the money spent on the poor does not directly reach the poor, but is absorbed by the salaries of officials, staffs, con-*

*sultants, and by other expenses of antipoverty organizations.* [23]

Third, *foreign aid actually widens the gap between rich and poor nations.* As we have seen, it inhibits those factors which would produce growth (e.g., by creating dependence rather than responsibility). More than this, it encourages explicit envy toward the rich, who are held to be responsible for the plight of those below them. Unfortunately, envy cannot be contained. Once directed against the rich in other countries, it soon focuses on people who are better off in one's own country. The idea that it is evil to make personal economic progress takes hold of the people, and fear of being envied prohibits growth and encourages poverty. Sociologist Helmut Schoeck writes:

*One of the decisive factors in underdevelopment or non-development is the "envy-barrier," or institutionalized envy among the population . . . Now when, as is quite patently the case, many of the politicians in developing countries make use of all their powers of rhetoric or persuasion for the crudest exacerbation of their people's envy of the rich industrial nations (even to the point of branding the latter as the cause of their own countries' poverty), these people's sense of envy — to which their cultures already make them overprone — is intensified. Thus the feeling and states of mind which inhibit development are not lessened but confined and given political sanction by the countries' leaders.* [24]

**BIBLICAL ALTERNATIVES TO FOREIGN AID** The Christian cannot support the unbiblical practices of government aid. But this does not mean we have nowhere to turn. There is much that we can do. *First,* we can support Christian missionary activity, to bring the gospel to the poor and build biblical principles into the lives of converts. This is the basic and indispensable requirement; without regeneration, true cultural transformation is ultimately impossible. As these peoples conform their lives to biblical standards, their societies will experience the economic growth promised in God's law. *Second,* we should oppose the really unjust patterns of both trade and aid in our world. We should abolish trade barriers of all sorts, and promote biblical law in all areas of government. *Third,* we may invest in those economies which abide by God's law enough to restrain from "nationalizing" our properties. Private capital, for many reasons, is more productive than foreign aid. It goes to producers, not governments, and thus does not concentrate political power; it is more personal and local; it is more likely to be handled responsibly, in terms of profitable production rather than prestigious superfluity; and it is related to specific market conditions, rather than the political goals of bureaucrats. *Fourth,* we can give to charitable causes for the relief of specific needs. As we saw in Chapter Two, biblical charity works toward responsibility in the recipient. And, being individual and uncoerced, it produces responsibility in the giver as well. Foreign aid is "charity" at gunpoint: our state officials force us to pay for it, through either taxes or inflation. It builds no moral character in either the "givers" or the receivers. Biblical charity is personal, prudent, and responsible. Because it is morally sound, it is economically sound as well. It genuinely enables us to "bear one another's burdens," and at the same time teaches the weak to be strong, so that "each one shall bear his own load."

## OVER-POPULATION

"THE CONSTANTLY GROWING DEMAND FOR FOOD MUST STOP—OR AT LEAST SLOW DOWN DRAMATICALLY. THAT MEANS . . . POPULATION CONTROL EVERYWHERE." [RONALD SIDER, *RICH CHRISTIANS IN AN AGE OF HUNGER*, P. 214]

---

"POPULATE THE EARTH ABUNDANTLY AND MULTIPLY IN IT." [GENESIS 9:7]

---

Perhaps the greatest contrived scare in the United States today is that of the alleged horrors of population growth. The Zero Population Growth advocates inform us that we are faced with a runaway population explosion that threatens to overwhelm the world with mass poverty and starvation. Ronald Sider wholeheartedly subscribes to this fraud—or at least he wants his readers to do so—and tells us that it is a "fundamental problem" of modern life.[1] We have already noted his prediction of a possible "war of redistribution" initiated by the overpopulated countries, and his warning is repeated again and again:

*Vast mushrooming famines in the poorer nations may tempt their leaders to unleash wars of unprecedented size and ferocity in a desperate attempt to demand a fairer share of the earth's resources. . . . As millions die and immi-*

*nent starvation stares tens of millions in the face, a country like India will have to seek some way out.*[2]

Naturally, something must be done about this, and Sider has the ever-present answer of state worship: "Foreign aid . . . is probably the only way to check the population explosion in time to avoid global disaster."[3] But he makes a fatal blunder. In his eagerness to increase our guilt over world hunger (too much emphasis on population might imply guilt on the part of the Third World), he makes a startling admission:

*It is simply incorrect to think that the population explosion in the poor countries is the sole or perhaps even the primary cause of widespread hunger in the world. Our ever increasing affluence is also at the heart of the problem.*[4]

Postponing for the present an examination of that last remark, notice the slight change of tune. First, the population explosion will lead to "global disaster." Second, the population increase isn't really the problem at all. This does not mean, however, that Sider is unconcerned about overpopulation. Even though he admits again that overpopulation is *not* "the main reason for continuing poverty," he makes this demand two paragraphs later:

*The right kind of aid—focused especially on promoting labor-intensive, agricultural development using intermediate technology—will help check population growth . . . the right kind of action could probably avoid disaster.*[5]

This is known in the language of Propaganda Chic as getting 'em coming and going: Population growth is not the problem— but if we don't stop it with foreign aid, we will have a global disaster on our hands, and it will be all our fault. If you're looking for logic here, don't bother. But there is a method to this madness. Remember, Sider's fundamental ethic is *plundering the rich*. At all costs, no matter how convoluted the argument, he wants to be Robin Hood. The fact that foreign aid is wrong, or that it doesn't work, or that reducing the size of population will not decrease hunger, will have no effect on his premise. His *a priori* principle is that of statism and egalitarianism (another example of his serious confusion, since you can't really have *both*). P. T. Bauer explains how the thinking runs:

*If the basis of the advocacy of aid is simply the need to reduce the allegedly wide and widening gap in incomes then such advocacy would not be affected even if it were recognized that* aid need not promote the material progress of the recipients as long as it impoverished the donors.[6]

This is the real point. This is why arguments in favor of aid do not have to be logical or factual. They are based on a religious presupposition that the riches of some are the cause of the poverty of others. The rich must be impoverished, regardless of the effect of such policy on the conditions of the poor. If legal plunder can be facilitated by using an irrelevant overpopulation argument, well and good. If the overpopulation argument gets in the way of producing guilt feelings among the rich, discard it. If the rich can be made to feel responsible for the overpopulation of others, better yet. But, whatever you do, *get their money.*

However, since Sider brought it up, it would be worthwhile to consider the population issue, in order to dispose of any remaining doubts in the reader's mind. It is clear that Sider himself is not being straightforward about the problem, in view of his obvious self-contradictions; but this need not deter us from dealing with it honestly and biblically ourselves.

**ADVANTAGES OF POPULATION GROWTH** It should be conceded at once by anyone claiming to be a "biblical Christian" that the Bible is not opposed to population growth as such. At the beginning, God commanded man to "Be fruitful and multiply, and fill the earth, and subdue it" (Genesis 1:28); and twice He repeated this command to Noah and his sons: "Be fruitful and multiply, and fill the earth. . . . Be fruitful and multiply; populate the earth abundantly and multiply in it" (Genesis 9:1, 7). God promises in the law that He will *cause* population growth among His obedient people, and they are clearly to regard this growth as a blessing (Leviticus 26:9; Deuteronomy 28:4, 11; cf. Psalm 127:3-5; 128:3-4). On the other hand, population growth is a definite *disadvantage* for the ungodly, since *population* is *people,* and a higher disobedient population means greater judgment

(Deuteronomy 28:18-19; Isaiah 49:19-20; Ezekiel 5:7-8). The answer to the population problems of the ungodly, however, is not population control but population *regeneration*. The issue is always spiritual and ethical, not biological. The ungodly culture suffers because it is under the Curse; and while we may engage in a certain amount of *ad hoc* treatment of symptoms, if we are serious about curing the disease we will attack the root problems, which have to do with man's depravity and rebellion against his Lord. And if our programs to relieve the needy ultimately reinforce rebellious cultural values—by applying the coercion of an omnipotent state and encouraging reliance on government to solve problems—we are merely aggravating the situation.

In an obedient culture, population growth is a marked advantage. It creates pressure for economic growth, and aids in that growth tremendously. A higher population means a greater demand for goods and services. "Isn't that just the point?" queries the ZPG advocate. "How can that increased demand be satisfied?" Don't forget that more people are around to do the work! Not only is there a greater demand, but there is also a greater supply of labor, a greater opportunity for division of labor, and hence more productivity. Increased population can provide a greater abundance of goods and services. And productivity—if people are willing to work, and not looking for handouts—increases at a *faster rate* than does population itself. This is because when there is manufacturing on a large scale, the overhead is reduced. Less capital is required for each unit produced, leading to a greater amount of real wealth per person. For example, suppose there is, in all the world, a "demand" for only *one pencil*. How much would it cost in labor and technology to produce one pencil? The price would be astronomical. But with our present population "problem," the cost of a pencil is minute. Why? Because of higher demand as a result of that higher population, *and* because more people are available to produce the pencils. That's important also, as we can see if we turn the illustration around. Let's say everyone in the world wants pencils, but there's only one man who knows how to make them (actually, as Leonard Read of the Foundation for Economic Education loves to point out, *nobody* really knows how to make a pencil—but let's pretend). From chopping trees to packing the product, only one man produces pencils. Again, how much would one pencil cost? But with the increasing division of labor provided by a growing population, prices fall, and real wealth increases. And that is not the end of the story. Citing a study by MIT's Everett Hagen, Robert L. Sassone reports:

*Rapid population increase "absolves" a country from many of the consequences of errors in investment decisions, both public and private, which are bound to occur. An erroneously judged investment, in a rapidly growing economy, stands a good chance of being able to be put to some alternative use; in a more nearly stationary economy it is much more likely to become a dead loss.*[7]

In addition, population growth increases technological knowledge. James Weber cites the fact that, "while world population has grown at rates of up to 2 percent a year, the international growth of new scientific knowledge has been booming at an annual, exponential rate of 7 percent."[8] New and more efficient resource development can also take place as the population swells, contributing further to the real wealth of the society. There is no conceivable economic reason for population control. The advantages to growth are so vast as to be virtually innumerable—as innumerable as the product potential of a creative population. Under the providence of God, a denser population puts pressure on individuals to fulfill their callings in subduing the earth, as agricultural economist Colin Clark observes:

*It is population growth which causes increased agricultural productivity, not productivity causing population growth. Besides the historical and geographical evidence, there is good reason why this should be so. The new methods of agriculture, at any rate at first, call for more effort, both physical and mental, than the old. We must recognize the fact that man, taken as a whole, is inherently lazy and conservative, and generally does not adopt productive improvements until he has to.*[9]

As I noted above, there is no biblical economic reason for compulsory population control. There are, however, *political* reasons for it—since "population control is *people* control," and statist rebels, abandoning their rightful dominion *over the earth*, seek instead *domination over men*. Weber convincingly argues that— provided the spiritual conditions for liberty exist in the first place—high population density acts to retard the centralization of political power, and promotes freedom from state control.[10] Would-be totalitarians thus have a very definite incentive to control population growth, and it is to this fact that we must now turn.

**OVERPOPULATION AND STATISM**   The foregoing discussion is not meant to imply that there is no such thing as overpopulation (although much of the rhetoric on the subject is long on discourse and short on evidence). A definition would help. Overpopulation in any meaningful sense must refer to a situation in which sufficient food is not available for the total number of people. Thus, "overpopulation" *cannot* refer to any *absolute* number of people, but only to the number of people relative to the food supply. In a word, what we're talking about is *famine*. If you have ten people stranded on an island with only enough food to sustain one life, you've got overpopulation. Before the arrival of the Europeans, North America was "overpopulated," since the Indians were not able to produce sufficient food for themselves—and, at most, there were only a few hundred thousand of them.[11] Yet the same continent, with the same natural resources, now supports hundreds of millions. What made the difference? *Christianity*. Pagan cultures, with a slave mentality, routinely see themselves as at the mercy of their environment, and are thus unable to cope with their surroundings. The Europeans, with a millennium's worth of Christian heritage behind them, saw it as their duty to develop the earth, to subdue their environment, making it serve man for the glory of God.[12] The problem lies not with population size, growth rate or natural resources. *The issue is the religious faith of the people*, and its outgrowth in cultural values, labor practices, and productivity.

India is another example. India's "sacred" cows eat enough food to feed 1,200,000 people.[13] That's not a misprint, and it doesn't count the sacred cows in India's bureaucracy, either. The rats at the docks consume up to 50% of India's food imports each year. If India were converted, the people would not be religiously restrained from getting rid of those cows — and a few bureaucrats as well — and there would be so much food they could export enough to feed everyone in Africa. India was a net exporter of food under British rule. One Indian leader estimates that if everyone in India worked diligently and intelligently — even if they kept the cows — "two-thirds of India's food produce could be exported."[14] The main problem is faith.

What causes famine (overpopulation)? Natural disasters play a very small part in famine, and even that would be extensively mitigated, were it not for the other causes. The most usual cause of famine is war.[15] Following that, the most significant causes of famine are:

1. *The prevention of cultivation or the willful destruction of crops;*
2. *Defective agriculture caused by communistic control of land;*
3. *Governmental interference by regulation or taxation;*
4. *Currency restrictions, including debasing the coin.* [16]

Am I wrong in seeing a pattern here? All five causes of "overpopulation" are entirely man-made. All five stem from man's sinful attempt to lord it over other men. All five, in other words, are reducible to one: statism. *Runaway population explosions are caused by runaway state controls over the population.*

Now let us return to Ronald Sider's "cure" for overpopulation: foreign aid. As P. T. Bauer states, "foreign aid promotes centralized and closely controlled economies."[17] And "closely controlled economies" produce overpopulation! There is a saying that some cures are as bad as the disease, but this is not the case here. Ronald Sider's cure *is* the disease.

E. C. Pasour, Jr., remarks that much of the cause of world hunger "can be attributed to the destruction or reduction of private property rights of food producers in countries where the hunger problem is most acute." He continues:

*Numerous examples can be cited where governments have weakened or destroyed economic incentives by confiscating private land, forcing farmers to work on collectivized farms, instituting price controls on food, and other such measures. India provides a good example . . . much of the food crisis in India can be attributed to actions taken by the Indian government affecting incentives of food producers. After her big electoral victory in 1972, Mrs. Gandhi's party reduced the amount of land that could be held by an adult male from 30 irrigated acres to 18 acres. . . . In addition to the direct effect of land confiscation on incentives, the policy also affected the profitability of tractors and implements. The reduced acreage was not enough to support the machinery.*

*The government also nationalized the wholesale grain trade, forcing farmers to sell their crops at fixed prices below the market level, whereas previously farmers were permitted to sell half of their grain to wholesalers at the higher market price. The impact of such actions on the quantity of food produced and marketed is predictable.* [18]

Overpopulation is virtually a necessary result of socialism. The only way to prevent wastes and shortages is to allow the free market to work. God's law is the sole foundation for success in every area of life. If our world increasingly turns away from obedience to biblical principles and toward state worship, we are indeed inviting "global disaster." We cannot remove the effect of the curse by violating God's laws even further. Overpopulation is famine, and famine is an aspect of divine judgment on deified states. If we would really work to abolish world hunger, we must work to establish universal obedience to the biblical faith. The biblical worldview, embedded in personal, family, community and state levels of society, will produce stunning economic growth, and increased population will be an important factor in this. By the multifaceted division of labor, as men work at their individual callings, the ground will yield God's blessings abundantly. The prophets wrote constantly of the very real economic results of obedience. God promises that the obedient nation will not suffer from overpopulation:

*And I will make a covenant of peace with them and eliminate harmful beasts from the land, so that they may live securely in the wilderness and sleep in the woods. And I will make them and the places around my hill a blessing. And I will cause showers to come down in their season; they will be showers of blessing. Also the tree of the field will yield its fruit, and the earth will yield its increase, and they will be secure on their land. Then they will know that I am the LORD when I have broken the bars of their yoke and delivered them from the hand of those who enslaved them. And they will no longer be a prey to the nations, and the beasts of the earth will not devour them; but they will live securely, and no one will make them afraid. And I will establish for them a renowned planting place, and they will not again be victims of famine in the land. . . . (Ezekiel 34:25-29)*

Population *density* can be a tremendous blessing; *over*population is a direct consequence of socialistic intervention. With typical blindness (or deceit, whichever you prefer), socialists wail and mourn over their own creations, placing the blame on others, and pleading for ever-increasing collectivism. Make no mistake: we *are* facing a global crisis, a blazing conflagration that threatens to destroy our civilization and our people. But Ronald Sider is asking us to fight fire with fuel.

# THE LAW AND THE PROFITS

"... A COMPANY BASED ON BIBLICAL NORMS RATHER THAN PROFIT." [RONALD SIDER, *THE WITTENBURG DOOR*, OCT./NOV. 1979, P. 13]

THUS SAYS THE LORD, YOUR REDEEMER, THE HOLY ONE OF ISRAEL; "I AM THE LORD YOUR GOD, WHO TEACHES YOU TO PROFIT, WHO LEADS YOU IN THE WAY YOU SHOULD GO." [ISAIAH 48:17]

The notion that there can be any such thing as "unfair profit" is one of the oldest socialist ideas, produced by two problems which are central to the very nature of socialism: *envy* and *ignorance*. Envy, because socialists assume that anyone who is successful must be wicked; and ignorance, because socialists do not understand economics.

In his brief section on profits,[1] Ronald Sider has fallen prey to both of these errors. The section is titled "Making a Fair Profit?"—the implication being, of course, that the high profits he goes on to cite are unfair. He lists examples of certain profit-making enterprises, and then states that "the returns on investments in poor countries are unjustly high."[2] His logic seems to be that "high" profits—or, at least, profits above a certain undefined percentage—are necessarily unjust. No proof is given for this assertion. He does not tell us just how high profits should be; he does not reveal his infallible source which determines what a "fair" return on investment is; he does not show that these profits were obtained in an unjust manner (in which case it would be not the profits but the entire enterprise itself that is unjust). To repeat: Sider says that certain profits are very high, and concludes that they are unjust. As long as you don't think *demonstration* is essential to an argument, you could say that Sider has put his case very nicely.

He seems to feel uneasy about this, however. Some uneducated readers may have missed the logical link which ties high profits to injustice. So for those of us who can't quite plumb the depths, he adds a helpful note:

*The reader without a degree in economics probably wishes international economics were less complex or that faithful discipleship in our time had less to do with such a complicated subject.*[3]

That was the whole problem, dear reader. You don't have a degree in economics. You didn't probe through the excretions of Keynes and Galbraith. That's why you don't understand. So let Father Sider take you by the hand, and he will lead you skillfully through the maze of economic theory.

He's got some competition, though. Solomon said you could study the Book of Proverbs. . . .

> *To know wisdom and instruction,*
> *To discern the sayings of understanding,*
> *To receive instruction in wise behavior,*
> *Righteousness, justice and equity;*
> *To give prudence to the naive. . . .*
> *The fear of the LORD is the beginning of knowledge. (Proverbs 1:2-7)*

According to Solomon, we can come to a capable understanding of what is fair and just simply by submitting to God's revelation and studying the biblical implications of God's law. Of course they didn't grant degrees in economics in those days, but even if they had, the Psalmist exclaimed:

> *I have more insight than all my teachers,*

*For Thy testimonies are my meditation. (Psalm 119:99)*

The Bible is the standard for every aspect of life. It tells us a great deal about economics. And it tells us that God's law alone is the standard of right and wrong, of justice and injustice. We might therefore expect that the Bible would have much to say about how to discern exactly when a profit rises above a "fair" level. But it does not. From this fact there are two possible conclusions. Either God was waiting for Marx or Sider to come along and do it for Him, or *there is no such thing as an unjust profit.* For the remainder of this chapter, I am assuming that the latter option is correct.[4]

The issue of profits centers on the problem of production. How does the entrepreneur know where to channel investments? Or, to put it another way, How can the wants of consumers be satisfied? The entrepreneur attempts to anticipate and meet constantly changing future consumer demands by directing the various factors of production in such a way as to make them provide what the people want in the most efficient and profitable way. If he fails to forecast the market correctly, he will suffer losses. If his decision is correct, he will make a profit. *The profit is the tangible sign of success in serving consumer wants.* A large profit means the entrepreneur has been very successful. He has not wasted resources, which are now released to the market to serve other consumer preferences.

It is commonly assumed that profits are arbitrary—that the entrepreneur says, "Well, let's see. Costs of production amounted to such-and-such; I will add on a profit of X percent and make a lot of money." But the entrepreneur cannot control demand. If the demand for his product is low, he will suffer losses. The entrepreneur does not "set" a profit. He does not know the future. The price (and hence the profit) will be determined by consumer demand in relation to the supply. If many consumers want the product, they will bid up the price in order to get the product. The profit comes from consumers who outbid *other consumers* in competition for it. The fact that profits are high means that many consumers are bidding, and this means that the entrepreneur has correctly discerned their needs. He makes a profit in direct relationship to how well he has satisfied their desires. Remember this law: consumers compete against consumers, while sellers compete against sellers. It follows that *the man who makes the highest profit is the man who is best serving the public*.

By "best," I do not mean that everything the public wants is good. Nor do I mean that a bubblegum producer who makes high profits is serving the public "better" than the man who sacrifices his life to care for the poor or the sick. But I do mean that the successful entrepreneur—assuming he has not defrauded or coerced his buyers—has satisfied *consumer demand* better than his competitors. You and I might wish consumer demand were directed toward other objects. I would like this book to be a best seller, but it probably won't be. So what? Unless we can demonstrate from Scripture that product X is *sinful*—not just luxurious or trivial or silly—we cannot say that the profit received from producing it is wrong. And if the item itself is wrong, we should stop talking about *profits* and start talking about prohibiting its *production*, since that's where the real problem is. Concern with profits as such betrays an envious mind, more disturbed that someone is successful than that the basis of his success may be wrong.

The average man probably associates high profits with high prices. This is not usually the situation in the free market. Henry Ford became a billionaire because he saw the truth of free market economics: high profits are associated with *low prices* and *high wages*. He redesigned mass production methods of manufacturing and applied them to automobile production. He then went out and offered to pay $5 per day to relatively unskilled laborers—an unheard-of wage in those days. He offered Americans the first low-priced automobile, the Model T, and he sold millions of them. It was the enormous volume of sales that made him rich. Price competition was the key to wealth, and still is. The method of selling to a mass consumer market, thereby reducing unit costs of production, is price competition. It helps make everyone rich.

How does the entrepreneur get his profits? By forecasting

accurately future demand and future costs of production. He is in competition with other producer-entrepreneurs. He tries to find special niches in the market where his competitors have failed to see an opportunity for profit. Because they have failed to see that consumers in the *uncertain future* will probably (he thinks) be willing to pay for a particular good or service, they have failed to enter the market for producer goods. Because they are not in there actively bidding up the price of raw materials, labor, and capital goods, the prices of these goods are low—for the moment. The competition has stayed out of the "producer goods auction," so the hopeful entrepreneur enters this market, buys up the goods, and diverts them into production. If he has been correct in his forecast, he will be able to sell consumers the goods they want at a price they are willing and able to pay. The man's profit comes from the discrepancy between the costs of production and sales revenue. But of course, these original conditions are unlikely to last very long. His competitors figure out what he has done, and they enter the producer goods market and start bidding up the prices, so that they, too, can profit by selling to consumers. Everyone's profit margin shrinks, which is as it should be.

Has the original entrepreneur exploited the consumers? Hardly. He saw what they wanted and provided it for them. If he had not seen their present preferences back when he started out, no one would have produced the consumer goods or services in question. The consumers would have had a smaller selection of goods to choose from. Far from having exploited the consumers, the entrepreneur who makes a profit has demonstrated his ability to serve the consumers well. Without his foresight, his willingness to bear risks, and his production and marketing skills, the consumers would have had fewer of their high-preference items to choose from. Not only that; his high profits (if above the rate of interest return and management fee return which he "pays to himself") will alert other entrepreneurs to enter the market and provide an even wider quantity of goods to select from. Why, then, are high profits so evil? It is the opportunity for making high, though admittedly temporary, profits that provides the consumers with the "carrot" with which they can lure entrepreneurs to meet their ever-changing, fickle demands. The profit motive, coupled with a social order which permits men to seek *and retain* profits, is the source of the *consumers' sovereignty* over national and even international production. Take away the opportunity to make and keep high profits, and you have turned the power of making production decisions over to the state's bureaucrats. The entrepreneur is a *middleman*, not a tyrant.

Production decisions have to be made by somebody. Either the "untouchables" in the state bureaucracies decide for the consumers, "in the name of the people," or else profit-seeking, risk-taking entrepreneurs will decide. An incompetent entrepreneur will soon be out of business. He will stop wasting the community's scarce economic resources in the production of items that the public prefers to skip. An incompetent, monopolistic, government-protected bureaucratic planning committee is a lot harder to remove. So take your pick: production by *compulsion* or production for *profit*. There is no third choice.

Seeing profits in this light helps us to understand something else about the high-profit complaint. If we say that someone's profits are *too* high, we mean one of two things. First, that *the entrepreneur was too efficient*. If he had done his job poorly, he would have directed the factors of production less efficiently, and the costs of production would have been higher, with the result that his profit margin would have been slimmer. But no—that wicked profiteer was able to allocate the scarce factors of production in the most careful and prudent manner, and thus he was able to reap high returns. The second thing we might mean by saying his profits are too high is that *he made too many people happy*. The only way to make high profits is by meeting a high demand. If someone makes a very high profit, it means that many people wanted that item, and were willing to pay high prices to get it. A more moderate man would not have tried to satisfy so many people. But that wicked profiteer is so despicable that he would please everyone in the world if he could.

God has structured the world so that those who are best at satisfying the public have the most control of production. This is the function of profits. The price system of the market transmits *information about consumer wants*, and the profits go to those who are most efficient in using capital to supply those wants. Complaints about profits really mean: "I disapprove of those consumer wants." Now that you realize what you actually meant, you can write a book—not about the evil of profits, but about why people should drink orange juice instead of Pepsi. And if lots of people like your book, you might make a high profit yourself, in addition to encouraging orange juice sales.

We should note further that high profits are *temporary*. High profits attract entrepreneurs and in hopes of making profits, they will begin producing the demanded item. As the supply increases in relation to demand, prices fall; and as competitors now bid up factor prices, profits decrease. Outside of a true monopoly— which means coercion to keep out competitors (e.g., the government monopoly of postal service)—it is impossible to continue a high profit; and even monopolists are not psychic. No one knows the future, and there can be no such thing as a "normal rate of profit." Profits are temporary. They simply reflect the market's readjustment to consumer wants. When the market readjusts, the profits disappear. (I am talking here about *pure* profit. What often goes under the name of "profit" is either remuneration for the managers of an enterprise or interest on invested capital.)

We must not try to restrict profit or hamper the ability of entrepreneurs to make profits. Profits show producers what consumers want. The existence of profits means that capital resources are continually being redirected in the most consumer-satisfying manner. As businessmen in search of profits increase the supply of goods demanded by consumers, prices fall, and thus— paradoxically, a socialist might think—*profits reduce the cost of living*! (That's Adam Smith's "invisible hand" at work.)

When government places restrictions on profits, the results are lower production, high costs, and waste. If businessmen cannot hope to receive a profit in a particular industry, they will turn their attention and capital elsewhere. This means that production will be lower for a good that is in demand, and thus prices will higher. (And remember, if the government seeks to alleviate this by controlling the price, there will be an even greater shortage of the good.) Furthermore, a controlled industry, which must not make more than a certain profit percentage, will thus try to appear to be not very successful. One way to *reduce profit* is to *increase cost*. Potential profits will be converted into activities that raise the cost of production, thereby disguising the actual profit from the government inspectors. Offices will become fancier, new typewriters will be purchased, along with more pencil sharpeners, copying machines, extra (and prettier) secretaries, more employees of the "preferred" racial background, fatter expense accounts, a fleet of company cars, and so on. If profits had not been restricted, the businessmen would have poured the new capital generated into the production of the desired good. But with profit restrictions, there is waste.[5]

Note again a basic lesson. Socialism cannot produce wealth; it can only destroy what wealth exists. It cannot generate; it can only confiscate. The only reasons for complaining about profits are *envy* and *ignorance*. But those who *truly* desire to be "biblical Christians" will learn to conquer their envy, and decrease their ignorance. Both goals will be achieved by submitting to God's authoritative revelation in His law, the standard of justice.

# ADVERTISING AND THE SLAVE MENTALITY

**"IF NO ONE PAID ATTENTION TO THESE LIES, THEY WOULD BE HARMLESS. BUT THAT IS IMPOSSIBLE."**
**[RONALD SIDER, *RICH CHRISTIANS IN AN AGE OF HUNGER,* P. 47]**

---

**"THE MATURE... HAVE THEIR SENSES TRAINED TO DISCERN GOOD AND EVIL." [HEBREWS 5:14]**

---

Of all the many imps populating Sider's imaginary Inferno, the archfiend of advertising is one of the worst—Old Nick incarnate. Sider has mounted a vigorous advertising campaign against advertising. His basic message is that advertising creates all kinds of desires in a gullible public, manipulating their wants.

*Advertisers regularly con us into believing that we genuinely need one luxury after another. We are convinced that we must keep up with or go even one better than our neighbors. . . . The purpose of advertising no longer is primarily to inform. It is to create desire . . . it attempts to persuade us that material possessions will bring joy and fulfillment.*[1]

One ad particularly censured by Sider is from his savings bank. The ad is characterized by him as "unbiblical, heretical, demonic." Here's the jingle:

*Put a little love away.*
*Everybody needs a penny for a rainy day.*
*Put a little love away.* [2]

Tacky, maybe. Crass. But heretical? Demonic? Sider must mean either that (1) saving money is demonic; or (2) the union of saving money with the sublime concept of love is demonic. (A third possibility would be that fractionally reserved banks themselves are demonic. He may have something there, but I won't take the time to explore it.) But thriftiness and saving are certainly biblical virtues (and many laws, e.g. inheritance, are meaningless apart from storing wealth); moreover, Jesus' parable of money investment (Luke 19:11-27) assumes the ethical validity of savings, and even banks are mentioned (of course, this was written before the Federal Reserve System came along).

Does advertising as such create desire? This is plainly not so. If it were true, it would mean that no business would ever suffer losses — it could just keep on "creating" a desire for its product. It would also mean that businesses would not waste their time in marketing research to find out what consumers want; if advertising could really *create* those wants, research is entirely superfluous (e.g., when God created the world, He didn't engage in research to find out what the creation would like to be). And how can we tell the difference between unjustly *creating* wants and *fulfilling* those desires that already exist? Sider does not tell us. He merely asserts that ads create wants. Presumably, therefore, no company really satisfies the wants of consumers. All consumer wants are fabricated by big business. And I thought the right wing had a corner on conspiracy theories! As well-packaged as Sider's anti-ad ad is, he doesn't give any proof. Maybe he should be federally regulated. We consumers need to be protected against such unscrupulous tactics.

Ludwig von Mises demolished this notion of the omnipotent advertiser:

*The consumer is, according to this legend, simply defenseless against "high-pressure" advertising. If this were true, success or failure in business would depend on the mode of advertising only. However, nobody believes that any kind of advertising would have succeeded in making the candlemakers hold the field against the electric bulb, the horsedrivers against the motorcars, the goose quill against the steel pen and later against the fountain pen. But whoever admits this implies that the quality of the commodity advertised is instrumental in bringing about the success of an advertising campaign. Then there is no reason to maintain that advertising is a method of cheating the public.* [3]

*Advertising is information.* The reason why it is often slick, sugary, gross, stupid or infuriating is because that is what the public wants. The advertiser's job is to inform potential buyers of his product. He must get the information to them in such a way that they will not miss it. This can mean the commercial use of beautiful sunsets, pretty girls, handsome men, cute kids, charming grandmothers, muscle-bound athletes, adorable puppies, and whatever else will attract consumer attention. *Information is useless if it is not communicated.* I know a man who wrote a gospel tract. On the cover were pictures of different-shaped noses, and the words: "Pick the one you want." The next page began: "Now that you're done picking your nose. . . ."—and the tract went on to share the gospel. Okay, it was gross. But it was read by many more people than would have read one beginning: "Are you saved?" The point is that he got their attention. This is not a defense of every attention-getting device. I am merely saying that this is a necessary function of advertising, and that *the public's taste determines what methods will be used.* Amos used a tricky advertising gimmick to get Israel to listen to his message, by telling them what they wanted to hear: how bad everybody else was (Amos 1:3-2:5). Advertising is wrong only when it breaks the law of God. Tackiness is not a sin.

But what about its effect upon impressionable minds? Sider claims that advertising "shapes the values of our children." [4] The only answer to this is: That's *your* problem. God has given you the responsibility to shape your children's values (Deuteronomy 4:9; 6:5-7). My wife and I have our three-year-old programmed for this. On the rare occasions when he watches TV, he will simply get up and turn it off whenever a distasteful advertisement comes on the screen. His level of discernment is pretty good. Television is not shaping his values. The word of God is, as it permeates the fabric of our home. Principles of godliness are discussed as naturally as are methods of cooking, decorating, using a screwdriver or throwing a Frisbee. It is part of life, and it forms the basic perspective through which the whole world is seen. There are problems, but the problems are met and conquered.

Advertising broadens the choices available to consumers, and enables us to "shop" ahead of time. Brand names make shopping more efficient, by enabling us to purchase goods of easily recognizable quality. When I buy jeans, I don't have to take the time to sort through a jumble of different types, analyzing each pair for durability. I just head for the Levi's. More than this, advertising enables us to discriminate differences we hadn't been aware of. The nationally-advertised "Pepsi Challenge" made consumers aware that Pepsi really *does* taste better to some consumers than its competitor. A product that fails to live up to its claims cannot succeed. We are responsible for testing everything (I Thessalonians 5:21). Christians aren't supposed to be gullible.

What then is the problem with advertising? Sider finally stumbles onto the point:

*Given our inherent bent for idolatry, advertising is so demonically powerful and convincing that most people persist in their fruitless effort to quench their thirst for meaning and fulfillment with an ever-rising river of possessions.*[5]

He's muddled it, but he's reached the basic issue: *idolatry*. People who are enslaved to the present, thinking only of immediate gratification, are seduced by advertising into buying the latest doodads and baubles. Their ethic is not one of saving, investment, and generous giving, but of consumption. And the central fact here is *not* the advertising. It is the *slave mentality* of the people, a condition that can be corrected only by regeneration and the deep cultural penetration of Christian values.

For example, let's consider the most blatant instance of false, unscrupulous advertising in all history: the temptation of Adam and Eve. God had placed the forbidden tree right in the middle of the Garden—not to tempt His creatures, but to give them strength as they daily grew in the ability to obey Him. But when the serpent handed them a line, they swallowed it. Why? Was the temptation too strong for them? To say that would be to charge God with deceiving them. No temptation is too strong (I Corinthians 10:13). The slickest ad campaign ever devised cannot in itself lead people into sin. The real problem lay in Adam and Eve's rebellion. They wanted to be like God, and that is why they gave in to pressure. They were judged. (Of course, the serpent was judged too, for misrepresenting the truth.) The basic problem is not advertising, but *depravity*. The only way to wipe out the consumption ethic is to convert the culture. We cannot legislate proper values; legislation should only penalize biblically evil external acts. Moreover, the same good may be right or wrong for different people. Is it right to own a Mercedes? Since sin is not in *things* but in people's hearts (Matthew 15:11, 17-20), the possession of a Mercedes may be perfectly all right for some, and wrong for others. Questions must be asked: "How does this affect your other financial obligations? Is it an idol? *Did you pay for it?*" Not all these questions are quantifiable; answers may vary for different individuals. It is a matter of faith and examination of one's own conscience—not legislation.

Sider does not *say* we should enact legislation against all the ads he dislikes. But that conclusion is likely, for two reasons. First, statist legislation is the thrust of his whole book—you can always hear the hum of an ax grinding in the background. Second, he says that the result of advertising is "structural injustice,"[6] and he constantly is after us to abolish structural injustice. Should advertising be regulated? No. There is no biblical warrant for a state regulatory board to oversee the advertising industry. But *proven, false advertising* (actual fraud) should be punished, since it constitutes theft. The one who engages in fraud must make full restitution for taking other people's goods under false pretenses. The

Bible does not give the state the authority to regulate anything. The state's function is to *punish criminals*. Biblical law is basically structured in terms of *ex post facto* punishments, not continual, daily regulation. I may not elevate my prejudices to equal standing with God's law. I may intensely dislike advertisements, but I must treat them as the Bible commands me to treat my enemies: with *justice*. Until someone breaks the law of God, I must not prosecute him. The state is given the authority to punish *evildoers* — not chuckleheads.

# CULTURAL BONE ROT

"ALL INCOME SHOULD BE GIVEN TO THE POOR AFTER ONE SATISFIES BARE NECESSITIES.... ANY 'CHRISTIAN' WHO TAKES FOR HIMSELF ANY MORE THAN THE 'PLAIN NECESSARIES OF LIFE,' WESLEY INSISTED, 'LIVES IN AN OPEN, HABITUAL DENIAL OF THE LORD.' HE HAS 'GAINED RICHES AND HELL-FIRE!' " [RONALD SIDER, *RICH CHRISTIANS IN AN AGE OF HUNGER*, P. 172]

---

"LET NO ONE ACT AS YOUR JUDGE IN REGARD TO FOOD OR DRINK.... LET NO ONE KEEP DEFRAUDING YOU OF YOUR PRIZE BY DELIGHTING IN SELF-ABASEMENT ... INFLATED WITHOUT CAUSE BY HIS FLESHLY MIND." [COLOSSIANS 2:16-18]

---

*Now Isaac sowed in that land, and reaped in the same year a hundredfold. And the LORD blessed him, and the man became very rich, and continued to grow richer until he became very wealthy; for he had possessions of flocks and herds and a great household, so that the Philistines envied him. Now all the wells which his father's servants had dug in the days of Abraham his father, the Philistines stopped up by filling them with earth. (Genesis 26:12-15)*

Envy is the greatest disease of our age. It is often confused with jealousy and covetousness, which have to do with wanting the possessions and privileges of others. Envy is much more insidious —and deadly. Envy is the feeling that someone else's having something is to blame for the fact that you do not have it. The principal motive is thus not so much to *take*, but to *destroy*. The envier acts against the object of his envy, not to benefit himself, but to cut the other person down to his own level—or below. The American Puritan divine Samuel Willard defined envy as "a man's repining at his neighbour's Prosperity, looking upon himself to be Hurt by it."[1] In his massive study of envy, Helmut Schoeck points up this central factor: "the envious man's conviction that the envied man's prosperity, his success and his income are somehow to blame for the subject's deprivation, for the lack that he feels.'[2] It can be summed up in Pierre-Joseph Proudhon's famous epigram: *Property is Theft!*[3]

This explains why "Envy and Malice are inseparable"[4]; as we can see from the example in Genesis quoted above, the envier's goal is destruction. Henry Hazlitt writes:

*The envious are more likely to be mollified by seeing others deprived of some advantage than by getting it for themselves. It is not what they lack that chiefly troubles them, but what others have. The envious are not satisfied with equality; they secretly yearn for superiority and revenge.*[5]

And it is this envious, destructionist mentality, nursing itself on the notion that *"your* wealth is the cause of *my* poverty," that is the basic ethos of socialism.[6] For socialism does not—and cannot—build up capital. It seeks only to expropriate or destroy the capital of others. It exalts a malignant, misanthropic disposition into an article of political economy, a machine for tyranny. *Socialism is institutionalized envy.*

Does Ronald Sider envy the rich? He would (I assume) deny the charge; we must examine his writings for the answer. The guilt-inspiring title of his book—*Rich Christians in an Age of Hunger*—certainly implies that the wealth of the rich is somehow to blame for the hunger of the poor. Is wealth a cause of poverty? Consider the following declarations:

*The ever increasing affluence among the rich minority is one of the fundamental causes of the present crisis.*[7]
*Our ever-increasing affluence is . . . at the heart of the problem.*[8]
*God casts down the wealthy and powerful—precisely because they became wealthy by oppressing the poor.*[9]
*The rich regularly oppress the poor and neglect the needy.*[10]
*The rich neglect or oppose justice because justice demands that they end their oppression and share with the poor.*[11]
*Frequently the rich are wealthy precisely because they have oppressed the poor or have neglected to aid the needy.*[12]

The envious man does not stop at merely bewailing the "fact" that the rich are to blame for the plight of the poor. He *nurtures* this hatred of his enemy. Regardless of his own advantages, he cannot bear to think of the object of his envy enjoying anything. The evil Haman, grand vizier of Persia, was able to recount many privileges granted him by the King (Esther 5:11-12): "Yet all this does not satisfy me every time I see Mordecai the Jew sitting at the King's gate" (v. 13). Thus the envier acts to destroy others, to hurt them in some way; it is of little concern whether he himself actually benefits. "One does not lift up the world," a revolutionary leader once remarked, *"one burns it."*[13] Therefore, as we have already observed, the primary aim of much "social" legislation today is not to benefit the poor, but to penalize the rich—or, more likely, the middle class.

When we envy, we rejoice in the misfortune of others (provided that they had some sort of perceived or assumed privilege). We like to think that they "deserve" to be brought down. Even when a bad man falls, we rejoice not so much because he was God's enemy, but because he was prosperous. An obvious example is the Watergate period, when many were less concerned with the actual violations of law than in watching the mighty dethroned. I constantly ran into people whose ignorance of the specific allegations was abysmal, but who nevertheless chortled with glee that "they finally got what was coming to them." Another example is the resentment of many toward Hugh Hefner, whose way of making money is certainly deplorable and unbiblical—but our indignation is doubtless fuelled considerably by the fact that he is rich in the first place, especially since we, who are pure, don't make as much money.

So envy is motivated toward destruction. Socialist policies are geared particularly toward plunder—and, notwithstanding Sider's seeming care for the poor, his specific suggestions have nothing to do with capital accumulation and the growth of real wealth, which are biblical means of overcoming poverty. Instead, he wants to steal. Well, that's not putting it charitably. He wants *other people* to steal. And the primary motive is to hurt the rich, by majority vote.

Consider, first, an apparently harmless statement on the duties of missionary activity in poor countries: "Why have missionaries so often taught Romans but not Amos to new converts in poor lands?"[14] In reply, it may be said that the book of Romans is a handy summary of Christian theology, and contains, in capsule form, practically all the major teachings of Scripture (and the last five chapters do speak a great deal about "community" and our duties to one another). Moreover, Romans was written for new converts; Amos was not. But Sider has a point: Amos is Scripture too. There's no reason why it *shouldn't* be taught, so long as it's not a cover for the Gospel according to Marx. (Erasmus, after listening to John Colet's lectures on the epistles of St. Paul, exclaimed: "I could hear Plato himself speaking!") Considering Sider's tendency to read social revolution into the prophets, that danger is very real indeed:

*Cross-cultural missionaries need not engage in politics. But they must carefully and fully expound for new converts the explosive biblical message that God is on the side of the poor and oppressed. The poor will learn quickly how to apply biblical principles to their own oppressive societies.* [15]

Especially if we drop a few hints. How does Sider think the "oppressed" should apply these explosive principles? Two concrete examples are *land reform* and *nationalization of foreign holdings*. (Love those euphemisms. "I'm not stealing your property. I'm reforming it.") Notice the moral twist in Sider's call for land reform, where he states that the poor want the land of the wealthy, but the wealthy don't want them to confiscate it. "Do we want to continue supporting that kind of injustice?"[16] (Did I miss something?) Theft is justice. Protection of property is injustice. An explosive message, to be sure. But I can't find it in my concordance. See if it's in yours.

Sider goes on to give Chilean President Salvador Allende honorable mention for expropriating copper mines owned by U.S. companies, on the basis that the high profits they earned had gone to the investors, resulting in the malnutrition of millions of children.[17] While we can sympathize with the condition of these children (and since the story came straight from the upright Mr. Allende, I see little reason to doubt its veracity), the issue here is *theft*. Concern for the poor has long been used as a justification for all sorts of crime. Judas Iscariot, who was a thief, is a prime example (John 12:4-6). Those who profess to be so high-minded that they can treat the law of God in this manner should at least have the honesty to abandon the facade of "biblical Christianity." But then a man who brazenly advocates theft won't flinch at lying.

But there is much more to Ronald Sider's tactics of envy than what we have already seen. A comparatively recent phenomenon, not envisaged by men such as Samuel Willard, is the use of envy *to manipulate the object of envy into feeling guilty for being envied*. He is made to believe that he really *is* responsible for the sufferings of others, that his wealth is actually a cause of poverty in other people. When envy is so pervasive in society, when it is positively encouraged by our leaders—and preachers in particular—we turn the envy back on ourselves and feel guilty for what we possess. A central motive of socialistic reformers is to cause an orgy of self-flagellation among property owners. A humorous example is that of a woman who is distressed because her grass is green. The following poem is not intended as a joke. It appeared quite seriously in *The Christian Century*:

**Priorities**
*My lawn*
*is green and lush,*
*By fertilizer fed.*
*The soil for the crops of the world*
*grows poor.* [18]

We can smile at such fertilized silliness. But the next example shows the awful lengths to which inverted envy can lead. I cannot even express my utter disgust—and deep sadness—at the moral blindness of a writer in a recent issue of *theOtherSide*. Randall Basinger, a philosophy teacher at a Christian college in Kansas, writes of his emotional turmoil at the successful delivery of his infant son. He admits that "Deep in my heart, I wanted to praise God for the beautiful event that had occurred. More than ever before, I felt the urge to utter a joyful prayer of thanksgiving. But the words wouldn't come."[19] Why not? Read on:

*I found my mind wandering from the plush, resort-like, suburban hospital in which I was standing to the crowded wards of inner-city institutions. I thought of parents and soon-to-be-born children who seldom reap the benefits of our advanced medical technology. Would husbands in the broken ghettos of the inner city experience the same joy I was experiencing? Would those unborn children have the same safe passage into the world as my son? Would their mothers come through the birth process as well as my well-doctored wife?*

*Then my circle of thought broadened to parents in other areas of the world. Enforced ignorance, poor sanitation, deficient diets, rank poverty, and scarce or nonexistent medical care—these were no doubt having their effect on many a mother and newborn child. What were the husbands of those wives and the fathers of those children experiencing? Was there joy at the birth of their firstborn?*

*I thought about those who lived before the onset of modern medicine. For my wife and myself, the threatening breach position of our unborn child had been no threat at all. Yet for countless parents through the centuries, the threat had been real—and often fatal. Those grieving fathers, far removed by time, were nonetheless a very real and quite disturbing presence in my mind.*

*In the face of all this suffering, both past and present, how was I to pray? Was I to praise and give thanks to God for what I had experienced?*

*To thank God for all that had happened was to presuppose that God had caused it to happen. At first, this seemed quite acceptable. But I cringed as I became aware of where this ultimately led, for if God had providentially caused these good things to happen in our lives, then must not God also be directly responsible for the misery, pain, and death experienced by so many others around the world?*

*Sure, I could praise God's goodness to me, but what would that imply about God's character, in view of the ugliness and evil that so many others experience?*

*And so I couldn't bring myself to utter that prayer. I couldn't thank God for being kind to me while ignoring the desperate needs of so many others. I knew that if that's the kind of God we have, then our God isn't just. If that's the kind of God we have, then somehow our God is at least indirectly responsible for the evil in the world. And that's not the kind of God I want.*

*Besides, I thought, such a prayer wouldn't even be very realistic. It sounds simple and pious to say, "Thank you, God, for what you have brought about in my life." But how well does that square with reality? Had not a host of "this-worldly" factors been instrumental in making my son's birth successful?*

*Why shouldn't my wife have given birth to a healthy child? She lives in a society and a time where tremendous medical knowledge and services are available. She is well educated. She knows how to take advantage of the best medical facilities. She has the money necessary for the best of medical care. And she is a member of a socio-economic class that gives her easy access to all of that.*

*The deck of life is stacked. My wife and I were among the lucky ones. An abundance of social and historical factors played a major role in our good fortune. And the lack of those factors often brings tragedy to others. To a large extent, we were simply at the right place at the right time. . . .*

*How easy and natural it would have been for me to thank God for causing my wife's delivery to turn out right. Pious, it would have been. But such a prayer would have also encouraged me to focus only on what was going on in my life—or in my own family's life, which is the same thing. And by so doing, I would have become less sensitive to the needs of others.*

*In addition, by emphasizing God's direct responsibility for our particular blessings, we ignore those social and economic factors that have made the blessings possible. And given the way our world is set up, those very same factors are often bringing untold hardships to others. By appealing to divine providence we ignore that reality. We don't have to deal seriously with the fact that so many of our blessings are built on the backs of the poor.* [20]

Usually, the articles in *theOtherSide* make me angry. This one made me weep as well—not so much for the guilt-manipulator who could write such trash, but for his son, now three years old, who has that kind of atmosphere to live in. The fact that this garbage is becoming more popular indicates that we are on the verge of cultural suicide.

Sider's whole "ministry" can be seen as one of guilt manipulation. His fable of the Indian prime minister threatening to blow millions into oblivion make *us* feel responsible. [21] The United States has "an unjust division of the earth's food and resources," [22] and our right to use them is superseded by the "human" rights of the rest of the world. [23] The poor nations suffer because *we* use more fertilizer, [24] eat more fish [25] and beef, [26] and generally consume more than other people do. [27] White schoolchildren are guilty of the "terrible sin" of getting a better education and thus better job opportunities, because their parents pulled them out of an inner-city school. [28] We are all guilty of Mexico's oppression of its farmers; [29] we all are guilty of the profits made by U.S. companies in other nations—profits which constitute "foreign aid" from poor people to us. [30] Profits from these countries are "unjustly high." [31] "Every North American benefits from these structural injustices . . . *you* participate in unjust structures which contribute *directly* to the hunger of a billion unhappy neighbors." [32] "The proper conclusion is that injustice has become embedded in some of our fundamental economic institutions" [33] —so much so that it is *"impossible to live in North America and not be involved in unjust social structures."* [34] If you're having trouble bearing the weight of all that guilt by yourself, Sider offers some comfort, hastening to make it clear that he does not "want to suggest that 214 million Americans bear sole responsibility for all hunger, starvation and injustice in today's world." No? Of course not: "*All* countries of the rich Northern Hemisphere are directly involved."[35] At least we're not alone. And, generously, Sider includes himself in all this flogging. He confesses that he paid $50 for an extra suit, and "that money would have fed a starving child in India for about a year."[36] Well, if you live on this continent, it's tough being righteous all the time. Come to think of it, the money I spent on Sider's book would have fed that kid for over a month.

> **A sound heart is the life of the flesh:**
> **But envy the rottenness of the bones.**
> (Proverbs 14:30, KJV)

Envy destroys the man who commits it. He does not work for the future and the glory of God. He cannot fulfill the purpose for which he was created. His frustration increases: he can't enjoy what he has, for he is eaten up by what others have or—when he turns the envy in upon himself—by what others do not have. We should take the verse literally to some extent: envy has very serious physical consequences. Because man is a whole person, God's curse on sin affects the whole man. You can quite literally be eaten up by envy.

More than this, envy is a rot on the foundations of society. If the cultural ethic is the destruction of anyone who owns something which others don't own, the result is chaos. And if you are fearful of your neighbors' envy, you won't produce. Success and productivity become dangerous, and the whole culture declines. *A civilization dominated by envy has rottenness in its bones: it is doomed to extinction.* "Wrath is cruel, and anger is outrageous; but who is able to stand before envy?" (Proverbs 27:4) The kind of cultural rot that sets in is terrifying, as described in Edward C. Banfield's *The Moral Basis of a Backward Society*.[37] George Gilder is right: "Rather than wealth causing poverty, it is far more true to say that what causes poverty is the widespread belief that wealth does."[38]

The only cure for this malaise is "a sound heart"—an attitude of contentment with God's providential government of your life. He is the one who raises up and puts down, and your advantages —or lack of them—are from Him. Samuel Willard said this in 1706:

*We are never the worse in our selves, because another enjoys a Prosperous Condition; it is of God that his State is such, and it in no way makes ours other than it is . . . to envy men the Prosperity which God bestows upon them, is to Hate them without a cause; or when they have offered us no real Affront or Provocation. It is an Affront offered to the Divine Sovereignty; it is God who lifts Men up, and puts them down; He is the Supream disposer of all the Affairs of the Children of Men. It implies a fault found with His Government of the World, as if He dealt Unjustly, and did not distribute His Favours, either in Wisdom or Righteousness. It Envys God His Glory in the World, in that it is Angry if He be Glorified by another; because he thinks that in so doing he out-shines him, and darkens his Light. It despiseth and reflects upon the Gifts and Favours of God, as if they were Lost, because they are not Concentred in him.* [39]

If you have needs, the Bible commands you to *pray* (Philippians 4:6-7), to *be content* (Philippians 4:5, 8, 12), and to *work* (I Thessalonians 4:11); and God, who hears the cry of the poor, will supply all your needs (Philippians 4:19). We have a wealthy Father, and under His care we can be at peace, regardless of our financial standing. But this requires obedience to Him, seeking Him as the Source of wealth (Deuteronomy 8:18), and finding our happiness in obedience to His law.

God's law does bring physical, material blessing to a culture. For one thing, the society's ethic is not envy, but obedience to God. This makes for both social *stability* and economic *growth*. The land prospers when people are at least externally obedient to biblical law; when they allow their neighbors to prosper; when they allow even wicked men—as long as they remain *externally* obedient—to develop the earth. God will catch up with the ungodly (Psalm 37:1-11), and if they in the meantime abide by His commands, we have nothing to worry about.

It is easy to point a finger at the culture around you. But don't forget: *you* are the culture: get the log out of your own eye, and don't seek legislation and the long arm of the state to rid your neighbor of the mote in his. Envy is a cheat. It will destroy you and your culture much more than any enemies — imagined or real — will do. The biblical ethic of contentment does not mean a lack of drive or ambition. It does not mean apathy or inaction regarding the *genuine* injustice in the world. But it does mean that we are not revolutionaries. We look neither to the *state* nor to *chaos* to achieve personal fulfillment or social improvement. Our aim is dominion under God's rule. We seek progress within a stable structure, fenced in by the law of God.

*Who among you is wise and understanding? Let him show by his good behavior his deeds in the gentleness of wisdom. But if you have bitter jealousy and selfish ambition in your heart, do not be arrogant and so lie against the truth. This wisdom is not that which comes down from above, but is earthly, natural, demonic. For where jealousy and selfish ambition exist, there is disorder and every evil thing. But the wisdom from above is first pure, then peaceable, gentle, reasonable, full of mercy and good fruits, unwavering, without hypocrisy. And the seed whose fruit is righteousness is sown in peace by those who make peace. (James 3:13-18)*

The politics of envy and guilt is nothing other than *class hatred and war*. It is a blight on the soul, a rottenness eating at the foundations of culture. No society can long survive it: the nation that fails to overcome it through faith and obedience will fall. As we have seen, it reduces man to impotence and frustration; the man who succumbs to it is rendered unable even to pray. And that, assuredly, is the sociology of Satan. It is but a step away from hell.

# THE JUBILEE PRINCIPLE

> **"THE ONLY LONG-TERM SOLUTION TO HUNGER AND MALNUTRITION IN THE THIRD WORLD IS INCREASED AGRICULTURAL PRODUCTIVITY THERE. THAT WILL MEAN LAND REFORM...."** [RONALD SIDER, *RICH CHRISTIANS IN AN AGE OF HUNGER,* P. 218]

> **"CURSED IS HE WHO MOVES HIS NEIGHBOR'S BOUNDARY MARK."** [DEUTERONOMY 27:17]

One of the most cherished myths of the "Christian socialist" movement is that the Old Testament law of the Jubilee Year (Leviticus 25) had something to do with redistribution of wealth. Because of what seems to be a *studied ignorance of Scripture among the evangelical community*, this utterly untenable interpretation has gone virtually unquestioned. Even those who, at a gut level, disagree with Sider still feel vaguely uncomfortable about the Jubilee. Granted, if the Bible really does command redistribution, we have no choice but to submit to it willingly and cheerfully. But the question must always be: What does the Bible say?

We have seen that Old Testament society lived in terms of seven-year cycles. The final year of each cycle was a year in which the land was to receive a rest, and debtors were to be released from their obligations. At the end of seven cycles (49 years), the 50th year also was to be proclaimed as a year of rest, and all believing slaves were released. More than this, however, was the fact that the lands which had been sold during the previous fifty years had to be restored to their owners. The land of Canaan had been parceled out to the various tribes and the families within those tribes. The property which they owned could not be permanently alienated from them. Because of debts, a man might have to put up his land for lease, but in the Jubilee Year the property had to return to him. It is this aspect of the law which is especially seized upon by those who would use the Bible to justify socialism.

What use does Sider make of the Jubilee law? First, he says, "at the heart of God's call for Jubilee is a divine demand for regular, fundamental redistribution of the means for producing wealth."[1] "God therefore gave his people a law which would equalize land ownership every fifty years."[2] The "Jubilee principle" is thus one of "massive economic sharing among the people of God."[3] In terms of this, we can see that God's word is opposed to laissez-faire economics,[4] and stands firmly on the side of "human rights" over against "property rights" (presumably, people who own property are not "human," and thus have no rights).

If the principle of the Jubilee is to be applied to the modern age, how does Sider envisage its implementation? Sider has several ideas about how Christians can "live the Jubilee,"[5] but two of his proposals deserve particular mention.

1) After calling for *tariffs* and *commodity agreements*, he observes that "the above suggestions seem just and desirable," although they are "very modest in comparison to the year of Jubilee."[6] We have already noted something of how just these practices are. But for Sider, they are only "modest" in terms of whatever it is he would really like to see: "We must discover new, concrete models for applying this biblical principle in our global village."[7] He longs for "a new generation of economists and political scientists who will devote their lives to formulating, developing and implementing a contemporary model of Jubilee."[8] If you had hoped

that Sider's ventures into international politics were simply temporary aberrations, think again—hard. He's only just begun.[9]

2) He suggests that we select a year in which to celebrate a modern Jubilee: "all Christians worldwide would pool all their stocks, bonds, and income producing property and businesses and redistribute them equally. . . . There would undoubtedly be a certain amount of confusion and disruption. But then good things are seldom easy."[10]

In comparing Sider's views with the biblical Jubilee laws, we should note at the outset that he is being somewhat hypocritical in all this, since he does not really believe the Jubilee laws are valid at all: "I certainly do not think that the specific provisions of the year of Jubilee are binding today."[11] And neither do I. But if we both agree that this legislation is no longer binding, why bring it up at all? Sider answers that "the basic principles, not the specific details, . . . are important and normative for Christians today."[12] This allows him to exercise his penchant for abstracting what he regards as *principles* and pouring his own content into them, in disregard for the biblical context. The Old Testament laws of land tenure for the twelve tribes of Israel are translated into price controls, redistribution of income, and whatever Sider's new generation of political scientists comes up with.

But Sider is correct about one thing. The Jubilee law is not binding today, on several counts. It referred specifically to the land of Israel, which God had divided among the tribes. By divine fiat, the Israelites became the "original owners." The previous owners—the Canaanites, Hivites, Jebusites, etc.—were forever dispossessed, because God had declared that the land belonged to His people. No other landowner can make this claim. I may buy or sell property, but I cannot claim a "divine right" to anything in the sense that the Israelites could. We cannot establish the Jubilee anywhere outside Palestine, for we have no starting point. Who is the *original owner* of *your* property? The Indians? Aside from the fact that the Indians had no sense of private property in land as we with our Christian heritage know it, the Indians aren't original owners either—they wrested it from people who were here previously. The "original ownership" of Israel was a creative act of God, and is simply inapplicable anywhere outside of the promised land. Until Sider gets around to claiming his own deity and decreeing original ownership, the Jubilee land laws have no relevance anywhere else. To abstract them from their context is to commit the same error as demanding the annihilation of modern "Canaanites." There are no biblical laws for original land tenure outside of Israel.

Moreover, the Jubilee laws about the land are invalid even in modern Palestine. Not counting the fact that the records of title holders were destroyed in A.D. 70—making it impossible to apply the law anyway—the land tenure laws are inapplicable after the coming of Christ. The Jubilee was *typological*: that is, it was a symbolic prefiguring of the work of Jesus Christ. The reasons for this take us back to God's original promise of the land to Abraham in Genesis 13:15 and 17:8. Paul, under the inspiration of the Holy Spirit, interprets these statements as in reality a promise of *Christ* (Galatians 3:14, 16), and says that Christians are inheritors of God's promise to Abraham (v. 29).

How was a guarantee of real estate a promise of Christ? This is because Palestine was no ordinary land. It was to be the scene of the most significant events in redemptive history, culminating in the birth, life, death, resurrection and ascension of our Lord. Therefore, when God pledged the *land* to Abraham, He was in reality giving him a capsulized promise of the *gospel* (Galatians 3:8), since the blessing of all nations was intimately tied up with Abraham's possession of the land. The promise was to Abraham's "seed" (i.e., believers; Galatians 3:29), "for an everlasting possession"; and this is immediately followed by the words: "and I will be their God' (Genesis 17:8). To truly possess the land was to truly possess *Jesus Christ*, God's holy seed, because He is what gave the land its definition and purpose. Without Christ, the promise of the land is empty and worthless: it is no gospel, and no real source of blessing to anyone, Jew or Gentile. But because

Christ came in fulfillment of the promise, the land—in its real meaning and significance—is ours forever.

In terms of this, the Jubilee required that the land could not be permanently alienated from godly heirs. This was a symbol that God would never leave or forsake His people—that, by His grace, His people would remain in the land, instead of getting kicked out as Adam and Eve were, and as were the previous heathen inhabitants of the land, who were spewed out of the earth (Leviticus 18:24-29). God's people have an atonement in Jesus Christ. The effects of the Curse, still visited upon those outside of Christ, are being reversed through the grace of God in the gospel. Therefore the announcement of the Jubilee was made on the Day of Atonement (Leviticus 25:9), after seven sevens of years, a perfect fulness (Leviticus 25:8), symbolizing Christ, who came in "the fulness of the time" (Galatians 4:4). The Jubilee was clearly ceremonial, pointing to our atonement, liberty and security in Christ, whose coming marked "the favorable year of the Lord" as he proclaimed "release to the captives" (Luke 4:18-19; cf. Isaiah 61:1-2). But Israel rejected liberty in Christ, choosing instead to be enslaved to Satan and the Roman antichrist. In spurning Christ, they thereby forfeited their right to the land; so the curses of the law were reinstated, the Jews were driven out, and their land was confiscated. Christ, like the land which spoke of Him, spews the ungodly out of His mouth (Revelation 3:16).

However, we must examine further the specifics of the Jubilee laws, in order to see just how much the actual principles conflict with Sider's version. In some ways, the Jubilee actually *furthered* inequality. For one thing, it did not equalize incomes. The "unlucky" Israelite who had to sell his land between Jubilee years to a more successful entrepreneur did not share in what might be high profits coming from the wise use of the property. The best man still won. The land was used by those who were best able to manage it, as demonstrated by their other successes that enabled them to purchase it in the first place. And when the original owner received it back, it would not exactly be in prime, income-producing condition, for it would have lain fallow, with no labor expended on it, for at least a year. This is obviously vastly different from pooling all "stocks, bonds, and income producing property" as Sider would like to see. The restored land was not producing any income at all. The income was already gone, in the hands of the wealthy businessman who had had the use of the land. The Jubilee constituted an extra Sabbath Year as well (Leviticus 25:11), so the one who received it back would not be able to plant it until the 51st year—in which case it would not be income-producing until after the harvest, about a year and a half after he repossessed it. It must be remembered, however, that these are merely inconsequential "details"; Ronald Sider stands for the *principles* involved: the expropriation of income-producing property and the control of prices at gunpoint.

But there's even more to the Jubilee law than this. The laws of *inheritance* are naturally involved with the question of just *who* is to receive the land. In biblical law, the first-born son receives twice as much as the other sons (Deuteronomy 21:17). As my second son will be happy to inform you, that is a significant inequality. Moreover, a father has the right to disinherit an ungodly son and pass an inheritance along to a godly servant (Proverbs 17:2); ultimately the godly will inherit all things, and the wicked are dispossessed entirely (Proverbs 13:22; 28:8; Revelation 21:7). Thus, even some Israelites did not receive land in the Jubilee Year.

Also, it must be remembered that immigrants were generally among the poorest members of society. They were not affected by the Jubilee provisions about land, nor were their interest-bearing debts cancelled. Many, if not most of the poor would be in this category, and the Jubilee did nothing for them. In this connection, we should consider the subtle shift Sider employs in his ax-grinding abstractions. He implies that the Jubilee was a complete redistribution of the means of production across the board: everything is equalized among everybody. As we have seen, it was not "the poor" who got land, but *the poor Israelite with the familial inheritance* who was restored to his ancestral land. Many poor were excluded—all non-Israelites and some Israelites who were disinherited. But Sider overlooks this completely: "The year of Jubilee envisages an institutionalized structure that affects everyone automatically."[13]

Again, Sider has blown his cover. He has no intention of submitting to biblical standards of justice. He uses the Bible to mask his real intentions with a superficial Christian flavor, but what he wants is *socialistic redistribution of capital*. The Jubilee, for a limited time and in a limited area, called for *restoration*—not "redistribution" or "equalization"—of specified, non-income-producing, ancestral lands to deserving heirs. It cannot be applied outside Israel. It cannot be applied after the resurrection of Christ. And it cannot legitimately be used as a smokescreen for socialism.

If Ronald Sider were really concerned for the poor, he would seek to implement the biblical Poor Laws we have studied. If he were concerned for the poor, he would seek to encourage the godly investment of private capital so that real wealth for all of society would rise. If he were concerned for the poor, he would encourage them to build, work, and save for the future, resisting the attempts of an ungodly state to enslave them. If he were concerned for the poor, he would try to prevent the state from playing god. If he were concerned for the poor, he would teach obedience to God's law as the means for obtaining God's blessings throughout our land.

The fact that he does the very opposite of these things raises an important question.

What *does* he want?

# 12 THE GOAL OF EQUALITY

---

"DOES THE NEED FOR 'PRIVACY' AND 'SPACE' MAKE IT RIGHT FOR ONE FAMILY TO OCCUPY A HOUSE THAT ... COULD EASILY MEET THE NEEDS OF TEN OR FIFTEEN PEOPLE?" [RONALD SIDER, *LIVING MORE SIMPLY FOR EVANGELISM AND JUSTICE*, P. 18]

---

"MY SON, IF SINNERS ENTICE YOU, DO NOT CONSENT. IF THEY SAY, 'COME WITH US. ... THROW IN YOUR LOT WITH US, WE SHALL ALL HAVE ONE PURSE'; MY SON, DO NOT WALK IN THE WAY WITH THEM, KEEP YOUR FEET FROM THEIR PATH. FOR THEIR FEET RUN TO EVIL, AND THEY HASTEN TO SHED BLOOD." [PROVERBS 1:10-16]

---

There are three dangers we face in reading the works of Ronald Sider, especially when he says something that closely approximates biblical truth. First we can fall into the trap of thinking he actually means what he says. Careful attention must be paid to the real focus of his thought, which is too often in opposition to his claims. Second, a casual reading might cause us to swallow the unbiblical ideas which he tends to fuse with the teachings of Scripture. And third, we can make the mistake of rejecting those things which are true, simply because Sider is usually so objectionable.

Does the Bible command "economic equality?" Sider says it does[1] and that since God "disapproves of great extremes of wealth and poverty,"[2] He "created mechanisms and structures to prevent great economic inequality among His people."[3] (One of these "equalizing mechanisms" is the Jubilee, examined in the preceeding chapter.)

God's word certainly tells us to care for the poor, as we have already seen. Even our enemies are to be given aid in distress (Proverbs 25:21-22). More particularly, Christian brothers and sisters who are needy should be helped out of our supply (e.g., I John 3:16-18). This is, in fact, the very meaning of Christian fellowship and communion (both words are translations of *koinonia*), as Sider points out very well.[4] For example, in Paul's description of the "body life" of the Christian assembly in Romans 12, he tells us that we should be "contributing to the needs of the saints, practicing hospitality" (v. 13). The word *contributing* there is the verb form of *koinonia*; in other words, if we are to have genuine fellowship in the body of believers, we must not be content with coffee and donuts on Sunday morning. We must be "fellowshipping to the needs of the saints," truly seeking to help them in their difficulties.

The primary symbol of this sharing ministry among believers is the communion service, which in modern churches has been almost entirely stripped of its meaning. Far from being the "pretend" meal of congregations today, the communion service of the New Testament was a continuation of the Old Testament Passover supper (see Matthew 26:19-30; I Corinthians 5:6-8). It was a "love feast," a common meal in which the Christians shared their food with one another. The participants did not get a little piece of cracker and a thimbleful of grape juice. They sat down and ate a meal. The danger Paul rebuked at Corinth was that the believers there were failing to discern the Lord's body (I Corinthians 11:29). This doesn't mean they failed to comprehend some mystical dogma regarding the precise relationship of Christ's physical body to the bread and wine. Paul was not rebuking a lack of intellectual understanding, but rather a lack of *moral* discernment. The Corinthians had been behaving sinfully, indulging themselves in gluttony and drunkenness, refusing to share food with one another (v. 21). The "body" they failed to discern was Christ's *congregational body*, their fellow believers. They came to have communion, and did not commune together; they did not share, yet they called it a "sharing service." Paul accused them of not eating "*the Lord's* supper," that each one ate "*his own* supper" (v. 20-21), with the result that "one is hungry and another drunk." And this is a problem with churches today—even though we've gotten rid of the alcohol in most cases (incidentally, we're supposed to *share* the wine, not abolish it). In many modern "communion" services, the participants receive a token meal, close their eyes and chew away, thinking spiritual, inward-type thoughts in total isolation from their neighbors. That's what the good ones are doing, anyway. Others of us are contemplating other sublime mysteries: What to do about the piece of wafer stuck in our throats and how sour the grape juice is. But is the service contributing to our mutual appreciation and loving relationship with each other as a body? Not usually, and not at all in the biblical sense of having the regular opportunity of sharing food with one another. And even the full communion service—which should be restored—is itself merely an emblem of what we are at all times: "We who are many are one body; for we all partake of the one bread" (I Corinthians 10:17). We should always be available to fellow believers, as members of one family in Christ.[5] James states this in strong terms:

*What use is it, my brethren, if a man says he has faith, but he has no works? Can that faith save him? If a brother or sister is without clothing and in need of daily food, and one of you says to them, "Go in peace, be warmed and be filled;" and yet you do not give them what is necessary for their body; what use is that? Even so faith, if it has no works, is dead, being by itself. (James 2:14-17)*

We should do what we can to meet the needs of our fellow

Christians who are truly in need. Does this mean equalizing our wealth? Sider says yes, on the basis of II Corinthians 8:13-15, where Paul requests the church at Corinth to give financial assistance to the needy Christians in Jerusalem:

*For this is not for the ease of others and for your affliction, but by way of equality — at the present time your abundance being a supply for their want, that their abundance also may become a supply for your want, that there may be equality; as it is written, "He who gathered much did not have too much, and he who gathered little had no lack."*

Paul is not speaking here of complete redistribution of income, but rather of *voluntarily* meeting the needs of the poor Jerusalem believers by the more well-to-do Corinthians. Sider tells us that "the norm . . . is something like economic equality among the people of God,"[6] and that "God desires major movement toward economic equality in the new society of the church."[7] This is a distortion. Paul is not asking that income be equalized, that Christians should "pool all their stocks, bonds, and income producing property and businesses and redistribute them equally."[8] The word for "equality" occurs one other time in the New Testament, where Paul commands: "Masters, grant to your slaves justice and *fairness*" (Colossians 4:1). This is not a demand for equal income between masters and their slaves. Paul is simply repeating the biblical mandate that a responsible owner's slaves should receive the necessities of life. The "equality" intended by Paul in II Corinthians is simply that Christians should try to meet the *needs* of destitute members of the body of Christ, giving them "what is necessary for their body" (James 2:16). Paul's mention of the gathering of manna by the migrant community of Israel does not constitute sumptuary legislation for all Christians for all time. The point of the quotation is to stress the ideal of even the poorest *members of the congregation* having sufficient food. The equality refers to provision for actual needs. We must not confuse the modern socialist notion with Paul's statement. In the specific sense of the Greek term, a wealthy master and his slave are *equal* if they both have enough to eat — even though the actual possessions of the master may be vastly disproportionate to those of the slave. The Bible requires me to help those in need of food and clothing. But this is a far cry from Sider's international egalitarianism.

Sider gives two New Testament examples of what he regards as "equalizing": Jesus' practice of sharing a common purse with His disciples (John 12:6; 13:29), and the "communism" of the early Christians in Jerusalem (Acts 2:44-46; 4:32-37).[9] Concerning the practice of Jesus and His disciples, it may be readily admitted that a small band of itinerant, full-time missionaries who are constantly living together and have no place of permanent residence (Matthew 8:20) would probably find this to be an efficient method of operating. But it was a special circumstance, for a limited time, and should not be considered normative for most Christians. Since Sider has not *yet* suggested that all Christians take up a nomadic existence as traveling preachers, we need not detain ourselves with this example any further.

The second example is the famous one. It has been used as a proof-text by Christian socialists for centuries. Yes, the early Jerusalem church practiced financial sharing. No, it is not normative for all Christians. The situation was this. On the day of Pentecost, when Jews from around the Roman Empire had gathered in Jerusalem, Peter preached a sermon which immediately added 3,000 new believers to the church (Acts 2:41). Shortly thereafter, 5,000 more were converted (4:4). *Because of the urgent necessity of receiving instruction in the faith, most, if not all of these new converts stayed in Jerusalem* (2:41-42). They had brought enough with them for their stay during the feasts, but they had not planned on staying in Jerusalem indefinitely. Nevertheless, there they were, and the early church was faced with an immediate economic crisis of gigantic proportions. God commands aid to needy brethren, and the Jerusalem Christians stepped in to supply for the needs. Many of the needy were apparently from Israel, but many also were "Hellenized" Jews from other nations (2:9-11; 6:1). It was a special situation, and required special measures to deal with it. So believers in Jerusalem who owned property liquidated it as the need arose, using the proceeds for charity. In addition, Jerusalem was "condemned property" anyway, because Jesus had promised to destroy it (Matthew 24; Mark 13; Luke 21), and *the Christians knew they would have to prepare to leave when the Romans surrounded it.* They sold knowingly to Jews who would lose everything in the city. In short, "tough luck" for the rebellious, crucifying Jews of that generation. God's new people used "inside information" about the future to "rip off" the Jews. As with the example of Jesus and his disciples, Sider's "Jerusalem Model" is no model at all. It was a special tactic designed to meet unique circumstances. And, obviously, if all Christians were to simply liquidate all their capital and redistribute it for immediate consumption, there would soon be nothing left. Selling property can continue only so long as there remains property to sell and buyers with assets to exchange. Certainly, the example of these early Christians rebukes our indifference and unwillingness to help needy brothers and sisters around us. But it does not demand that we do what they did, unless we get a load of 8,000 jobless Christian immigrants dumped on our community too—and even then, capital consumption should be a last resort. We will also need *rich nonbelievers* to sell to—economically productive people who can put our capital to good use.

Sider's reasons for wanting Christians to practice economic equality are not really related to the church. His goal is to use Christians to appeal for governmentally enforced economic equality, and he feels that the demand for this would be more credible if the church were to observe it as an example. *This is the basis for everything he is demanding from the church—it is all a means to his very political ends.* This can be seen in the title of his article, "Sharing The Wealth: The Church As Biblical Model For Public Policy."[10] He sees the church as "the most universal body in the world today";[11] thus if he can control the church, he will be well on his way to controlling the world. Here is his reasoning:

*To ask government to legislate what the church cannot persuade its members to live is a tragic absurdity. . . . Only as groups of believers in North America and Europe dare to incarnate in their life together what the Bible teaches about economic relationships among the people of God do they have any right to demand that leaders in Washington or Westminster shape a* new world economic order . . . only if the body of Christ is already beginning to live a radically new model of economic sharing will our demand for political change have integrity and impact.[12]

Now, contrast that with his statement that economic sharing among Christians—the means to his goal of *centralized power*—is to be "voluntary," and that "Legalism is not the answer."[13] Not, that is, until it is *legislated*. Then, armed officers will come to collect our donations, and the texts exegeted as the basis for it will come from the *Federal Register*. If you think Sider was simply outlining a plan for a wonderful paradise of voluntary sharing among Christians, you've been conned. He has no intention of stopping with voluntarism. He wants to manipulate the church with envy and guilt, to provide a model for public policy, and later, when his proposals are enacted into laws, voluntarism be damned. You *will* share, whether you like it or not. Again he says: *Certainly we should work politically to demand costly concessions from Washington in international forums working to reshape the International Monetary Fund, as well as new policy in trade negotiations on tariffs, commodity agreements and the like. Certainly we must ask whether* far more sweeping structural changes *are necessary. However, our attempt to restructure secular society will possess integrity only if our personal lifestyles . . . demonstrate that we are already daring to live* what we ask Washington to legislate. . . . *If even one-quarter of the Christians in the northern hemisphere had the courage to live the . . . vision of economic equality, the governments of our dangerously divided global village might also be persuaded to* legislate the sweeping changes *needed.*[14]

What sort of "sweeping changes" in public policy would Sider like to see? He suggests for his "model" the church, that it should be "the norm, rather than the exception, for Christians to . . . evaluate each other's income-tax returns and family budgets, discuss major purchases, and gently nudge each other toward lifestyles more in keeping with their worship of a God who sides with the poor."[15] Thus, using this as a model, a government officer can sit in on your next family budget-planning session and discuss major purchases with you. He might have to bring his billy club along in case you need a "gentle nudge."

Actually, Ronald Sider has nothing but *contempt for private charity*. He would rather have state-enforced "institutional change." Here are two of his reasons:

*First, institutional change is often more* effective. . . . *The cup of cold water that we give in Christ's name is often more effective if it is given through the public health measures of preventive medicine or economic planning.*

*Second, institutional change is often* morally *better. Personal charity and philanthropy still permit the rich donor to feel superior. And it makes the recipient feel inferior and dependent. Institutional changes, on the other hand, give the oppressed rights and power.*[16]

Now, if only the Lord had thought of that. But it's too late. That morally inferior personal charity is encoded into biblical law, and we're stuck with it until heaven and earth pass away. Darn! However, at least we have learned something significant about Sider's views. The power of the state, restricted by biblical law, should be aggrandized. God's law is less effective. State intervention, forbidden by Scripture, is morally better than the eternal word of God. *Personal charity*—which we all thought was the whole point of his book—is really just a *model* for the *omnipotent state*, and the model, morally substandard as it is, will probably be scrapped once we get the state programs going full blast. There will be less money for charity after taxes.

The professed goal of economic equality has long been used by tyrants as a cover for the most brutal kinds of intervention. It is a fetish, held up before the poor to excite envy, dangled in front of the rich to induce guilt. Revolution and statist oppression are facilitated thereby: the envious will rebel, and the guilty will have been rendered impotent. Sider does not want the biblical idea of *equality before the law*—which assumes that there are distinctions among men, and guarantees justice for all, and freedom to fulfill one's calling under God. Sider instead wants a *state-enforced egalitarianism*, a deliberate, coercive policy of levelling all men to conform to arbitrary, man-made canons of "social justice." *Equality before the law is incompatible with egalitarianism.* The socialist doctrine of economic equality requires the stealing of property and the prohibition of economic freedoms. It ignores the fact that "the LORD makes both poor and rich" (I Samuel 2:7), and that if men desire to improve their economic standing they must submit themselves to Him, work hard, and call upon Him for blessing: "Humble yourselves, therefore, under the mighty hand of God, that he may exalt you at the proper time, casting all your care upon Him, for He cares for you." (I Peter 5:6-7). But the socialist does not humble himself; he envies. He does not work; he steals. Sider's plea for "equality" is in reality a grasp for *power*:

*The constantly growing demand for food must stop — or at least slow down dramatically. That means reduced affluence in rich nations* and population control everywhere.[17]

We have already taken notice of several of his other goals, all to be implemented by the state, and all in the name of equality: "Just prices," tariffs, commodity agreements, land "reform," nationalization of private industries — and, in a passage quoted already, "a new world economic order" — in other words, "equality" imposed by a world government.

Sider denies that he wants a "wooden, legalistic egalitarianism." We may concede that it is not wooden. It is lead bullets and steel bayonets and iron chains and concrete cells. His "public policy" programs for "structural change" *require* policemen with very physical clout. If he did not intend coercion by armed thugs, he would not be pressing constantly for *legislation*. If he merely wants to be a "moral" force, he can preach, lecture, and write books. But we have seen that those activities are merely preliminary stage-settings for the main event. He has stated, again and again, that the voluntary equalization of his followers is designed to give credibility for their demand that the *state* enforce equalization. And that can be done only through violence, theft, and prohibition of men's freedoms. The possessions of some are expropriated and given to others. The force of law is directed against the rich. And thus economic equality is nothing other than *legal inequality*. This is not justice, it is tyranny. It is legislated lawlessness. "Thou shalt not steal," even by majority vote.

And because it is lawless, it cannot succeed in its professed intentions. As we have seen, biblical law commands charity, but only as a stop-gap measure, and never enforced by the state. The only way for the economy to grow is by progressively creating new capital. As labor becomes more productive through the continual investment of ever-increasing capital, real wages—i.e., genuine purchasing power—for workers must rise. This is the only method of increasing the economic status of the poor in any lasting way. Consumption of existing capital is nothing other than "eating the seed corn," enjoying benefits in the present at the expense of the future. And this, as Ludwig von Mises said, is the very character of socialism:

*Socialism is not in the least what it pretends to be. It is not the pioneer of a better and finer world, but the spoiler of what thousands of years of civilization have created. It does not build; it destroys. For destruction is the essence of it. It produces nothing, it only consumes what the social order based on private ownership in the means of production has created . . . each step leading toward Socialism must exhaust itself in the destruction of what already exists.*[18]

The real goal of equalization, motivated as it is by envy, is thus neither equality for all men before the law, nor the genuine benefit of the poor. Notwithstanding the rhetoric, the true goal of "economic equality," enforced by the state, is something very different indeed. As P. T. Bauer states:

*Comprehensive planning does not augment resources.* It only concentrates power.[19]

And now we know the answer to the question posed at the end of Chapter Eleven. Ronald Sider's concern is not with the poor, not with justice, not with equality, not with growth in terms of God's law. *Ronald Sider wants power.*

# STATISM

---

To virtually every problem raised in his writings, Ronald Sider's answer is state intervention. Even where he appeals to the "private sector," his motive is to have the uncoerced actions of individuals serve as "models" for coercive actions of government. As we have seen, he regards the biblical method of charity to be morally inferior to the biblically forbidden methods of statist expropriation and redistribution. Are prices "unjust"? Have the state lower them—or raise them, judging solely on the basis of economic class, siding with the poor, providing for their needs, creating more and more dependence upon government. Do we need jobs? Let the state provide them. Are profits too high? Let the state slice them down to size. Do we eat too much meat? Let us have a national food policy. What about health care? That is the business of the state. Is there inequality in the world? Let us ask our Father in Washington to make us all equal in economics. Of course, when other inequalities arise—not *differences*, mind you, but *inequalities*—the state will have to level them too. Until— *In the not very distant future, after the Third World War, Justice had made great strides. Legal Justice, Economic Justice, Social Justice, and many other forms of justice, of which we do not even know the names, had been attained; but there still remained spheres of human relationship and activity in which Justice did not reign.*[1]

So begins L. P. Hartley's futurist novel, *Facial Justice*, in which facial beauty must be equalized, to ensure that justice is complete. We may smile, but the possibility of it seems daily less remote. Where does the "justice" of statism stop? If we have abandoned the biblical limitations on the power of the state, there is no logical boundary to its activity. Of one thing we may be sure: If Hartley's nightmare ever comes true, it will no doubt have been brought about, to a great extent, through the tireless and diligent efforts of a dedicated group of "biblical Christians"—the Evangelicals for Facial Action.

The only functions allowed to the state by the Bible are *defense of its people* and *punishment of criminals*. To go a step beyond this is forbidden. Biblical law works to prevent power being concentrated in any one institution, by creating and sanctioning many institutions—family, church, community, voluntary associations, and the state—all of which have legitimate but limited powers, all acting as buffers against the other powers, in a system of counter-balanced authorities. Gary North writes: "No one institution should be regarded as sovereign outside of its own legitimate, but strictly limited, sphere. Society in this perspective is a matrix of competing sovereignties, each with certain claims on men, but none with total claims in all areas."[2]

Statism is thus the infringement of God's limits on the state. It is *sin*, defined by the Westminster Shorter Catechism as, "any want of conformity unto, or transgression of, the law of God." For the state to *fail to conform* to God's law (e.g., by refusing to execute those who should be executed) is statism, because it is the state playing god by attempting to relax God's standards. For the state to *transgress* God's law (e.g., by interfering with the price mechanism of the market) is statism, because the state is claiming omniscience and omnipotence over the creation. God has given the state certain legitimate and necessary functions; but ruling the world is not one of them. The state's only duty with respect to the market is to guard against and punish what the Bible defines as public crime — which, as we have seen, is not absolutely identical with sin. I may have sin in my heart in refusing to do business with red-haired people, but it is not a crime legitimately punishable by the state. God will deal with me. Again, if my prices are "too high," the search for bargains will induce people to patronize the business of a competitor whose prices more closely are in line with the reality of demand. God's imposed scarcity (Genesis 3:17-19) induces men to become less wasteful. The free market is free only with respect to state intervention. It is never free from the providence of God. And this is as good a point as any to consider Sider's objections to the free market and its alleged inventors, the 18th-century economists:

*During the eighteenth century, Western society decided that the scientific method would shape our relationship to reality. Since only quantitative criteria of truth and value were acceptable, more intangible values such as community, trust and friendship became less important. Unlike friendship and justice, GNP can be measured. The result is our competitive, growth economy where winning and economic success (and they are usually the same) are all-important.*[3]

*From the perspective of biblical revelation, property owners are not free to seek their own profit without regard for the needs of their neighbor. Such an outlook derives from the secular laissez-faire economics of the deist Adam Smith, not from Scripture.*

*Smith published a book in 1776 which has profoundly shaped Western society in the last two centuries. (Since the Keynesian revolution, of course, Smith's ideas have shaped Western societies less than previously, but his fun-*

*damental outlook, albeit in somewhat revised form, still provides the basic ideological framework for many North Americans.) Smith argues that an invisible hand would guarantee the good of all if each person would pursue his or her own economic self-interest in the context of a competitive society. Supply and demand for goods and services must be the sole determinant of prices and wages. If the law of supply and demand reigns and if all seek their own advantage within a competitive nonmonopolistic economy, the good of society will be served. Owners of land and capital therefore have not only the right but also the obligation to seek as much profit as possible.*

*Such an outlook may be extremely attractive to successful North Americans. Indeed laissez-faire economics has been espoused by some as the Christian economics. In reality, however, it is a product of the Enlightenment. It reflects a modern, secularized outlook rather than a biblical perspective.* [4]

Thus, with one fell swoop, St. Ronald lops the head off the mighty capitalist dragon. Minus the logical fallacies and historical errors, that's really quite an argument: "I don't *like* capitalism." That aspect of his thesis is, in fact, unanswerable. Rather than tackle it, therefore, I will concede his victory, and deal with the more vulnerable parts of his statement.

Was Adam Smith a deist? That may depend on the definition of deism, a difficult task to begin with. If by deism is simply meant the "absentee landlord" view of the world—that God has nothing to do with it—then Smith was no deist, as can be abundantly proven by reference to his works. He certainly believed in heaven and hell, and in God's providential and loving oversight of the world. As examples of the latter, consider these statements:

*Every part of nature, when attentively surveyed, equally demonstrates the providential care of its Author; and we may admire the wisdom and goodness of God even in the weakness and folly of men.* [5]

Thus, when we are oppressed by evil men, Smith says:

*The only effectual consolation of humbled and afflicted man lies in an appeal to a still higher tribunal, to that of the all-seeing Judge of the World, whose eye can never be deceived, and whose judgments can never be perverted.* [6]

Because of this, there is a final remedy for injustice:

*The justice of God . . . requires, that he should hereafter avenge the injuries of the widow and the fatherless, who are here so often insulted with impunity.*[7]

I am not defending Smith as an evangelical Christian. He certainly tended toward empiricism and natural theology. But "deism" is a rather ambiguous term — and muddies the water with *ad hominem* arguments. If Smith *was* a deist, that alone does not invalidate his whole economic thought. Why, if I were to play dirty like that, I would mention that Sider's beloved Lord Keynes was an atheistic homosexual with a marked taste for young Tunisian boys, which proves that *his* economics is fallacious.

As for the charge that the laissez-faire economists cared little for "intangible values" — incidentally, all values are intangible — "such as community, trust and friendship," the answer is to *read* them. Adam Smith's *The Wealth of Nations* assumes the existence of the moral order provided by a Christian culture. For him, the growth of wealth was not in the least incompatible with concern for the welfare of others. But he also knew that such an atmosphere required the rule of law. "Commerce and manufactures can seldom flourish long in any state which does not enjoy a regular administration of justice, in which the people do not feel themselves secure in the possession of their property."[8] Whatever may be said against him, he did not, in contrast to both Keynes and Sider, advocate theft as a matter of public policy. He saw community, trust and friendship in terms of *lawful* behavior.

Sider's confused argument against the view that "supply and demand . . . must be the sole determinant of prices and wages" seems to imply that the "biblical perspective" requires some *other* determinant. What would that be? He offers no Scripture for this — understandably, since there is none — but simply asserts it. His position, of course, is that *the state* must be the sole determinant of prices and wages; but that view cannot be supported by the Bible. Sider is simply using the arguments of a socialist demagogue, attempting to use the church as a means to increase the oppressive power of the state. When it suits him to use a superficially "biblical" argument, he does; but he is by no means tied to Scripture.

The law of supply and demand has no "ought" about it. It cannot be repealed or contradicted by any government action whatsoever. The law of supply and demand *always* operates. It is inescapable, since God's imposed curse of scarcity is inescapable. If the government raises the price of an item, it creates a surplus of that item. Why? Because demand falls: fewer people are willing to pay the higher price. If the government lowers a price, it creates a shortage, because consumer demand rises in excess of the supply. The law of supply and demand has not been thereby avoided. It is just that the market price is now illegal. The law of supply and demand is still true. The only difference is that now there is injustice and the resultant surplus or shortage which is God's curse on those who defy Him.

Is laissez-faire economics *Christian*? That all depends on the meaning of the term. If "laissez-faire" means anarchy, the answer is *No*. The Bible does not want the government to stand idly by while Murder, Inc. negotiates a "market price" for its service. The *market* is to be free from government regulation, but criminal activity in the market must be abolished. Laissez-faire, in the Christian sense, means that the state enforces God's laws, and leaves men free to make choices. The duty of the state is not to save men from the consequences of their own irresponsible decisions. The duty of the state is to guard men from *criminal activity*. This is not to say that the free market is paradise, or that the concern in Christian economics is only freedom from price controls. What we desire is a Christian commonwealth, wherein the choices of men will flow from devotion to the glory of God. But we are saying that such a culture will not be produced by attempting to legislate men's scales of value. The state must *punish lawbreakers* and *protect the law-abiding*. The culture itself can be transformed only by the regenerating and sanctifying grace of God. The state is not the agency of regeneration. And, in spite of Sider's contempt for the "invisible hand," let us remember that he would replace it with the very visible, armored fist of a coercive state. He would substitute bureaucratic compulsion for voluntary exchange.

The whole point of the invisible hand thesis is that the only way of determining equitable prices is to allow free men to make free choices. Contrary to popular myth, producers do not set prices. Consumers do. Every time you buy or do not buy an item, *you* are casting a vote on its price. You aren't the only one voting, certainly; but you are voting nonetheless. The producer wants as much money as possible for his product, and the buyer wants as much product as possible for his money. The price will thus tend toward a point at which the supply will equal the demand; there will neither be shortages nor surpluses. If a producer makes a mistake by producing a good for which there is insufficient demand (at a price which would reward the producer for producing it), he will see his mistake in the loss column, and will either redirect his investment entirely or find a way to produce the item at a lower cost, enabling him to sell at a price which consumers are willing to pay. This operation of the free market means that *mistakes in investment tend to be quickly corrected*, consumer demand is satisfied, and producers are rewarded only when they fulfill the wants of consumers. The market price determines profit and loss, and this means that, even though both consumer and producer are pursuing his own interests, each is helping the other. The producer supplies what the consumer wants at a price the consumer is willing to pay, and the consumer tells the producer he is on the right track by rewarding him with his payment for the product. The wants of society are supplied at a price which gives producers the incentive to supply them. If the price is too low, there will be a great demand, but not sufficient incentive to produce. If the price is too high, demand will fall, and the producer will suffer losses. The market system is a giant auction, where profit, loss, and the freedom of buyers and sellers to mutually bid the price up and down are the only ways to get a "clearing price"—an equality of supply and demand. Any "tampering with the machinery" by a non-market factor—whether it be a syndicate's "protection" racket or governmental price control—will inevitably disrupt the system. The reason for this is that God curses disobedience.

Statism cannot succeed, for God's word and His world are against it. We will now examine some of Sider's statist proposals and see how God's curse is inflicted upon them—that they result in the very opposite of their professed goals, and produce a lower standard of living.

**PRICE CONTROLS**    Let's say the government decides that the price of milk is too high. Instead of $2 per gallon, it should be $1 per gallon. At this price many people will be willing to buy more milk, and they will be very grateful if the government controls the price at this level. But many of the milk producers will be unable to sell at this price, because their costs of production are too high. They will drop out of the market, and the supply of milk will fall drastically. The government, in its misguided charity, had intended that *more* people would be able to buy milk, but the result of the price control is that *fewer* people are actually able to buy it. So the government steps in again, and decrees that the costs of production—machine parts, fuel, feed for the cows, milk cartons, and so on—be lowered. Now the producers who had dropped out will be able to supply milk for the $1 price . . . except that those who had been producing the factors of milk production are now beginning to drop out of *their* markets. Milk producers are now more than ever unable to produce the required milk, because although the factors of production now cost less, they are unavailable. The milk price is still officially low enough for many people to buy it, but there is less milk to buy. And no matter what the government does to further reduce costs, the result will still be the same: a shortage of the controlled product. Price controls are biblically unlawful, and thus they cannot work.

Consider rent controls. The state planners decide that housing is too expensive, so they set a limit on the amount of rent a landlord may charge. Because profits are now less available in housing, entrepreneurs will reduce their investments in building houses and apartments, and some landlords will find other uses for their properties. In a free market, investment would flow in the direction of housing to meet the demand. At first, with a high demand and low supply, prices would be high. This would attract more investors who would compete for the money of consumers — and as competition increased, prices would fall. A free market — including the absence of compulsory zoning laws — will supply the demands of consumers. But statism cannot bring supply and demand together. Moreover, price controls will reduce not only the *supply* of goods, but the *quality* of goods as well. Landlords will try to reduce their costs by cutting down the quality of their housing, since there is no market incentive for them to retain high standards. They will not seek to keep up the plumbing facilities and so forth, because with the shortage of housing due to the controlled price, they do not have to compete for renters. They will always be able to find people so desperate for housing that anything will do. So improvements are not made and breakdowns are not repaired. If costs are prohibitive and losses are high, many landowners will simply disappear, abandoning their properties altogether. This is happening daily in New York City. The planners do not intend any of this, but it has happened again and again. It will always happen. God curses those who disobey Him. Their plans cannot succeed.

Sider writes constantly of "just" and "fair" prices. What is a fair price? Where are we to go for an authority which can infallibly determine it? Personally, I think a just price for my book would be around $50, but you didn't think so, and the publisher figured you wouldn't. Should I scream about this obvious injustice? The notion of a just price is based on the fallacy of intrinsic value — that there is a specific, quantifiable, objective and eternal market value in a good or service. Sider holds to this view, and complains that "one pays much more for a haircut in New York than in an Indian village. But it probably is worth no more."[9] This utterly meaningless statement is supposed to produce guilt in New Yorkers, but that is the extent of its possible use. For the customer in New York, the haircut is worth *more* to him than he pays for it. If it were not, he would take the risks of having his wife do it instead. If Sider means that barbers in India are as technically proficient as American barbers are, he may be right; but that has little to do with the variations in price between the two countries. As we noted in Chapter One, exchange takes place because each party values the other's good or service more highly than he values his own. This means that value is not intrinsic. Value is *imputed*. Each of us forms consumer preferences on a scale in his own mind. With changing conditions, these preferences also change. Men's preferences cannot be measured in money or anything else. They can only be compared. Whenever you make an exchange, you do it in terms of your scale of values, deciding if a certain good is worth what you must give up for it. Meanwhile, the other person is doing the same; and if the exchange is completed, that means that each of you valued the other's good higher than you did your own. If the goods were truly valued *equally*, there would be no exchange: neither one of you would be anxious to buy or sell. You exchange because you would rather have the other good than that which you trade for it. This means that there can never be a "just price"—but prices can be just. Prices are just when there is no fraud or coercion in the market—when God's laws are obeyed. It follows that *a price set by the government must always be unjust.* Instead of allowing free men to buy and sell in terms of their own scales of value, the state applies coercion—necessarily backed by potential violence—in order to force people to comply with its arbitrary justice. Always, this is done in favor of one class or pressure group against another, in direct violation of God's command:

*You shall do no injustice in judgment; you shall not be partial to the poor nor defer to the great, but you are to judge your neighbor fairly. (Leviticus 19:15)*

How does Sider get around this verse, seeing that it condemns his class-warfare ambitions? He answers: "The God of the Bible is on the side of the poor just because he is *not* biased."[10] That is slick. It must be a gift.

**MINIMUM WAGE LAWS**  In one of his most amusing state-ments, Sider defends minimum wage laws against those who stand for the biblical mandate of personal charity:

*Personal charity is too arbitrary and haphazard. It depends on the whim and feelings of the well off. Many needy people fail to meet those who can help. Proper institutional change (e.g. a minimum wage) on the other hand automatically benefits everyone.* [11]

Again—to be repetitious—such statist intervention is com-pletely unbiblical. God's law *commands* personal charity. If we do not obey God's word with regard to this command, God promises to destroy us. Biblical law is the standard of righteousness. But now a new Prophet has arrived, with a new word. He tells us that God's law can't get the job done. God's law is not only morally in-ferior to statism, but it is also "too arbitrary and haphazard" in practice.

More than this, the specific example of a proper means of charity is the minimum wage law—"which automatically benefits everyone." Sider is guilty of either ignorance or duplicity, but in any case, he is not telling us anything about justice or compas-sion. The minimum wage law is unjust, and serves as a powerful tool of *statist oppression.*

When the state does not intervene into the market, all those who wish to work will find jobs. Labor is always scarce. At some price, producers will hire labor. Unemployment is a limited and temporary phenomenon. But when the state mandates a minimum wage, that suddenly changes. Each employer must now pay his *least productive* workers this wage, plus the legal fringe benefits which amount to 25-35%. At the present minimum (1981) of $3.35, this means that the marginal worker costs his employer well over four dollars per hour. Thus, no one whose productivity is lower will be employed. The minimum wage law creates *institutional unemployment*, where people who are willing and able to work are legally prohibited from selling their labor at its market price. Hans Sennholz points out that "at least three million idle Americans owe their unemployment to this labor law.

Teenagers and uneducated, unskilled minority workers are its primary victims."[12] It is striking that this law is spoken of as *just* by a man who claims to be on the side of the poor. It "automatically benefits everyone"—everyone, that is, except: *employers*, who must cut production because of the rising costs; *consumers*, who are hurt by the lower productivity and high prices; and, especially, *the poor*, who are legally unemployable. But there is hope. If those who are unemployed by this law will cry out to God, He will hear them and avenge them. He will come and destroy their oppressors who support such an unjust, unbiblical law.

**A NATIONAL FOOD POLICY**    Americans eat too much, and we eat all the things Ronald Sider doesn't like, such as sugar and grain-fed meat. Therefore, he says, all industrialized nations, "especially the United States and Canada," should immediately devise a national food policy, in which the government would tell us what's best for us to eat. Aside from the fact that nutrition experts disagree widely on "what's best" (e.g. the cholesterol debate), any real implementation of such a program necessitates *tyrannical state controls over food production and distribution.* Such controls are not allowed by the laws of the Bible. Any "Yes, but . . ." arguments are invalid, and demonstrate an unwillingness to submit to biblical law. It is true that some people do not eat good food. That is no argument for disobeying God's law by giving the state the power to change their eating habits. Some people do not brush their teeth. On Sider's principles, we should enact laws, provide free toothpaste and brushes to every citizen, and send bureaucrats to each home every morning and evening, armed with dental floss (unwaxed), to enforce oral hygiene on the population. Dental Justice For All. Smile!

Sider does not appeal to Scripture for this plan. Instead, he says, "Norway has proven that a national food policy can make a difference."[13] No argument on that point: Norway, one of the most heavily socialistic nations in the world, is in deep financial trouble. Norway suffers the highest production costs in the world. Its social welfare system eats up about 55% of its gross national product. Every industrial worker receives high government subsidies (shipbuilders are subsidized to the tune of $10,000 per year), and it multiplies its problems by strictly inhibiting all private investments.[14] Give Ronald Sider the controls, and you too can have a Worker's Paradise. Bauer pinpoints the problem: *The state cannot create new additional productive resources. The politicians and civil servants who direct its policy dispose only of resources diverted from the rest of the economy. It is certainly not clear why overriding the decisions of private persons should increase the flow of income, since the resources used by the planners must have been diverted from other productive public or private uses.* [15]

Thus, "the controls imposed under comprehensive planning generally have nothing to do with raising popular living standards. Indeed, they usually depress them."[16] Mises summed it up: *There is no other alternative to totalitarian slavery than liberty. There is no other planning for freedom and general welfare than to let the market system work. There is no other means to full employment, rising real wage rates and a high standard of living for the common man than private initiative and free enterprise.* [17]

If this is true—and it has been demonstrated again and again that *socialism does not work*—why do intelligent men such as Sider persist in believing it? The answer is found in Romans 1:21-23: *For even though they know God, they did not honor Him as God, or give thanks, but they became futile in their speculations, and their foolish heart was darkened. Professing to be wise, they became fools, and exchanged the glory of the incorruptible God for an image in the form of corruptible man. . . .*

*Socialism is a religious faith.* Its foolishness—its inability to cope with the real world—stems from the fact that its adherents have "exchanged the truth for a lie, and worshipped and served the creature rather than the Creator" (Romans 1:25). Socialism is the religion of man. It is the product of humanism. It is nothing but state-worship, seeing the state as Lord and Savior. Rejecting

God's word, it thus rejects reason as well. Facts are seen in terms of presuppositions, and the socialist has a vision of reality completely determined by his adoration of the omnipotent state. He is hypnotized by power.

Adam Smith, that great champion of liberty, had a phrase to describe the statist — *the man of system*. His characterization is particularly fitting: we are pawns in the bureaucrats' chess game.

*The man of system . . . is apt to be very wise in his own conceit, and is often so enamoured with the supposed beauty of his own ideal plan of government, that he cannot suffer the smallest deviation from any part of it . . . he seems to imagine that he can arrange the different members of a great society with as much ease as the hand arranges the different pieces upon a chessboard; he does not consider that the pieces upon the chess-board have no other principle of motion besides that which the hand impresses upon them; but that, in the great chess-board of human society, every single piece has a principle of motion of its own, altogether different from that which the legislature might choose to impress upon it.* [18]

This is the core of all socialist policies. Socialism does not treat men as *men*, created in the image of God. Socialism is a power theory. We must not look merely at Ronald Sider's alleged ideals — that the poor should have enough to eat, that we all should be healthy, that we should not covetously spend our money on every trifle we see advertised, and so on — but we must look closely at how he intends to accomplish these things. He wants to see the state empowered to enforce his goals in every area of life. Let us never forget that this means the use of weapons to ensure compliance on the part of the people. I am not implying, of course, that there will be a shootout every time the state moves in on an offender. The threat, however, always exists. But the only ultimate reason for asking the state to enforce something is that the state possesses the legal right of coercion — and practically speaking, as Chairman Mao said, political power grows out of a gun barrel. Nor am I implying that the state's use of violence is always wrong. But that power of coercion must be used only where God has given the state the authority to do so. Any other use of it is abuse. It is the exaltation of the state into the place of God.

It is conceivable that Sider has not thought of the implications of his demands. He may be only very ignorant, and not as evil as I have suggested. He has, indeed, called for a "nonviolent revolution," and seems to deplore the use of physical force.[19] We can hope that he is sincere, but that does not change the fact that his policies require all sorts of *violent intrusions upon liberty*. We have already noted that comprehensive statist planning means nothing other than the concentration of power. And this concentration of power is forbidden by the law of God. It is therefore doomed to failure. It cannot increase resources, capital, or productivity. It cannot ultimately do anything for the poor. The only thing statism will ever produce is the judgment of a jealous God upon its presumption. Sider's appeal for state controls will result only in tyranny and destruction.

# THE PROPHETIC MESSAGE

**"MOST SERIOUS IS THE UNJUST DIVISION OF THE EARTH'S FOOD AND RESOURCES." [RONALD SIDER, *RICH CHRISTIANS IN AN AGE OF HUNGER*, P. 18]**

---

**"BEHOLD MY SERVANTS SHALL EAT, BUT YOU SHALL BE HUNGRY.**
**BEHOLD, MY SERVANTS SHALL DRINK, BUT YOU SHALL BE THIRSTY....**
**BECAUSE HE WHO IS BLESSED IN THE EARTH**
**SHALL BE BLESSED BY THE GOD OF TRUTH."**
**[ISAIAH 65:13-16]**

---

The Old Testament prophets are often used by socialists to justify their statist policies. "After all, the prophets were against the oppression of the poor; so are we," they say. On the surface, this might seem convincing. The prophets were often at cross purposes with the rich people, and warned continually against the dangers of covetousness and materialism. They spoke out against the very real oppression and victimization of the poor, and told the people that such practices would result in the judgment of God. Since there are similar elements in the ravings of the socialists, their identification of themselves with the prophets might appear to be valid. But as we shall see in this chapter, the difference between the biblical prophets and the "biblical socialists" is indeed vast—and, as Sider says in another context, "the chasm widens every year."

The prophetic function was one of restating the law of God and applying it to the contemporary situation. The prophets served as messengers of the covenantal law-order to Israel's theocracy, demanding a return to the principles of the social structure, personal behavior, and worship outlined in the books of Moses. They were, as E. J. Young said, "guardians of the theocracy."

*The prophets were to build upon the foundation of the Mosaic Law, and to expound that law unto the nation. They would thus be the preservers and defenders of the principles upon which the theocracy had been founded by God.* [1]

Meredith Kline has rightly characterized the prophets as prosecuting attorneys, messengers from God sent to remind God's vassals of their covenantal obligations, and warning the people of the consequences of disobedience.

*The mission of the Old Testament prophets, those messengers of Yahweh to enforce the covenant mediated to Israel through Moses, is surely to be understood within the judicial framework of the covenant lawsuit.* [2]

The prophets therefore took their stand firmly in terms of biblical law. They did not go beyond it, but simply applied it to the problems of the society, and commanded the people to repent of their sins and return to the way of obedience under the law of God. Everything they said was in complete accordance with the law. This means that, while they were very concerned over the oppression of the poor—incidentally, that was not their only concern—they never advocated statist policies to remedy the situation. You will never read of an Old Testament prophet calling for rent controls, minimum wage laws, or guaranteed jobs. They never demanded that the government print more money or expand credit. They did not plead for foreign aid, national health care, or restriction of profits. They did not try to institutionalize envy or legalize theft. Instead, they worked to reestablish the law of God in every area. This is the fundamental difference between the prophets and the socialists. While they both speak about the poor, their content, methodology and goals are completely at odds.

This could be amply demonstrated by a thorough survey of all the prophetic literature, but that would itself constitute an entire book. So we will narrow our field of inquiry to one prophet, who, above all others, seems to be a socialist favorite. This is the prophet Amos. If there was a single man in all of Scripture who spoke out against the sins of oppressions and economic injustice, it was Amos. For this reason, socialists seize upon his little book to justify statist remedies of every kind—yet, as we shall see, with not one whit of actual support from the prophet.[3]

Amos began his ministry around the middle of the eighth century B.C. Sent by God from the southern kingdom of Judah, where he had been a shepherd and farmer, he went to the northern kingdom of Israel to warn them of approaching judgment. Israel at this time was in a period of great wealth and prosperity, but it was also in the stage of "covenantal forgetfulness" spoken of in Deuteronomy 8:11-20:

*Beware lest you forget the LORD your God by not keeping His command-ments and His ordinances and His statutes which I am commanding you to-day; lest, when you have eaten and are satisfied, and have built good houses and lived in them, and when your herds and your flocks multiply, and your silver and gold multiply, and all that you have multiplies, then your heart becomes proud, and you forget the LORD your God who brought you out from the land of Egypt, out of the house of slavery . . . otherwise, you may say in your heart, "My power and the strength of my hand made me this wealth." But you shall remember the LORD your God, for it is He who is giving you the power to make wealth, that He may confirm His covenant which He swore to your fathers, as it is this day. And it shall come about that if you ever forget the LORD your God, and go after other gods and serve them and worship them, I testify against you that you shall surely perish. Like the nations that the LORD makes to perish before you, so you shall perish; because you would not listen to the voice of the LORD your God.*

This is exactly what happened in the days of Amos. The Israel of the eighth century had forgotten God as the source of wealth. As a result, both church and state were corrupt, the rich were oppressing the poor, the courts were controlled by bribes, and political leaders were emphasizing military might over godliness as the means of security. Society had become so perverse that the people could no longer distinguish between good and evil. Amos came to them with a message of the abiding authority of God's law, His judgment upon the disobedient, and the urgent need for repentance.

After getting their attention by thundering against the sins of the surrounding nations (1:3-2:5)—a fact which shows the law's validity *outside* the theocratic kingdoms of Israel and Judah— Amos then turned his guns toward Israel, and dealt immediately with its sins in the area of economics. Righteous men were being condemned because their wealthier enemies had bribed judges, and poor men were sold into slavery over trifles (2:6). Instead of obeying the laws commanding mercy on poor brethren (Leviticus 25:25-28), the rich men of Israel were trampling them into the dust. Gross immorality, perhaps even ceremonial prostitution, was taking place (2:7). In violation of the laws on debt (Deuteronomy 24:10-13), the poor man's collateral was withheld from him—and all the while, the people were claiming to be devout and pious men, daring even to display the "profits" of their sins in the house of worship (2:8). Their response to those who brought God's word was to attempt to corrupt them, and where that failed, to silence them (2:12).

Amos included in his denunciation the wealthy women of Israel (4:1-3), calling them "cows of Bashan." Bashan was a well-watered, fertile region, and the cattle of Bashan were, understandably, quite fat—which is just Amos' point about these women. He accused them of oppressing the poor and crushing the needy. This charge was *not* because they had actually done anything personally against the poor, for they probably rarely ever came in contact with the poor people at all. The basis for the charge was their expensive demands on their husbands. Their self-indulgence crushed those who were below them. How is this possible? The socialist myth—that wealth *per se* is a cause of poverty—is not supported here. There are several possible ways that their affluent lifestyle could have caused oppression. Since the poor were ignored in Israel, the luxuries of these women were probably bought at the expense of the Tithe, zero-interest loans, gleaning, and the like. Their weak husbands were unable to provide for the needy because their wives' greed made it impossible to obey God's laws in these areas. In addition, they were forcing men into slavery unnecessarily, in the interests of making a quick shekel, rather than being merciful. Perhaps they took a poor man's tools of production as collateral, in violation of God's law (Deuteronomy 24:6). They probably charged interest on charity loans as well.

There are many possibilities of making short-run financial gains by defying God's law and oppressing the poor. In our day, we have devised methods that are even more sophisticated. One way middle-class Americans oppress the poor through their affluent lifestyles is in their methods of payment. When the average man wants a new stereo, car, or refrigerator, what does he do? Does he go out and pay for the item with the fruits of his labor? Not on your MasterCard. He "buys" it on credit (i.e. debt). *This is covetousness*, and covetousness is idolatry (Colossians 3:5). The economic result of this widespread practice is inflation, because the bank credit is made possible through the absolutely unbiblical practice of fractional reserve banking (the banks lend out *many* more times what they actually hold in reserves). With a blip of the computer, Poof! Brand-new money! As this newly created money is injected into the market, the supply and demand schedule receives false data, and prices begin to rise. These higher prices are uncomfortable, but affordable, to middle-class and upper-middle-class debtors. But those who are poor cannot buy at the inflated prices caused by their neighbor's covetousness. We can blame the government's Federal Reserve System for allowing this ungodly practice, and also the banks for making money from what is essentially theft. *But the government wouldn't allow it if we didn't want it.* For example, if the government provided free dinners of lice and maggots to middle-class Americans, there would be no takers, because we don't *want* to eat that stuff. Any government service would fold if no one accepted it. But because of our covetousness, we *want* credit expansion, so the government provides it. Thus we wallow amidst our financial luxuries, contentedly oblivious to the fact that we have stolen from our neighbors and crushed the poor. The prophetic rebuke to the fat cows of Israel is quite applicable to us today. God judged them for their oppressive covetousness, and He will judge us too.

The fractional reserve banking system can work against any group, depending on which group succeeds in gaining access to the newly created money first. For example, if the Federal government runs a massive deficit—if!!! (a little humor)—and the Federal Reserve Board steps in and buys a portion of the government's bonds by creating fiat money, the government will spend the newly created money in subsidizing its patrons. If this should be welfare recipients or Social Security pensioners, then these groups can benefit temporarily (at least until inflation destroys the value of the currency, not to mention the social order). Those hard-pressed middle-class people who are on tight budgets may not choose (or be able) to indebt themselves. Thus, they see their savings go down the inflationary drain, while the poor, who have no savings, maintain their living standards by means of their ready access to "indexed" welfare payments. They get the fiat money first, spend it before it depreciates, and leave the middle class businessmen and families holding the bag—the "bag" being a savings account, or pension program, or annuity, or cash-value life insurance savings full of worthless paper money.

Under fractional reserve banking, which is universal today, it pays to be the favored group which gets access to the fiat money first, before its purchasing power deteriorates. We can expect class war eventually, such as Germany experienced in the years of mass inflation, 1921-23. Everyone wants to be the favored person in the race against price inflation, which is in turn caused by monetary inflation. Thus, by looking at the short run, and voting for a debt-based monetary system, today's middle-class voter is sealing the doom of the social order which has permitted the economic benefits to flow to the middle class—a social order based on voluntary exchange, contract, social peace, and honest money. Ignorance of economics, when coupled with envy, and motivated by a false sense of guilt, can produce a devastating social crisis.

Amos also attacked these people for their empty religion (4:4-5; 5:4-7). While it is commonly held that religion is man's attempt to approach God, this is not true. No one seeks after God (Romans 3:11), and Paul tells us that the real purpose of much of man's religious activity is to cover his flight from the true God (Romans 1:18-25). This was the case with Israel. The Israelites were using their worship to try to escape from God and the demands of His law. They were tossing worthless scraps of religiosity to God, when what He had demanded was *justice*. The oppressive men of Israel had become experts in certain externals of religion—much like the heroin smuggler who is scrupulous in his observance of traffic laws. But God was not fooled. With all their religion, they were still trampling on the poor, extorting bribes from them, not giving them justice in the courts, and living off of the income from their thefts (5:11-12). Men who opposed these practices were silenced when they spoke out, and so many did not openly show their disapproval (5:10, 13). The pious actions of these oppressors —festivals, assemblies, offerings and hymns—were an abomination to God, and He expressed His complete disgust for them: "I hate, I reject. . . . I will not even look. . . . Take away. . . . I will not even listen. . . ." (5:21-23). What God wants is not our sacrifices, but our obedience (I Samuel 15:22-23; Isaiah 1:11-20). He demanded, "Let justice roll down like waters, and righteousness like an ever-flowing stream" (5:24).

But Israel's worship was not only hypocritical. It was also *syn-*

*cretistic*, mixed with heathenism (5:25-27). The people had a history of apostasy: even during the forty years' wandering they had continually fallen into idolatry, and their worship of the true God had been mixed with falsehood. Apparently, Israel had actually carried heathen shrines with them throughout the journey — and after all these years, they had not changed. Their "sacrifices" were not genuine sacrifices at all. God can tell the difference between true worship and our baptized secularism. We can't take *Rich Christians in an Age of Hunger*, bind it in leather, and call it "Christian Economics." Nor can we sprinkle holy water on our ungodly contempt for the poor and afflicted, refusing to give needed help, and call it "Christian Stewardship." Both are lawless.

Amos went on to denounce the men of Israel for their godless trust in "the mountain of Samaria" (6:1). They were complacent in their apostasy because of their supposedly impregnable fortress there (and it *was* strong; when the Assyrians invaded, the siege lasted three years). True national security can come only from the gracious hand of God: it is a blessing He grants in response to national obedience (Deuteronomy 28:7). Disregarding their accountability to God, Israel "put off the day of calamity" (6:3), arrogant in their deistic belief that God is not concerned with economics, presumptuously assuming that "the LORD will not do good or evil" (Zephaniah 1:12). The court, the seat of justice, had instead become a place of violence and oppression (6:3). The rulers saw this as an accumulation of power, but in reality it sealed their doom. God had seen.

In his final list of Israel's crimes (8:4-6), Amos again spoke of oppression of the poor. The businessmen of Israel chafed and fretted over the Sabbath laws; they wanted to get back to work — but their "work" was lawless. They were cheating customers by falsifying their measures. They were also inflating the money supply by debasing their currency. Their whole goal in business activity was to enslave others and bring men under their control. Remember, God's laws were structured compassionately: slavery was a merciful means of enabling a poor debtor to get back on his feet—and even then, slavery was a last resort. God commanded the wealthy to restrain their demands over those who are helpless, to refrain from squeezing the last dime out of the needy. But many businessmen in Israel refused to listen. The whole of their economic activity was calculated to trample on those below them.

For all these things, Amos pronounced judgment: Israel would be destroyed by Assyria and taken into captivity. None would escape (2:13-16; 4:2-3; 9:1-4), and only a tiny remnant would survive (3:12; 5:3). Moreover, since they had continually rejected God's word, He would send them a "Bible-famine": God's word would be withdrawn, and people would be unable to hear the saving message of God's revelation (8:11-13).

The message of Amos had a great deal to do with economic transgressions of God's law. The Israelites were not merely guilty of failing to have morning devotions—indeed, their religion was very devotional. Amos speaks powerfully to us today. We cannot take refuge from the demands of God's law. Ironically, in the final announcement of judgment (9:1), the Lord appears beside the altar in the very place Israel was seeking to hide from Him. We can never hide. We cannot make up our own kind of god—a god who will be so comfortably "spiritual" that we can get away with any kind of crafty economic oppression we like. God is who *He* says He is. If we flout his laws while claiming to be His loyal people, we will only incur greater judgment. Israel rejected God's word through Amos, and Israel was soon destroyed. And if we continue in our faithless, uncharitable religion, we will be destroyed as well.

But Amos never appealed to socialism or statism for the answers. He never said that it was wrong to make a profit, or unjust to have possessions. The wrong in these things was the fact that they had been obtained by violating the specifics in God's law. He did not try to incite envy by comparing the incomes of rich and poor and then *assuming* that the wealth of the rich was unjust. He *named* their sins: extortion, partiality in court, falsifying weights and measures, debasing the currency, disobedience to the Poor Laws, false advertising, fornication, religious syncretism, hypocrisy, and so on. He did *not* say that profits were unjust simply because they were high. He did *not* ask that foreign aid be sent to those heathen nations that were about to become impoverished through God's judgment on their ungodliness. And, most emphatically, he did *not* request state intervention into the market. In all of his condemnation of Israel's sins, he never lost sight of God's law. He represented the law symbolically as a plumbline (7:6-9), the standard of measurement in terms of which the nation was to be judged (cf. Isaiah 28:17). For Amos, the standard of judgment was not himself, or the feelings of the poor, or the theories of either popular or dissident economists. He knew that "sin is *law*lessness" (I John 3:4).

Ronald Sider and others profess to be reviving the message of the prophets, in calling for compassion on the poor. But the difference on this point is crucial. The modern socialist prophets have rejected the plumbline, the yardstick of scripture. While Sider's plea for justice is commendable, his *standard* for justice is in fact lawless. He does not, with the biblical prophets, demand a return to the biblical laws which mandate *personal* care for the poor. Instead, he demands statist intervention, a socialistic concept which the Bible opposes completely. He also advocates majority-vote theft, thinking that the poor will be helped by plundering the rich. But God's blessings do not come from compounding crimes. That can only bring swifter destruction, for both rich and poor.

Amos wanted justice. But he defined it as obedience to God's law. He wanted the hungry to be fed. But he saw that this would come about solely through a return to God's word. And he held out the hope that this will someday come to pass. If men will obey God's laws, He will bless them in every way — and one of those blessings (which is impossible in a socialist state) will be *increased productivity*:

*"Behold, days are coming,"* declares the LORD,

*When the plowman will overtake the reaper*
*And the treader of grapes him who sows seed;*
*When the mountains will drip sweet wine,*
*And all the hills will be dissolved." (Amos 9:13)*

When godly business activity is left unhampered, and men devote themselves to glorifying God through developing the earth's productive potential, obeying His laws and caring for the needy, remembering that God gives the power to get wealth — He will open the windows of heaven for them, causing the earth to yield its fruit in astonishing abundance. Amos' prophecy of productivity will come true, but only when our nation returns to his God and the laws of scripture. And by distorting the message of the prophets, Ronald Sider is only postponing that day of abundance. He is actually helping to bring about another prophecy of Amos instead:

*"Behold, days are coming," declares the Lord GOD,*
*"When I will send a famine on the land. . . ."*

# 15 PREPARING THE CHURCH FOR SLAVERY

"...THE KIND OF TENSION [FEELINGS OF GUILT] YOU MENTION IS INHERENT IN THE MESSAGE...." [RONALD SIDER, *THE WITTENBURG DOOR*, OCT./NOV. 1979, P. 15]

"YOU SHALL NOT BEAR FALSE WITNESS AGAINST YOUR NEIGHBOR." [EXODUS 20:16]

The policies of state intervention do not attain their professed goals. They cannot do so, for they are in violation of God's commands, and this is His world. Foreign aid does not help the poor; price controls create an imbalanced, chaotic market; minimum wage laws result in unemployment; profit restrictions increase consumer costs; enforced economic equality means a radical political inequality; in short, all attempts by the state to abolish poverty serve only to intensify it in one way or another. We have also seen, however, that statism has another, often unprofessed, goal: domination over men. This urge for power is the only thing that statism can satisfy—and that lasts only so long as God withholds His judgment. The demand for statism is a demand for control—nothing more or less. The real goal of increasing government intervention is totalitarianism.

What part does Ronald Sider play in the establishment of a totalitarian state? While he does call repeatedly for statism, that is not the main thrust of the books published under his name. There are many in our day who would try to convince us that we need a bigger Big Brother. But Sider's function in the Revolution is much more specialized. Whether he is a calculating propagandist or merely an ignorant tool in the hands of others (the evidence points strongly toward the former), he nevertheless is serving the cause of totalitarianism in a way in which, for example, Marx and Keynes were unable to do so. This is because of two factors: his *sphere of activity* and his *message*.

Ronald Sider's semi-official standing as a theologian gives him unique access to positions of influence denied to other statists. He claims to be a Christian, and his writings are dotted with Bible quotations. He teaches at a school which trains men for the ministry. He is invited to speak at Christian churches, colleges, seminaries, and conferences. His books are distributed by an important Christian publishing house, and I have not yet seen one Christian bookstore that does not carry his books. (One store near me refuses to stock any books that uphold biblical law, while Sider's books advocating theft are prominently displayed.) His articles are printed in the leading Christian magazines; clearly, he has a powerful platform from which to speak. His message is being heard, and is increasingly accepted. (In speaking to a Christian schoolteacher whom I had just met, I happened to use the word *biblical*. She immediately assumed, for no other reason, that I was talking about Sider and the Evangelicals for Social Action).

Sider's specific message is one of guilt. In a previous chapter, we noted some of the many ways he attempts to cause us to be ashamed, embarrassed and humiliated because of the blessings we enjoy under the hand of God. Envy is directed at us from all sides by his skillful manipulation of fallacies, distortion of facts, and misinterpretation of Scripture. Envy is then inverted, and becomes guilt—not in the biblical sense of actual, moral transgression of God's law, but psychological, sociological guilt, the feeling of being responsible for the envy of others. And perhaps no tool of totalitarianism is as significant as the ability to induce guilt feelings.

How is this so? It is because of the relationship of *guilt* and *the loss of freedom*. If a man is enslaved to guilt, he is rendered powerless. The child who feels guilty for not completing his homework is unable to face his classmates and teacher with confidence. The businessman who feels guilty for having made some error is unable to fully direct his concentration to the tasks at hand. When we are ashamed—"guilty"—for failing to remember someone's birthday or anniversary, we are less able to deal with him personally. I have known several college students whose sense of guilt because of one or two instances of tardiness was so great that they would begin cutting classes to avoid facing the professor; eventually, they would drop the course altogether. Guilt is an extremely powerful force; when we feel it, we become distracted, confused and incompetent. We fail to recognize our valid responsibilities, and are much more likely to be manipulated by others. We become overly dependent upon others to make decisions for us, and begin to avoid necessary confrontations and independent actions. We become *slaves*. Our external, social slavery is produced by our slavery of heart and mind.

One of the most striking examples of the power of guilt—an incident that changed the course of history—is in the life of King Harold of England during the Norman Invasion of 1066. Harold was an inspiring leader, a man unusually able to inflame others with intense loyalty and obedience. During his brief reign, he faced two major crises—and they occurred less than three weeks apart. The first was the Battle of Stamford Bridge, in which Harold successfully repulsed the attempted takeover of England by the King of Norway. The second crisis was the Battle of Hastings, which he lost to the Normans led by William the Bastard (later known as William the Conqueror—which shows what happens when winners write the history books). One important reason for the difference in outcome between the two battles was King Harold's state of mind, which underwent a drastic change just before the conflict with William. While preparing for the battle, he received word that the Pope had excommunicated him and had given his blessing to William. It turned out to be a self-fulfilling prophecy: Harold acted as if the life had been sucked out of him. When he went into battle against William, he was unable to lead his men. David Howarth writes that, in marked contrast to the encounter at Stamford Bridge,

*. . . the English army never moved. It never acted as if it had received a general order: it stood where it was all day, only shrinking in on itself as its numbers fell. It never made a concerted attack, nor in the end did it make a concerted retreat. Either Harold never gave a general order, or else it was never carried out . . . the strangely passive battle he fought seems to fit a mood of fatalism, as if he scarcely fought for victory but simply awaited the expression of God's judgment. His behavior at Stamford Bridge and Hastings was utterly different. Both battles were equally long and equally hard fought, between armies almost equally matched; but in the first he was always in attack, and in the second never. In the first, and in the whole episode of York, he undoubtedly inspired everyone; but in the second, he left no evidence of leadership at all. He acted like a different man: something had changed him in the eighteen days between . . . he was behind the line, and most of the men in front, one can only suppose, stood facing death all day without a word of encouragement or command from the King they were fighting for.*[1]

Guilt produces *passivity*, and makes a man *programmed for defeat*. The importance of this for totalitarianism cannot be overemphasized. If a whole *society* can be made to feel guilty, it will be unable to withstand an enslaving state: it is ripe for conquest. This has long been recognized as the most successful method of rendering men passive and pliable, incapable of resistance to statist domination and control. A major aspect of the Communist takeover of China was the manipulation of envy and guilt by the organization of community discussions "around leading questions, such as, 'Who has supported whom?' and 'Who has made whom rich?', and the encouragement of the aggrieved to 'spit out their bitterness'. . . . the Communist exploitation of grievances was probably more systematic than anything in the past."[2]

This is precisely what Sider is doing. He piles on the guilt fast and thick: we are guilty for eating meat, sugar, fish, bananas; for drinking wine and coffee; for making profits; for having extra clothing in the closet; for having green lawns; even for living in North America. He approves of the heretical, legalistic position that anyone who lives on more than the bare necessities of life risks going to hell.[3] He encourages groups to examine and evaluate each other's expenditures in terms of his envious standards. The practical results of such tactics can be observed in any issue of *theOtherSide*, as writers regularly flog themselves for their failure to be "totally committed" to the ideal of economic and population stagnation, confessing their occasional cravings for steaks and other wicked goodies.

As guilt produces impotence, it also leads people to call for more and more controls from the state. The passive population is not only malleable, yielding, submissive; it positively *welcomes* state intervention. Sider's cleverness in this is diabolical. First, he tells us that a billion people are starving because of our eating habits. Next, he urges his guilt-absorbed readers to reduce their quotas of beef. But this is not enough, because "unless one also changes public policy, the primary effect of reducing one's meat consumption may simply be to enable the Russians to buy more grain at a cheaper price next year or to persuade farmers to plant less wheat"[4]—and just think how much *more* guilty we would be then! And so the pliant masses who read Sider—having been primed by a dozen years of statist indoctrination in the public schools—are manipulated by this alternation of envy, guilt, and hopelessness into asking for stricter controls, broader legislation, increasing intrusions, more bondage. The guilty, unable to solve life's problems, will be *saved by the state.*

And Sider's goal of establishing an oppressive regime is working. Christians have become obsessed with their own imagined wrongdoings (while entirely ignoring their real violations of God's law), agonizing over their criminal inability to feed the hungry, glutted with remorse and shame because of their secret love for ice cream, suffering nagging worries about just how much their vacations contribute to world poverty, wondering how many children die on their account—longing for the day when the government will be empowered to decide all these questions, taking the growing burden off their shoulders.

The churches also have become enslaved. Regardless of all the hoopla over Moral Majority, most pastors are toeing the government line. When was the last time your minister spoke out against unbacked paper money and the expansion of credit? Does he even want to know what those words mean? A well-known pastor in Southern California holds strong personal beliefs against homosexuality, abortion, the Equal Rights Amendment, and other modern examples of our national apostasy. You would never know that from his sermons, because he never utters a peep about them. He's worried about the tax-exemption for his heavily mortgaged, shiny new temple. He doesn't want it taken away, so he keeps quiet. Essentially, he is an *agent of the state*, terrified about the consequences of resisting tyranny.

Men overcome by fear and guilt are unable to fight. The more the church is enslaved, the harder it will be to resist the state's tyrannical invasions. The more we become preoccupied with these fantasy-world sins—these "transgressions" of which the Bible says not a word—the less able we will be to obey God's command to exercise dominion over the earth. Under the vain delusion of false guilt, the church will retreat, leaving already-conquered territory for the devil's illegitimate sway. His emissaries seek to distract God's people from their true mission of world conquest and full development of the earth's resources, by sending us off into vacuous campaigns against illusory windmills. Sadly, many in the church, with a cultivated ignorance of Scripture, are heeding the lies of their enemies.

The captivity of the church is essential to the strategy of the statists. If the church can be persuaded to abandon its calling, nothing on earth can prevent the domination of power-mad government. The people of God have been freed from their slavery to sin—thus, ultimately, from slavery to all but God—and are not easily dominated by men; *there is no inherent slavery in the believer* as there is in the unbeliever. Moreover, the people of God have been raised up with Christ (Ephesians 2:6); He as our representative is seated on the throne of all power, above the principalities and powers, as supreme Lord over all who have rule and authority (Ephesians 1:20-22). Jesus is the King of all kings, the Lord of all lords (Revelation 17:16); and we rule with Him, waging war and overcoming. No state—*none*—can successfully lord it over God's people. We are kings, and those who oppose us must be crushed to powder: the nation that will not serve us will perish (Isaiah 60:12).

> For the LORD Most High is to be feared,
> A great King over all the earth.
> He subdues people under us,
> And nations under our feet. (Psalm 47:2-3)

It is thus of crucial importance to Satan's plan that he delude the church into thinking she is powerless. And if the church is bemused by guilt-manipulators and sapped of her vigor, our nation is lost. Christians alone have the power of dominion over the Evil One; we alone can provide the moral force to prevail against the enslaving state, for the principle of liberty in Christ has set us free from the bondage of men; we alone can preserve our land from destruction, for we are the salt of the earth. But if the day comes that we lose our savor, we will be cast out with the heathen.

We would like to tell ourselves that this can never happen to God's people, but that is a devilish lie to keep us secure in the very mouth of destruction. It happened to the churches of France in 1789; of all Europe in 1848; of Russia in 1917; of Germany in 1933. In every case, *the churches had been rendered impotent*—by guilt, by fear, by benefits; and always because the church departed from the word of God as the only standard for every area of life. Do not say it cannot happen here. That is to say that we can do all things *without* Christ. Do not say that we will somehow muddle through the crisis of the hour: Christ did not call us to muddling, but to victory. Life is a battle — no, more: *it is a war to the death* with the forces of evil. We cannot merely hold our ground. If we do not conquer we will be conquered. If we do not gather with the victorious Christ, we are scattering abroad. There is no middle ground, no possible moderation or compromise. If Ronald Sider and his ideological colleagues have their way, my sons could be slaves to a ruthless bureaucracy before they reach manhood. Your children will join them.

This is no ivory-tower issue; it is not an airy, inconsequential debate between abstract theologies. Sider states himself somewhat vaguely with respect to the specific political programs he prefers, the means employed to enforce them, and the limits of state power. He is vague about just how much personal wealth constitutes immoral wealth. But he is clear enough: we need more compulsory wealth redistribution. We have too much wealth. Vague standards of righteousness, coupled with emotional generalities, can produce a lot of guilt. That, of course, is the whole point.

Nor is this a political or economic contest alone, as if we may leave the job to the professionals. Dominion is the task of every man and woman in the kingdom. God holds *you* responsible for the future of your children. You must do the work. If you abandon your calling, you are bringing down God's judgment on your seed. There is no escape. And never, never assume that you will raptured out of the earth before the trouble begins. That is the retreatist's dream, and it blinds us to the truth. It is presumption: why should God do for you what He did not do for others? Were Christians raptured from the Inquisition? Were the 10,000 men, women, and babies who were slain in their beds on St. Bartholomew's Day in Paris raptured? Are Christians who suffer tribulation from statists around the world being raptured daily? Consider Jesus' prayer to His Father:
*I do not ask Thee to take them out of the world, but to keep them from the evil one (John 17:15).*

Our Lord did not pray for us to be raptured away from the

problems of life, before God's confrontation with Satan in this world is over. He prayed that we would not be overcome by the devil. And it is to be feared that those who think only of escape have already been overcome. *There is no escape except death.* We must choose between victory or defeat, conquest or flight, dominion or slavery, in time and on earth.

Ronald Sider's mission is to hobble the church from fulfilling her divine calling, for he is enough of a theologian to understand that history follows the church. If God's people are impotent, the world is enslaved to sin; when they are free, the world finds liberty in Christ. The key to statist control is to keep blinders on the church so that she knows neither her calling nor the puny weakness of her foes.

Victory belongs to the people of God. If we retreat, God will smash us and raise up another generation that will follow Him in His conquest of the nations. Our commission will succeed; the nations will be discipled to the obedience of the faith. If we do not do it, others will. But if we do not do it, we will be thrown away and trodden under the feet of men—men who will make us their slaves. If we are obedient, we need have no fear. We rule with Christ. We have the almighty power of the Lord God at our disposal, and He will move heaven and earth for His obedient people. He calls us not into battle alone. He calls us to go with Him through the battle into victory.

PART II | THE FUTURE OF POVERTY

# 16 THE BASIS FOR ECONOMIC GROWTH

As we have seen, the only way to achieve real wealth for everyone is to increase productivity through capital investment. Where the market is not hampered by restrictions on investment and income or by inflation of the money supply, increased production for consumer wants will result in rising real wage rates and lower prices for everyone. Gustavo R. Velasco of Mexico wrote:

*The fundamental obstacle which prevents Mexican workers from enjoying the ample wages that American working men receive . . . consists simply in the fact that our production per head is many times lower than that of our neighbors, because the latter do not work alone, but aided by the greatest accumulation of capital in history.* [1]

But this capital accumulation and investment did not just spring out of nowhere. Because man is created in God's image, he is an innately religious being: every aspect of his life will reflect his relationship to God. Man's culture, therefore, is necessarily religious and covenantal, as Henry Van Til has stressed:

*Since religion is rooted in the heart, it is therefore totalitarian in nature. It does not so much consummate culture as give culture its foundation, and serves as the presupposition of every culture. Even when faith and its religious root are openly denied, it is nevertheless tacitly operative as in atheistic Communism. A truly secular culture has never been found. . . .*[2]

The religious basis for the culture always bears fruit in the economic sphere. Long-established habits and traditions do not change as quickly as does theoretical speculation. When the religious basis of a culture is transformed, it takes *time* for that change to work itself out into the cultural life. The religious shift in the Renaissance period, separating nature from grace, produced the statism of the Reformation era; the Reformational return to the principles of biblical law eventually worked out in political liberty and free enterprise under the rule of law; and the Enlightenment saw its fulfillment in the essentially pagan politics of revolutionary statism and anarchy. Culture is produced by religion, and to some degree lags behind it. (This is why, as we have seen, some ex-heathens were prohibited from exercising full civil status in Israel for up to ten generations.) But the cultural fruit of the religious root eventually comes to maturity, which is why, as John Chamberlain says, "Christianity tends to create a capitalistic mode of life . . . capitalism is a material by-product of the Mosaic law."[3] The laws of the Bible work to restrain both *statism* and *anarchy*. It must be admitted that many modern "capitalists" think in terms of Enlightenment principles; hence, the tendency toward statism among Conservatives, and towards anarchy among Libertarians—both groups trying to base the product of Christianity upon pagan principles, and thus both groups doomed to failure.

The Christian framework of freedom within law cannot be simply imposed upon a heathen culture. The bare economic structure of capitalism cannot be imported into a culture successfully. We cannot talk about the mere fact that India needs free enterprise and capital investment. The issue is: *Why* does India resist freedom? The answer is to be found in India's religious and philosophical persuasions. Mises says:

*India lacks capital because it never adopted the pro-capitalist philosophy of the West and therefore did not remove the traditional institutional obstacles to free enterprise and big-scale accumulation. Capitalism came to India as an alien imported ideology that never took root in the minds of the people.*[4]

The ideology of pagan countries is ably summarized by P. T. Bauer as:

*lack of interest in material advance, combined with resignation in the face of poverty; lack of initiative, self-reliance and of a sense of personal responsibility for the economic fortune of oneself and one's family; high leisure preference, together with a lassitude often found in tropical climates; relatively high prestige of passive or contemplative life compared to active life; the prestige of mysticism and of renunciation of the world compared to acquisition and achievement; acceptance of a preordained, unchanging and unchangeable universe; emphasis on performance of duties and acceptance of obligation, rather than on achievement of results, or assertion or even a recognition of personal rights; lack of sustained curiosity, experimentation and interest in change; belief in the efficacy of supernatural and occult forces and of their influence over one's destiny; insistence on the unity of the organic universe, and on the need to live with nature rather than conquer it or harness it to man's needs, an attitude of which reluctance to take animal life is a corollary; belief in perpetual reincarnation, which reduces the significance of effort in the course of the present life; recognised status of beggary, together with a lack of stigma in the acceptance of charity; opposition to women's work outside the household.*[5]

Bauer goes on to emphasize that these attitudes "are not surface phenomena," but are "an integral part of the spiritual and emotional life" of hundreds of millions of people.[6] This situation can only be aggravated by foreign aid and irresponsible charity. It cannot be helped by the capitalist cure-all of investment. Make no mistake: these economies *do* need free enterprise and enormous capital investment. But the point is that those things alone will not change the face of heathen economies in a lasting way. Autonomous capitalism is a washout. It is an attempt to grab the blessings of God by secularist methods. The fact that Robert J. Ringer's *Restoring the American Dream* spent five months on the New York Times Best Seller List should be no cause of rejoicing to those who desire a return to biblical free enterprise. His book should be retitled *Anarchist Nightmare*. It is a libertarian lawlessness. Its basic thrust can be guessed from the titles of his other hits: *Looking Out for #1* and *Winning Through Intimidation*. That kind of "capitalism" can produce only cultural disintegration. Nothing will change a spiritually enslaved culture apart from freedom in Christ. No course in economic principles, divorced from their Christian base, will be able to lift a society out of the practically dead-end stagnation described by Bauer. The task is completely hopeless.

Ludwig von Mises discovered this in pre-World War II Austria and Germany, as he and a small group of free-market economists labored mightily to convince their contemporaries of the fallacies and dangers of statism. Mises was an extraordinarily lucid writer; communication itself was not the problem. But he was speaking to a generation determined to fling itself into slavery. Nothing he said or did was to any avail. (One Nazi economist even informed him that he had no interest in the problem of inflation, since it had nothing to do with economics!) Later, as a newly-arrived immigrant to America, Mises penned the most poignant lines in all economic literature:

*I have come to realize that my theories explain the degeneration of a great civilization; they do not prevent it. I set out to be a reformer, but only became the historian of decline.*[7]

Salvation, in this world and the next, is not found in economics. Regeneration is the only foundation for social stability and growth. Slaves need liberty, but they cannot be legislated into it. If men are not bound to Christ, they will be slaves to Satan, and there will be no escape from the whirlpool of cultural decomposition. At least totalitarianism, for all its faults, acts as a temporary buffer of semi-law before the final end in complete dissolution. Edward Banfield's study of a backward society has already been cited; but he wrote another book which was much more upsetting to sociologists, for it was based on his research among social classes in America, and shows the fundamental causes of institutional poverty in this country:

*At the present-oriented end of the scale, the lower-class individual lives from moment to moment. If he has any awareness of a future, it is of something fixed, fated, beyond his control: things happen to him, he does not make them happen. Impulse governs his behavior, either because he cannot discipline himself to sacrifice a present for a future satisfaction or because he has no sense of the future. He is therefore radically improvident: whatever he cannot use immediately he considers valueless. His bodily needs (especially for sex) and his taste for "action" take precedence over everything else—and certainly over any work routine. He works only as he must to stay alive, and drifts from one unskilled job to another, taking no interest in his work. . . .*

*Although his income is usually much lower than that of the working-class individual, the market value of his car, television, and household appliances and playthings is likely to be considerably more. He is careless with his things, however, and, even when nearly new, they are likely to be permanently out of order for lack of minor repairs. . . .*

*The lower-class individual has a feeble, attenuated sense of self; he suffers from feelings of self-contempt and inadequacy, and is often apathetic or dejected. . . . In his relations with others he is suspicious and hostile, aggressive yet dependent. He is unable to maintain a stable relationship with a mate; commonly he does not marry. . . . He feels no attachment to community, neighbors, or friends (he has companions, not friends), resents all authority (for example, that of policemen, social workers, teachers, landlords, employers), and is apt to think that he has been "railroaded" and to want to "get even." He is a non-participant: he belongs to no voluntary organization, has no political interests, and does not vote unless paid to do so.*[8]

Banfield concludes:

*So long as the city contains a sizable lower class, nothing basic can be done about its most serious problems. Good jobs may be offered to all, but some will remain chronically unemployed. Slums may be demolished, but if the housing that replaces them is occupied by the lower class it will shortly be turned into new slums.*

*Welfare payments may be doubled or tripled and a negative income tax instituted, but some persons will continue to live in squalor and misery. New schools may be built, new curricula devised, and the teacher-pupil ratio cut in half, but if the children who attend these schools come from lower-class homes, the schools will be turned into blackboard jungles, and those who graduate or drop out from them will, in most cases, be functionally illiterate. The streets may be filled with armies of policemen, but violent crime and civil disorder will decrease very little. If, however, the lower class were to disappear — if, say, its members were overnight to acquire the attitudes, motivations, and habits of the working class — the most serious and intractable problems of the city would disappear with it.*[9]

In a word: *regeneration.* The issue is not poverty or hunger, but faith and ethics. The present-oriented slave cannot be helped by mere capitalist moralizing about pulling himself up by his own bootstraps—he does not *want* to. Nor will he be helped by handouts—they will only reinforce his moral defects. This is not to say that we shouldn't give him "charity" when it is needed. But it is to say that, if we are *genuinely charitable,* we must give much more than money and food, and that our charity must not be focused on mere money and food. And, particularly, we must not do what Ronald Sider does in his book. Banfield warns against the use of rhetoric which tends "to encourage the individual to think that 'society' (e.g., white racism), not he, is responsible for his ills."[10] Increased envy will only aggravate the problem: as Solomon said, "the compassion of the wicked is cruel" (Proverbs 12:10).

Again, the poor need free enterprise, capital investment, and rising productivity in order to attain better living standards. Socialistic transfers of wealth—even assuming funds went to the poor, and not to bureaucrats and politicians—can only reduce differences in incomes by reducing the incomes of the wealthy, not by increasing productivity; thus, even at best, socialism cannot sustain higher living standards among the poor (and besides, it's theft). But neither can a decadent, amoral capitalism produce an appreciable change in the poor. What they need cannot be reached by capital. Bauer and Banfield's descriptions of the chronically poor of East and West are horrifying. They completely undermine all current theories of "doing something" for the needy. Apart from the deep penetration of God's word into the basic ethos of society, nothing can be done. Even the biblical laws of charity are only temporary, short-term measures. We are commanded to give generously, and we must do so. But if we are going to do more than subsidize poverty, we had better not stop there.

First, there must be *evangelism*. Sider reports that American churchgoers "tithe" about 2.5% of their income,[11] and that is indeed a tragedy. Personally and by our giving, we must bring the gospel to the poor. And it must not be the lawless, cheap "evangelism" of the antinomian. Our hearers must be presented with the full-orbed demands of the covenant in every area of life. The biblical gospel teaches Christ as Savior and Lord. His law must be obeyed. The poor must learn the relationship of salvation to family life, work, debt, responsibility, thrift, savings, and everything else. The working of the Spirit in their lives, combined with the practical standards of biblical law, will give them the power to exercise increasing dominion as God opens up new opportunities to His obedient people. Evangelism among the poor in the United States and abroad is a crucial priority.

Flowing from this should be *Christian schools* in poor neighborhoods. Tithes should go to support those institutions that are centered firmly in the application of God's laws to the various disciplines, including the learning of trades. We must work diligently in this area; and if we are faithful, the godless, theft-financed public schools will fold under, allowing Christian mission schools to have a monopoly in more and more areas.

In addition, we do need to support *political action* in order to change the truly unjust structures that hurt the poor. We must seek to *abolish:* the minimum wage, fractional reserve banking, the government monopoly of the mint, compulsory education laws, rent controls, zoning restrictions, tariffs, price supports, price ceilings, closed-shop union laws, taxation of property and inheritance, immigration restrictions, "windfall profits" taxes, restrictions on energy development, and so forth. We need to do everything we can to increase the productivity of God's world. Poor countries should be made aware that true development will occur, not by envious political expropriation, but through increasing capital supply and investing it in terms of market demand. National, state, and local governments must be forced to retreat into their rightful spheres of authority. Capital punishment and restitution laws must replace the unbiblical prison system—which will also free up resources for investment. In every area, men must be allowed the responsibility to fulfill their callings under God.

Am I dreaming? How could this happen? That brings us back to the first point—*evangelism.* As men are regenerated by the grace of God, learning to take on the responsibilities which the law commands, they will give up their idolatrous dependence upon the state. The key to cultural transformation is the gospel. Envy will steadily disappear—not by appeasing it, but by the dissemination of biblical ethics throughout the society. Those who obey will be blessed with more dominion, while those who disobey will be cursed. With increased responsibility, productivity will increase. The culture will grow, in numbers and in wealth.

The issue is not poverty. The issue is not even capital supply. "Abundant food is in the fallow ground of the poor, but it is swept away by injustice" (Proverbs 13:23). Resources are not infinite. But they are vastly more than we can imagine. The earth was made by God, and He is capable of bringing forth tremendous prosperity. Even the undeveloped land of the poor man can support a great deal of production. But it is presently swept away by injustice—by ungodly structures and practices which God curses by withholding abundance. And the only real issue is faithful obedience to the law of God. Capital can grow. Productivity can increase until the Last Judgment. But the basis for such economic growth is biblical law.

The religious and economic history of England provides a good illustration of this. Early in the eighteenth century, a high-society lady once joked that Parliament was "preparing a bill to have 'not' taken out of the *Commandments* and inserted in the *Creed*."[12] It was not far from the truth. By all descriptions of the period, it was characterized by rampant ungodliness and almost complete disregard for biblical standards in every area of life. J. C. Ryle wrote:

*Christianity seemed to lie as one dead . . . There was darkness in high places and darkness in low places—darkness in the court, the camp, the Parliament, and the bar—darkness in country, and darkness in town—darkness among rich and darkness among poor—a gross, thick, religious and moral darkness—a darkness that might be felt.* [13]

The government and the courts were corrupt: open bribery was a continual practice, and the poor were flagrantly oppressed— which is not to say that the poor were any better. Crime was abundant, and the attempt of the authorities to suppress it (by making 160 offenses punishable by death) was to no avail. Whole districts were sunk in abject heathenism, ignorant of the most basic principles of the gospel. And what were the churches doing? Says Ryle: "They existed, but they could hardly be said to have lived. They did nothing; they were sound asleep."[14] In short, England was well down the road which, for a nation just across the Channel, climaxed in the orgy of horror known as the French Revolution.

Yet, within a few years, the situation changed entirely. Thousands were converted to vital Christianity; the slave trade was abolished (in a manner vastly different from the Unitarian-inspired abolitionist movement in America); widows, orphans and poor were cared for; hospitals were established; missionary and tract societies flourished. What made the difference? To a great extent the change can be traced to the labors of George Whitefield and his companions, who spearheaded one of the most far-reaching evangelistic movements in history. England heard and believed the gospel of Jesus Christ, and began to obey the laws of God. This flowed out into every aspect of culture, including economics and politics. Those results are described by Ludwig von Mises:

*In the middle of the eighteenth century conditions in England were hardly more propitious than they are today in India. The traditional system of production was not fit to provide for the needs of an increasing population. The number of people for whom there was no room left in the rigid system of paternalism and government tutelage of business grew rapidly. Although at that time England's population was not much more than fifteen per cent of what it is today, there were several millions of destitute poor. Neither the ruling aristocracy nor these paupers themselves had any idea about what could be done to improve the material conditions of the masses.*

*The great change that within a few decades made England the world's wealthiest and most powerful nation was prepared for by a small group of philosophers and economists. They demolished entirely the pseudo-philosophy that hitherto had been instrumental in shaping the economic policies of the nations. They exploded the old fables: (1) that it is unfair and unjust to outdo a competitor by producing better and cheaper goods; (2) that it is iniquitous to deviate from traditional methods of production; (3) that labor-saving machines bring about unemployment and are therefore an evil; (4) that it is one of the tasks of civil government to prevent efficient businessmen from getting rich and to protect the less efficient against the competition of the more efficient; (5) that to restrict the freedom and the initiative of entrepreneurs by government compulsion or by coercion on the part of other powers is an appropriate means to promote a nation's well-being. In short: these authors expounded the doctrine of free trade and laissez-faire. They paved the way for a policy that no longer obstructed the businessman's effort to improve and expand his operations.*

*What begot modern industrialization and the unprecedented improvement in material conditions that it brought about was neither capital previously accumulated nor previously assembled technological knowledge. In England, as well as in the other Western countries that followed it on the path of capitalism, the early pioneers of capitalism started with scanty capital and scanty technological experience. At the outset of industrialization was the philosophy of private enterprise and initiative, and the practical application of this ideology made the capital swell and the technological know-how advance and ripen.* [15]

The only ultimately productive economic system will be the

result of two critical factors: *future orientation* — the assumption that progressive development and productivity are possible and desirable; and *the rule of law* — the widespread obedience of the culture to the commands of the Bible. As the gospel spreads throughout society, the biblical worldview will become the framework of economic activity. Slavery of all types — including statism and consumerism — will disappear, as ethics become conformed internally and externally to the word of God.

The only hope for the real elevation of the poor is capital accumulation and productivity. And the only hope for capital accumulation and productivity in the long run is cultural obedience to God's law in all human action.

# THE CONQUEST OF POVERTY

**THERE SHALL BE NO POOR AMONG YOU, SINCE THE LORD WILL SURELY BLESS YOU IN THE LAND WHICH THE LORD YOUR GOD IS GIVING YOU AS AN INHERITANCE TO POSSESS, IF ONLY YOU LISTEN OBEDIENTLY TO THE VOICE OF THE LORD YOUR GOD, TO CAREFULLY OBSERVE ALL THIS COMMANDMENT WHICH I AM COMMANDING YOU TODAY. [DEUTERONOMY 15:4-5]**

*Will poverty ever be eliminated?* As Moses suggests, we will be able to answer that question when we have answered these: *Will God's people ever be obedient?* Will there be a truly Christian culture, in which Christ is recognized as LORD over everything? Many Christians today would say *NO*. After all, we are living in the last days. Christians will soon be "Raptured" out of this world, and Christ will then descend in judgment. Some are even saying the Rapture will happen this year. But, whenever it happens, we know one thing for sure: Christians are fighting a losing battle. The forces of evil will triumph until the return of Christ to set up His kingdom. We can rescue a few brands from the burning; but in this age, the preaching of the gospel will fail to convert and disciple the world. Satan's power will increase.

If this outline of the future is correct, we can expect certain political and economic consequences to flow from such increasing depravity. Both statism and local anarchy will rise to unprecedented heights; wars will increase; government monetary policies will continue to produce soaring inflations and ravaging depressions; fraud will abound; self-seeking, piggish consumption will be the norm; men will be lazy, improvident, and undependable; the productivity of the earth will decline; the food supply will dwindle away. The outlook for conquering world poverty is bleak, to put it mildly. As ungodliness dominates the world, long-term, chronic poverty will expand. Billions will starve. There will be no hope. Poverty will never be alleviated, for all we can expect is for it to grow dramatically until the return of Christ. *If* this outline of the future is correct . . .

But what if it isn't correct? What if the Bible holds out the promise that, *before* the return of Christ, the world will see a truly Christian culture? If that is what the Bible teaches, we can expect that under His blessing, the rich potential of the earth will unfold, and that "there shall be no poor" among us. It's a nice thought, but not worth much unless there is a truly biblical basis for it. What does the Bible teach? We have seen that the Bible does teach *one* of the two requisites for long-term productivity: *the rule of law.* But there is another thing necessary: *future orientation,* optimism about the future possibilities of economic growth. The Bible teaches this as well. Christ will be victorious in this age. The gospel will convert the nations and disciple them to the obedience of God's law. And God will bless that obedience by giving worldwide peace and economic abundance. Let's consider some of the biblical evidence which leads to this conclusion.

**THE PROMISE OF WORLDWIDE BLESSING** God gave Abraham the promise of the gospel in these words:
> *Your Seed shall possess the gate of His enemies.*
> *And in your Seed all the nations of the earth shall be blessed.*
> (*Genesis 22:17-18*)

The "Seed" spoken of here is Jesus Christ (Galatians 3:16).

The coming of Christ was to result in the blessing of all the nations. The specific blessing mentioned here is that He will possess the "gates"—the centers of rule and jurisdiction—of His enemies. The blessing that comes to the world through Christ must result in political and economic change, and this means social transformation. This promise is repeated again and again in different ways:

*All the ends of the earth will remember and turn to the LORD,*
*And all the families of the nations will worship before Thee.*
   *(Psalm 22:27)*
*Cease striving and know that I am God;*
*I will be exalted among the nations, I will be exalted in earth.*
   *(Psalm 46:10)*
*All the earth will worship Thee*
*And will sing praises to Thee. (Psalm 66:4)*
*All nations whom Thou hast made shall come and worship before*
   *Thee, O LORD;*
*And they shall glorify Thy name. (Psalm 86:9)*
*So the nations will fear the name of the LORD,*
*And all the kings of the earth Thy glory. (Psalm 102:15)*
*In the last days,*
*The mountain of the house of the LORD*
*Will be established as the chief of the mountains,*
*And will be raised above the hills;*
*And all the nations will stream to it. (Isaiah 2:2)*
*The earth will be full of the knowledge of the LORD*
*As the waters cover the sea. (Isaiah 11:9)*
*"From the rising of the sun, even to its setting, My name will be great*
   *among the nations, and in every place incense is going to be offered to*
   *My name, and a grain offering that is pure; for My name will be*
   *great among the nations," says the LORD of hosts. (Malachi 1:11)*

The true God will receive genuine worship from all the nations. This is certainly not to say that all men who have ever lived will be saved. Nor does it suggest that at some point in the future every single individual alive will be a Christian. But it does say that the time will come when Christianity will be the universal religion, when social structures and personal ethics will conform to biblical standards. The ruling disposition among most men will be Christian. As Abraham and the prophets contemplated this, it probably seemed even more astonishing than it seems to us. In our day, Christianity is known throughout the world; Bibles are translated into virtually every language; we are well on the way toward accomplishing God's goal of blessing all nations. But in the days of the Old Testament, such a goal would have appeared unattainable to many.

One event made all the difference. That was the coming of Jesus Christ. By His life, death, resurrection and ascension He definitively won the victory over Satan and the forces of evil. He wrested the earth from the Destroyer, and extends the blessings of salvation to every nation. It is this strand of biblical evidence which we shall now examine.

**THE VICTORY OF JESUS CHRIST**   The very first promise of the coming Redeemer foretold His victory through suffering. God said to the serpent:

> *On your belly shall you go,*
> *And dust shall you eat*
> *All the days of your life;*
> *And I will put enmity*
> *Between you and the woman,*
> *And between your seed and her Seed;*
> *He shall bruise you on the head,*
> *And you shall bruise Him on the heel. (Genesis 3:14-15)*

Christ's victory over the serpent would be total; and its ramifications would spill over, the prophets proclaimed, into all of life. It would mean victory over the nations, and even earth's natural order would undergo significant change:

> *Nations will see and be ashamed*
> *Of all their might.*
> *They will put their hand on their mouth,*
> *Their ears will be deaf.*

*They will lick the dust like a serpent,*
*Like reptiles of the earth.*
*They will come trembling out of their fortresses;*
*To the LORD our God they will come in dread,*
*And they will be afraid before Thee. (Micah 7:16-17)*

*"The wolf and the lamb shall graze together, and the lion shall eat straw*
*like the ox; and dust shall be the serpent's food. They shall do no evil*
*or harm in all My holy mountain," says the LORD. (Isaiah 65:23)*

The destruction of Satan's power began during the ministry of
Christ, as He cast out demons and healed the sick. One of the
striking aspects of the Gospels is their record of the sudden,
violent outburst of demonic activity during this period. All-out
warfare was being waged. Our Lord gave to His disciples the
powers of dominion over the devil, and on one occasion, as they
returned to Him, flushed with victory, He said:

*I was watching Satan fall from heaven like lightning. Behold, I have given*
*you authority to tread upon serpents and scorpions, and over all the power of*
*the enemy, and nothing shall injure you. (Luke 10:18-19)*

But it was Christ's work in His death and resurrection which
effectively sealed the fate of the Satanic hordes. This theme runs
through the apostolic letters to the early Christian assemblies.
Paul wrote that when Christ "had disarmed the rulers and authorities, He made a public display of them, having triumphed over
them in Him" (Colossians 2:15). Jesus *disarmed* the demons! Can
we really suppose that the world is still the Devil's territory—that
we can do nothing to stop his activity? He is still active, certainly;
but he has been disarmed. The devil was *rendered powerless*
(Hebrews 2:14). Satan is alive on planet earth, but he's not well.
He doesn't even have a Triangle to his name. "The Son of God
appeared for this purpose, that He might *destroy* the works of the
devil" (I John 3:8). Note: this is speaking of Christ's First Coming, not His Second Coming. On the basis of Christ's victory, His
people are promised, in this age, the same power over Satan that
God foretold at the first. Paul wrote to the persecuted believers in
Rome that "the God of peace will soon crush Satan under your

feet" (Romans 16:20). Our all-too-common timidity as we face the forces of evil is entirely unjustified. The basic victory has already been won, and our Lord has committed to us the power to shake Satan loose from his hiding places. All that hinders us from dominion is our sinful unbelief in the work of Christ and the promises of God. Marcellus Kik wrote:

*To say that the defeat of Satan will only come through a cataclysmic act at the Second Coming of Christ is ridiculous in the light of these passages. To think that the church must grow weaker and weaker and the kingdom of Satan stronger and stronger is to deny that Christ came to destroy the works of the devil; it is to dishonor Christ; it is to disbelieve His word. We do not glorify God or His prophetic word by being pessimists and defeatists.* [1]

Can we be sure that it is Christ's work in this age to establish His victory throughout the world? A currently popular theory among evangelicals holds that the kingdom of Christ awaits His return, when he will set up His throne in Jerusalem and reign for 1000 years. This thoroughly unbiblical idea is refuted by the passages in the following section.

**THE COMING OF THE KINGDOM**   The Psalmist wrote of the opposition between God and the heathen nations, in which "the kings of the earth take their stand, and the rulers take counsel together against the LORD and His Anointed" (Psalm 2:2). Many are in despair today as they look on a world ruled by Nimrods, Caesars, Hitlers, and Ayatollahs. Often, evil conspiracies are viewed by both Right and Left as omnipotent forces over which there is little hope of victory. This is to place our faith in man, not God. He is the ruler of history, and the Psalm goes on to celebrate the coming dominion of Christ over all the nations as universal King. God told his Son:

*Ask of Me, and I will surely give the nations as Thy inheritance,*
*And the very ends of the earth as Thy possession.*
*Thou shalt break them with a rod of iron,*
*Thou shalt shatter them like earthenware. (Psalm 2:8-9)*

Kings and rulers are advised by the Psalmist to submit to the rule of Christ. If they do not, they will be destroyed (Psalm 2:10-12). The reign of the Messiah is not pictured by the Old Testament writers as confined to Jerusalem; instead, it will be universal, in which all nations will serve Him (Psalm 72). This necessarily means the acceptance of His law as recorded in Scripture. The notion that Christ's kingdom has nothing to do with politics and economics is altogether false. Isaiah announced that "the *government* will rest on His shoulders . . . There will be no end to the increase of His government or of peace" (Isaiah 9:6-7).

When will Christ's kingdom begin? The prophet Daniel was given the answer. Interpreting Nebuchadnezzar's dream, Daniel foretold the future of four great world empires, symbolically represented by a statue. First there was the Babylonian empire; it would be followed by the Medo-Persian, the Greek, and the Roman empires. But during the last empire, a stone would strike it, bringing it to destruction, and becoming a mountain which would fill the earth. The stone represented the kingdom of Christ, which would endure forever (Daniel 2:31-45). Because of the obvious connection of the beginning of God's kingdom with the Roman Empire, those who wish to deny it have invented the myth that we would see a "*revived* Roman Empire" in the last days. The Bible says nothing of this; but as someone has remarked: Dispensationalists believe in the revival of the Roman Empire; we believe in the revival of Christianity.

Daniel goes on to show Christ ascending in the clouds to His Father and receiving everlasting dominion, in order that "all the peoples, nations, and men of every language might serve Him" (Daniel 7:13-14). This theme is picked up by Zechariah, who connects Christ's triumphal entry into Jerusalem, just before His crucifixion, with His universal rule. Premillennialists arbitrarily and quite high-handedly insert a gap of 2000 years between these verses, but, again, without a word of biblical support:

*Rejoice greatly, O daughter of Zion!*
*Shout in triumph, O daugher of Jerusalem!*
*Behold your King is coming to you;*

*He is just and endowed with salvation,*
*Humble, and mounted on a donkey.*
*And I will cut off the chariot from Ephraim,*
*And the horse from Jerusalem;*
*And the bow of war will be cut off.*
*And He will speak peace to the nations;*
*And His dominion will be from sea to sea,*
*And from the River to the ends of the earth. (Zechariah 9:9-10)*

Constantly, the prophets told of Christ's kingdom beginning with His first coming. If this is really the case, we would expect it to be the message of the Apostles as well. As a glance at your concordance will reveal, Christ's kingdom is a primary topic of the Gospels. A study of these references alone should convince you that He had no intention of "postponing" it at all, contrary to the claims of Scofield and others. The authoritative interpretation of Christ's kingdom was given by Peter on the Day of Pentecost. He reminded the Jews of their father David's prophecy. "Because he was a prophet, and knew that God had sworn to him with an oath to seat one of his descendants on his throne, he looked ahead and spoke of"—the Second Coming? No!—"the *resurrection* of Christ" (Acts 2:30-31). Christ became the King at His resurrection, after which he declared: "*All authority* has been given to Me in heaven and in earth" (Matthew 28:18). Jesus is King *now*, not in some future earthly reign. He is on "David's throne" *now*, for that merely symbolized His heavenly throne. If Christ now has "all authority in heaven and in earth," what could possibly be added to that authority in the future? Paul tells us that when God raised His Son from the dead,

*He . . . seated Him at His right hand in the heavenly places, far above all*
*rule and authority and power and dominion, and every name that is named,*
*not only in this age, but also in the one to come. And He put all things under*
*His feet . . . (Ephesians 1:20-22).*

The kingdom of Jesus Christ is now being extended over all the earth. God has "delivered us from the domain of darkness, and transferred us to the kingdom of His beloved Son" (Colossians

1:13). As members of His kingdom, Christians are ruling with Him now: "He has made us to be a kingdom, priests to His God and Father" (Revelation 1:6). In His messages to the churches of Asia, Jesus exhorted each one to overcome the powers of evil in terms of their high calling as kings and priests; and He made a promise to those who obeyed, using the language of Psalm 2:

*And he who overcomes, and he who keeps My deeds until the end, to him I will give authority over the nations: and he shall rule them with a rod of iron, as the vessels of the potter are broken to pieces, as I received authority from My Father (Revelation 2:26-27).*

Jesus is King *now*, in *this* age; and His obedient people have every reason to expect *increasing victories in this age*, as they confront the nations with the omnipotent authority of their Lord. This will not come without a struggle, as the ungodly seek to retain their illegitimate hold on the world. But victory is ours, in principle, as we are to march forth into all the world and into every field of life, conquering in Jesus' name.

Matthew 16:18 — Christ's promise that "the gates of hell shall not prevail against the church" — is often watered down to mean only that the church will be divinely protected against attacks by the forces of evil. Come now. When have you ever heard of *gates* attacking anything? Gates do not attack. Gates *defend*. The picture here is not that of the church besieged by the forces of evil. It's the other way around. *The church is the one on the offensive.* God's people are attacking the forces of evil, and Jesus promises that the ungodly will be defenseless under our attack. We will win! We share Christ's dominion now, and we are to extend that dominion throughout creation, confident of victory.

Marcellus Kik said:

*It is true that we must not underestimate the influence and power of the Evil One; but it is also true that he can be easily overcome by those who believe in the power of the blood of Christ and are not ashamed to testify of it. They are the overcomers.*[2]

How will the kingdom of Christ be established in this age? How will the prophecies of His universal dominion be fulfilled in every nation? These questions are addressed in the section below.

### THE PROGRESS OF THE GOSPEL     Just prior to His death, Jesus spoke of Satan's defeat:

*Now judgment is upon this world; now the ruler of this world shall be cast out. And I, if I be lifted up from the earth, will draw all men to Myself (John 12:31-32).*

The victory over Satan is based upon the atoning work of our Savior on the cross. The proclamation of the gospel—the "good news" of salvation in Christ—is the means of defeating the power of the devil in every sphere of life. The combination of *Christ's death* and aggressive *evangelism* will completely rout the forces of evil. It has always been so. John was told of how Christians would win the war against Satan: "They overcame him because of the blood of the Lamb and the word of their testimony, and they did not love their lives even to death" (Revelation 12:11). Christ's death and resurrection are the basis of victory, the foundation of His kingdom. And as we testify of Him to the world, we will see the world gradually subdued by His power. It is *gradual*; books such as Daniel and Revelation show us that it is a fierce struggle that often claims the lives of believers. Just as Canaan did not come without a fight—many fights, in fact—so the gospel conquest of the world will require battles. It will take time. But we will win. Jesus said, "The kingdom of heaven is like leaven, which a woman took, and hid in three pecks of meal, until it all was leavened" (Matthew 13:33). The woman didn't use dynamite, to get the job done quickly; she used yeast. Similarly, God doesn't want to blow up the world; He wants to transform it. This is why Christianity is not revolutionary. Even in the face of manifest injustice, we do not overthrow the system, but overcome it by the gospel. The early Christians did not start a liberation movement against the "structural injustices" of the Roman Empire. They converted the Empire instead. *Then* they changed the structures.

For example, I do think it's a tragedy that worthy people do not own land. I think every Christian ought to own property—and, someday, I believe every Christian *will* own land (as we shall see further in this chapter). But socialistic "land reform" is not the answer. Regeneration is the answer. As men become responsible, they will inherit the earth — *meekly*. Meekness does not mean spinelessness. It means obedience to God, and submission to His providence.

Hilaire Belloc wrote of the "abolition" of slavery that took place as Europe was Christianized:

*In general you will discover no pronouncement against slavery as an institution, nor any moral definition attacking it, throughout all those early Christian centuries during which it nonetheless effectively disappears.*[3]

Slavery disappeared because *a majority of men stopped being slaves to Satan.* Christianity works like leaven: from the inside out. Laws — *biblical* laws — are important to the security of society. But if men are not ruled by law internally, the external controls will break down. Our work to establish God's laws in society may, and should, accompany our evangelistic efforts. But apart from those efforts, we are laboring in vain and striving after wind. Dominion will come through proclaiming God's word and obeying it ourselves. The world will be transformed by the faithful preaching and living of God's people. On the basis of His sovereign authority, Jesus commanded: "Go therefore and make disciples of all the nations" (Matthew 28:19). That command is usually misunderstood. Jesus did *not* say: Witness to the nations. He said: *Disciple the nations.* The great commission is not exhausted when we have brought the gospel to the attention of all nations. That is not even half the battle. It is only the beginning. We must disciple all nations to the obedience of His commands, and that can come only as we ourselves are discipled to God's law. Only disciples can make disciples. Hybrids cannot reproduce. But as we ourselves submit to Christ, the nations will also.

The subduing of the nations to the discipleship of Christ will take place as we are faithful. That is the crucial issue, and that is why Christians have lost ground over the recent past. It is not due to the advance of paganism (remember, gates can't advance). It is due only to the *retreat* of Christians.

*That there is still a remnant of paganism and papalism in this world is chiefly the fault of the Church. The Word of God is just as powerful in this generation as it was during the early history of the Church. The power of the Gospel is just as strong in this century as in the days of the Reformation. These enemies could be completely vanquished if the Christians of this day and age were as vigorous, as bold, as earnest, as prayerful, and as faithful as Christians were in the first several centuries and in the time of the Reformation.*[4]

Thus we must work diligently and patiently for the kingdom. It has come and it is still coming. In the meantime, we are not to envy even the wicked who are in power. They will fall, and the meek will inherit the earth (Psalm 37). The gradual growth of Christ's kingdom was stated beautifully by Benjamin Warfield:

*Through all the years one increasing purpose runs, one increasing purpose: the kingdoms of the earth become ever more and more the kingdom of our God and His Christ. The process may be slow; the progress may appear to our impatient eyes to lag. But it is God who is building: and under His hands the structure rises as steadily as it does slowly, and in due time the capstone shall be set into its place, and to our astonished eyes shall be revealed nothing less than a saved world.*[5]

**THE BLESSINGS OF NATIONAL OBEDIENCE**  We have noted the cultural effects of obedience so often in our study that it would be superfluous to recount them all here. But this chapter is on the elimination of poverty as the result of obedience to the law, and I want to use that subject to bring together the various strands of biblical revelation which we have considered here.

We have seen that worldwide blessing is promised in Christ; that when He came He was victorious; that His victory continues throughout the earth as His kingdom expands; and that the expansion of His kingdom follows the fearless delivery of the gospel into all nations. From what we have studied in previous chapters, it should be clear that the reign of Christ in the hearts and social structures of men will produce responsibility and freedom under the law of God. As men mature in this responsibility and freedom, they will be granted more (Matthew 25:21, 23). With increased work, savings, and capital investment, productivity will rise, creating more capital for investment, and so on. *There will be uninterrupted growth over time until the Last Day*, and poverty will disappear. Those who remain ungodly will be disinherited, as God's providential forces in history work against them. The wealth of the sinner is laid up for the just (Proverbs 13:22). God's people will inherit *land* as we mature, as we submit ourselves to biblical law and extend its implications all through society. The biblical statement of the elimination of poverty is found in Micah 4:2-4, which speaks of the blessings on the nations that are converted, and thus submit to the law of God:

> *And many nations will come and say*
> *"Come and let us go up to the mountain of the LORD*
> *And to the house of the God of Jacob,*
> *That He may teach us about His ways*
> *And that we may walk in His paths."*
> *For from Zion will go forth the law,*
> *Even the word of the LORD from Jerusalem.*
> *And He will judge between many peoples*
> *And render decisions for mighty, distant nations.*
> *Then they will hammer their swords into plowshares*
> *And their spears into pruning hooks;*
> *Nation will not lift up sword against nation.*
> *And never again will they train for war.*
> *And each of them will sit under his vine*
> *And under his fig tree,*
> *With no one to make them afraid,*
> *For the mouth of the LORD of hosts has spoken.*

As obedience to biblical law spreads, capital will be shifted from warfare to more productive endeavors; and as productivity rises, we find each man on his own property, sitting under his vine and fig tree. This is the direction of history. Men will become more obedient, hence more responsible, hence more productive, hence more capitalized. . . . The Bible shows that poverty will be abolished through godly productivity and rising real wealth. The biblical answer is not, as the saying goes, to redistribute the pie, but to make a bigger pie.

It can happen. Moreover, it will happen. Ultimately, poverty has no future, except for the ungodly who are dispossessed. Ezekiel's vision of the kingdom's growth throughout the world (symbolized by the gradually rising stream flowing from the temple, Ezekiel 47:1-12) showed the blessings of God affecting virtually everything in life, bringing health and prosperity to the world. Even the salty Dead Sea, symbol of God's curse upon Sodom and Gomorrah, will become fresh—but some few places will be "left for salt" (v. 8-11), still under the judgment of God. The Bible looks forward to the time when none of God's people will be poor, when by God's gracious providence the land will be distributed to all those who are obedient.

This will never come about through ungodly acts of expropriation. It will never happen as long as the church continues to heed unbiblical philosophies which seek to turn her away from obedience to God's law. Institutional poverty will never be cured by socialism and statism. Ungodliness can only extend the Curse. The conquest of poverty is not really based on the issue of poverty at all. It is an issue of obedience, of godliness, of submission to the Lord Christ at all points.

Our nation has a Christian heritage. While they had their flaws, the Puritans and the leaders of the young United States knew the importance of biblical laws, and that "righteousness exalts a nation" (Proverbs 14:34). Their adherence to God's word was blessed by God, and our land became one of increasing wealth. But we fell into the snare warned of in Deuteronomy 8. We looked at our peace and prosperity and convinced ourselves that our strength had come from ourselves. We began to seek growth for ourselves, and not for the glory of God. We rejoiced in the gifts, and ignored the Giver. We used His tools to build idols. While we boasted of freedom, we became enslaved.

When God's goodness does not lead to repentance, He chastises. He sent judgments to our nation, to turn us from our sins—and as we felt our power eroding, we turned more and more toward sin as a means of strength. We allowed our rulers to lead us into wars, in order to achieve a supremacy that is denied to all but the obedient. We increasingly deified the state, ascribing to it creative powers, abandoning biblical standards in one area after another. We coveted goods, and got credit expansion; we wanted business booms, and the state provided them. Our demands increased, and the dominance of our new god was enlarged to keep up with them. And as our nation became enslaved, the Christians ran—some to the security of fundamentalist retreat, some to the comfort of liberal compromise, some to the heretical moderation of hovering somewhere in between. Every avenue was tried but the way of obedience.

And everything backfired. Our wars reduced our population; our foreign aid produced contempt and envy; our foreign policies generated revolutions abroad and riots at home; our welfare resulted in poverty and dependence; our economic booms terminated in racking depressions; our energy policies caused shortages; our evangelistic campaigns strewed a generation of "carnal Christians" across the land. And inflation accompanied it all. The Curse became a part of everyday life.

So we sought for new solutions, in a fruitless attempt to avoid the consequences of apostasy without repenting of sin. And our new solutions have bound us in chains stronger than those we had before. From national pride we have sunk into national guilt. We once bragged about God's blessings; we now feel ashamed of them. Our freedom has become an unstable anarchy; our stability has resulted in stagnation. God has judged.

And in the midst of all this, Ronald Sider and the Christian socialists have appeared as God's scourges of further chastisement, and a disobedient, antinomian church has blindly followed them into the ditch. Christian circles, departing God's law, have endorsed statism as the cure for our diseases. The moral fiber of our country—made strong by obedience—has rotted away in envy and guilt. Culturally and psychologically, we have committed suicide, and our sins will be visited upon our great-grandchildren. The wrath of God is evident in our seduction by shoddy, morally-bankrupt misanthropes. Our future—if the spokesmen for salvation-by-suicide are any indication of it—will be a downward spiral into self-absorption, slavery, despair, and damnation.

And yet we still have our Bibles, we still have our homes, we still have a considerable remainder of the rule of law; capital of all kinds with which to build. Will we repent? I am just enough of an optimist to hope that we will yet turn to God and begin again the construction of a Christian culture based on biblical law.

*What can be learned from the experience of the revolutionary era? That man, without God, even with the circumstances in his favour, can do nothing but work his own destruction. Man must break out of the vicious revolutionary circle; he must turn to God whose truth alone can resist the power of the lie. Should anyone consider this momentous lesson of history to be more sentimental lament than advice for politics, he is forgetting that the power of the Gospel to effect order and freedom and prosperity has been substantiated by world history. Let him bear in mind that whatever is useful and beneficial to man is promoted by the fear of God and thwarted by the denial of God. He should bear in mind especially that the revolutionary theory was an unfolding of the germ of unbelief and that the poisonous plant which was cultivated by apostasy from the faith will wilt and choke in the atmosphere of a revival of the faith.*[6]

That is the reason for this book. It is written to encourage a return to Scripture; to stir into flame the embers of godly principles which form our great heritage, and which will lead again to dominion under God's law. The statists cannot ultimately prevail; and, dark as it looks, they have not yet won the present battle. By the grace of God, we can still change the drift of our culture. God has given us the tools, and guaranteed our success if we obey. As Hilaire Belloc observed,[7]

*There is a complex knot of forces underlying any nation once Christian; a smoldering of the old fires.*

# GLOSSARY

The following list of terms is intended to clarify the meanings of expressions used in this book. Several of the definitions have been adapted from *Mises Made Easier*, by Percy L. Greaves, Jr. This work by Greaves is an excellent source for understanding free-market economics. (Free Market Books, P. O. Box 298, Dobbs Ferry, NY 10522; $10.)

**Anarchy** literally means "no civil government," a utopian condition of lawlessness which results in social chaos and disorder, followed by warlordism or statist tyranny (the reaction). See *Antinomianism*.

**Antinomianism** is "anti-law-ism," the belief and practice of rejecting God's law as the standard for every area of life. See *Sin*.

**Autonomy** means "self-law," the belief and practice of determining the standards of life for oneself. No one can truly be autonomous from God, for "in Him we live and move and exist" (Acts 17:28). The man who attempts to live autonomously will be cursed.

**Biblical** has two usages. As I use it, it means *ruled by the laws of God's word*. As Ronald Sider uses it, it means *statism*.

**Black markets** are markets for buying and selling in violation of governmental price controls and rationing regulations. Free-market thinkers prefer to regard black markets as "alternative zones of supply," since the government regulations and controls are biblically illegal in the first place.

**Blessings** are bestowals of goods. God's blessing of His people is first of all the giving of salvation through His Son. This results in long-term material blessing as the believing culture is obedient to God's law (Ephesians 1:3; Deuteronomy 28:1-14; Proverbs 10:22; 28:20; Malachi 3:10-12). God's people are blessed with increasing dominion over the earth, and the land yields abundant fruit under the godly development of its resources.

**Capital** is the net wealth of goods and savings owned by a person who participates in a market. Capital can be accumulated only by saving and increasing the supply of capital goods. See *Saving*.

**Capital goods** are things such as tools, machines, and buildings —already produced "factors of production"—which make labor more productive by reducing the time and energy necessary to reach the goals of production. (Sider subscribes to the fallacy of regarding "labor-intensive"—i.e., less efficient—production as morally superior; see *Rich Christians*, pp. 54, 230. In reality, increasing the productivity of labor means increasing per capita wealth and employment opportunities. Money that is saved by hiring fewer workers will be spent elsewhere, thus employing the workers in another industry. See Henry Hazlitt's *Economics in One Lesson*, ch. 10).

**Capitalism** is the Marxist term for *Christian Society*. It is the system of private ownership and control of the means of production as well as the fruits of production, and stands against policies of govenmental ownership or control. See *Free enterprise.*

**Capitalists** are people who either invest in an enterprise or defend and advocate the system of capitalism.

**Commodities** are *things,* real goods which people value. For example, paper money is not a commodity: you don't value the money in your wallet for the actual worth of the *paper,* but for what you hope the paper *represents* (ability to purchase goods). But *commodity money* (gold or silver) is valued because of what it is as a commodity. See *Money* and *Value.*

**Commodity agreements** are contracts in which various nations establish cartels to control the sale of "primary products" (raw materials and foodstuffs) at specific prices that are "stabilized" above the market price. They are "price floors." See *Price controls.*

**Communism** is generally synonymous with socialism, in which all economic activity is controlled by the state. Since 1928, it has been used by Communists to refer to the professed goal of socialism, when all property will be held in common by all, and there will be no need for civil government. It is an unbiblical and unrealizable goal, and no socialist state seriously attempts to achieve it. See *Socialism.*

**Competition** is the action of individuals attempting to reach the most favorable position in society's division of labor. It is not "competitive" in the sense of warfare, but simply in the sense that goods and services are distributed in the least wasteful way. Sellers compete with each other by offering better and cheaper goods; buyers compete with each other by offering higher prices; workers compete with each other by offering better and cheaper labor; employers compete with each other by offering higher wages. The result of this process is that supply and demand tend to equal each other by means of freely fluctuating prices, and consumers are presented with the best and cheapest goods that are consistent with the level of demand. In statism, competition degenerates into attempts to curry the favors of those who are in power in civil governments—legal monopolies of violence.

**Credit expansion** is the most common modern form of inflation, and takes place when banks lend out more money than they actually hold in reserves. Borrowers are allowed to write checks for more money than depositors have deposited. (See *Fractional reserve banking* and *Inflation.*) The expanding credit in effect creates new dollars, which are then spent or invested. Those who get this new "magic money" first bid up prices for goods. This causes latecomers to suffer, and gives false information to businessmen, who think that the increased buying of their products means that they should produce more—not realizing that the "money" spent on their products has been recently counterfeited (legally). Credit expansion is a totally dishonest practice. It steals by diluting the purchasing power of everybody's dollars. Early spenders win; others lose, especially the gullible patriots who trust the governments' money. See *Sin.*

**Currency** is money or money-substitutes. The only way to have an *honest* currency is when the money is *real* money (see *Money*). Paper is easier to carry than coins and bars are, but a sound currency will be solidly backed by "hard" money (gold or silver) and fully redeemable in that hard money. Paper money should be a "warehouse receipt" for a given commodity: 100% reserves. There is no biblical justification for government monopoly of currency. Many kinds of coins, bars, and warehouse receipts (fiduciary media) should be allowed in voluntary exchange at freely fluctuating exchange rates (prices).

**The Curse** is God's judgment upon those who disobey Him. As described in Deuteronomy 28:15-68, the Curse can take many forms. While we cannot assume that an *individual's* relationship to God is always reflected in his external conditions, we can observe the *general regularity of God's law* in the absence of a *society's* material blessings, and we observe natural disasters within a culture that has engaged in long-term disobedience. The Curse is lifted only by the grace of God in response to cultural repentance and obedience (II Chronicles 7:13-14).

**Debasement of currency** is the practice of falsely increasing the money supply by cheapening the monetary unit. Before paper currency, this was done by mixing precious metals with baser materials, and passing the result off as pure gold or silver (Isaiah 1:22). With paper money, this is done by simply printing unbacked bills; and with computers it is done by credit expansion (q.v.). When private persons do this, it is called counterfeiting. When governments do this, it is called progressive monetary policy. The Bible calls it theft no matter who does it (Amos 8:5). See *Inflation, Keynes,* and *Sin.*

**Deism** is incipient atheism. It is not a strictly defined school of thought, but a general tendency (especially among some 18th-century European thinkers) to deny the biblical principles of revelation, God's providence, prayer, and biblical ethics. Man's autonomous reason was regarded as the determiner of truth, and the world was viewed as running according to "natural" laws rather than by God's continual government. In disregarding the revealed social laws of God, Ronald Sider manifests a strong deistical tendency.

**Demand** is the *willingness* and *ability* of consumers to spend money. I may wish to have a fleet of yachts, but that is not a *demand* unless I am willing and able to purchase them. By their demand (production), consumers dictate what goods will subsequently be produced, and at what price. If the demand is not expected to be sufficient to pay producers to produce a good, the good will not be produced. Thus, the goods that are available are the ones producers believed would be most wanted by the aggregate of consumers. Moreover, consumer demand determines the wages of workers in each industry, by showing the market worth of labor's product, and therefore the market worth of the labor expended in producing it. It is not possible to "exploit" labor for long, since rival producers will not allow one firm to profit by paying below-market wages. Rival employers bid up wages.

**Depression** is a lot like the condition of a heroin addict when he tries to kick the habit. When business gets "high" from the boom caused by monetary inflation, the market eventually has to go through "withdrawal symptoms": greatly reduced business activity, mass unemployment, and much misery, as the market readjusts to reality: uninflated demand. Depressions are not caused by the free market but by government intervention, especially through central bank inflation and commercial bank credit expansion (people making investments with phony "magic money"). Inflationary booms necessarily end in depressions. A depression is a painful but necessary procedure; any attempt to interfere with it will only prolong the agonizing inflationary symptoms. Wait around a few years, and you'll get to see what it's like.

**Division of labor** is an indispensable requirement for exchange, in which each member of the economy works in the area in which he can be most productive. God has distributed various gifts to individuals, and the demands of the market draw men into those activities that they expect will be the most productive for the society as a whole, and therefore most profitable personally. Each man then trades his product or service for those of others. As men specialize in what they do best, the overall productivity of the society increases.

**Dominion** is man's responsibility to subdue the earth for God's glory. For Adam, this involved three general tasks: production of goods, scientific investigation, and aesthetic endeavors. By the division of labor, the work of dominion can be greatly furthered as each person learns to specialize in a particular field within these areas. By rebelling against God's law, man abandoned this responsibility; and the more externally rebellious a culture is, the less dominion it will have. This is the biblical explanation for so-called "primitive" cultures: they are not chronologically primitive but decadent and degenerate. Their forbears turned away from God's law as it was known to Noah and his sons; and the more they apostatized, the less able they were to cope with their surroundings (see *Curse*). Dominion is restored to the people of God as they are re-created in God's image, and the subduing of earth again becomes possible. See *Blessings*.

**Economics** is the study of people's actions as they purposefully use means to attain desired ends. The starting-point of Christian economics is not what "works,"—pragmatism—but the commands and prohibitions of God's law. All human action stands under the judgment of God. Lawful activity is blessed by God, in this life *and* the next; unlawful activity is cursed by God, in this life *and* the next. Unbiblical economics does not work because it is morally wrong and therefore is cursed. Biblical economics acknowledges scarcity (Genesis 3:15-17), the dominion covenant (Genesis 1:28), and personal responsibility (Philippians 2:12).

**Egalitarianism** is the ungodly desire, provoked by envy, to reduce all men to an arbitrarily conceived "equality," at least in those matters that the state can supposedly control. Egalitarians are statists: they want the government to enforce equality upon society. This results in an *inequality before law*, since the relatively wealthy are legally discriminated against in favor of the relatively poor. This kind of inequality is condemned by biblical law. It violates the principle of the *tithe*: fixed proportion taxes.

**Empiricism** is the unbiblical notion that experience is the only source of knowledge. John Locke and David Hume were notable exponents of this view. The Bible tells us, on the other hand, that God's word is the source of knowledge. Our experience can test truth only insofar as our experience is subject to God's word. Christians begin their search for knowledge with the assumption that the Bible is true. See *Presuppositions*.

**Entrepreneurs** are those who act in the present to produce a more desirable situation in the future. They act because they believe that doing nothing new, would not be as beneficial. In this sense, everyone is an entrepreneur, engaging in speculation about, and action toward, the unknown future. In business terminology, an entrepreneur is one who directs the factors of production in order to achieve a desired result in the most efficient and profitable way. But we should remember that the "professional" entrepreneur's function is not qualitatively different from that of anyone who allocates his resources in anticipation of the future. Entrepreneurs are specialists in *risk-taking* and *economic forecasting*.

**Envy** is the belief that one person's wealth is the cause of the poverty of others. The envious man blames others for his own want. His primary desire is not so much to obtain their property as to see *them* deprived of it. This is one reason why socialists cannot be convinced of the undesirability of socialism's inefficiencies, even when they admit that their policies will not result in the benefit of themselves or the poor; for the main goal of socialism is to confiscate and destroy. *Socialism is institutionalized envy*. When envy dominates a culture, progress is impossible: the envious will hate those who are successful, and everyone will do his best not to appear successful, in fear of being envied. When envy is inverted and turned in upon oneself, it becomes guilt (q.v.). You can sell a lot of copies of books that encourage guilt in an envy-dominated culture. Christians who do not tithe constitute a strong potential market for such books.

**Exchange** is involved in *every* human action, for people act in order to trade a less-desired condition for a more-desired condition. Within a free market, every morally legitimate exchange will benefit both parties, since both are exchanging less-desired goods for more-desired goods. See *Profit.*

**Factors of Production** are three: (1) the natural resources of the earth (land), (2) the human work in developing those natural resources (labor), and (3) time. These three factors of production are usually summed up as *land, labor* and *capital.* Capital is the combination of land and labor over time. They receive rent, wages, and interest (time-preference payment).

**The Federal Reserve System** is the central bank of the United States, created by the Federal Reserve Act of 1913. (Over 100 amendments have since been added to the Act, vastly increasing the power of the "Fed.") The Fed controls the supply of money and credit, in line with the general policies of the administration in power. It creates money out of nothing and buys up federal debt. Then the government spends this new money. Its actions have caused the increasing worthlessness of the dollar. See *Credit expansion, Fractional reserve banking* and *Inflation.*

**Fiat money** comes from the biblical account of creation, when God said (in the Latin translation), *"Fiat lux,"* which means "Let there by light." The government says, *"Fiat bucks!* Let there be *money!"* This is done by printing paper money or expanding credit beyond actual gold or silver reserves. It is a modern form of alchemy, in which the government magicians try to turn base materials into gold. The government, knowing that its magic money is really worthless, backs it with "legal tender" laws, forcing people to accept it. Fiat money is theft. See *Inflation.*

**Fractional reserve banking** is the commercial banks' practice of lending out more money than is actually held in their vaults. This is the most powerful tool of inflation. The present reserve requirement (set by the Federal Reserve) is *eight percent*. This means that, theoretically, banks could lend out up to $12.5 million for every $1 million they really possess. It is a sophisticated, legal means of theft. It is also quite profitable for banks. Why do civil governments allow it? Because they enjoy access to less expensive loans. See *Credit expansion*.

**Free enterprise** is the freedom to buy and sell at will, without government intervention. The civil government's biblical function is to *protect* the market from private coercion or fraud. State intervention is legitimate only where the "enterprise" is forbidden by Scripture. Government control of trade is a practice of Antichrist (Revelation 13:17).

**Free trade** is free enterprise on an international basis—the exchange of goods and services among citizens of many nations, unhampered by national commodity agreements, tarriffs, or any other barrier to trade. Assuming nations are not at war, trade should be unhampered. If any trade is lawful, then it should be completely free trade.

**Future orientation** is an attitude of optimism about the possibility and desirability of progress. It is a necessary requirement for expanding the real wealth of society. Only a Christian culture, holding the firm promise of God's blessings for the future, can sustain a long-term future orientation. Such a future orientation produces lower interest rates. God has commanded us to develop the earth and to disciple the nations, and He has guaranteed the success of our mission. See *Dominion*.

**The Gospel** is the "good news" of the kingdom of God. It is not merely the bare message of how to be justified before God, or of how to go to heaven. It is "the whole counsel of God" concerning our salvation in Christ—including His lordship over us and His commands for *every* aspect of our lives. Thus, the gospel message involves a call to repentance from ungodly economic and political practices, and the explanation of what God demands in these areas. The Roman Emperors were designated *Savior, Lord,* and *God*; the application of those titles by the early church to Jesus Christ constituted a declaration of war on the cult of statism. The gospel is the whole teaching of Scripture as it affects *all* of life, and it is centered on Jesus Christ as Lord.

**Guilt** is, in biblical usage, not primarily related to feelings, but rather the objective, real condition of having committed sin. As it is used today, the term refers more to the *feeling* of having done wrong (psychological guilt). Ronald Sider's message creates guilt feelings in people by directing envy toward them and encouraging them to feel somehow responsible for the envy of others. It is a false guilt, and threatens to produce inaction, passivity, dependence, and slavery. The manipulation of guilt is an important weapon in the arsenal of modern socialism.

**Humanism** is a system in which self-proclaimed autonomous man's values and interests are presupposed as the basis of right and wrong. It is a refusal to abide by the standards of God's law, and is generally synonymous with antinomianism and autonomy (q.v.). See also *Sin*.

**Inflation** is the government artificially increasing the supply of money. In popular usage, inflation means an increase in prices. This is misleading, and a convenient way for politicians to direct attention away from the real problem, namely, central bank financing of national government's budget deficits. High prices are an *effect* of inflation. When the government increases the money supply (through either the printing press or credit expansion), the purchasing power of each dollar falls, and businesses must charge higher prices to keep up with their own higher costs. Inflation also falsifies economic calculation: bad investments are made with "money" which—in real terms—does not exist. The only beneficiaries of inflation are those who are first to receive the new money, who can extend their purchases before prices go up. As inflation proceeds, prices begin to rise faster than the volume of money does. This eventually leads to the final stage of inflation: a frenzied rush to get rid of money in exchange for real goods of any kind. To cure inflation, the government needs only to abolish the central bank, require 100% reserves for all commercial banks, and repeal its own legal tender laws.

This happened to Germany in 1923, when the German mark fell to one-trillionth of its 1914 value. In Hungary after World War II, the purchasing power of the pengo fell to a low probably unequalled in all history: prices rose by $399.62 \times 10^{21}$ in a little over a year. The government began printing notes denominated *one hundred quintillion pengos*, the buying power of which was still far below that of *one* pengo before the inflation. The point is that *inflation is always caused by government expansion of the money supply* coupled with fractional reserve banking, a government-licensed system of counterfeiting.

**Institutional unemployment** happens when government interferes with voluntary wage agreements. Rather than being a temporary matter, unemployment becomes a permanent phenomenon, because the government decrees that wages must start at a certain level. All those whose labor is worth less than that amount are made legally unemployable. See *Labor unions, Minimum wage laws* and *Surpluses*.

**Interventionism** is the government practice of *intervening* into the market by making rules and regulations (e.g. price and wage laws) or by providing a service which the Bible doesn't allow it to do (e.g. tax-financed medical care, education, and welfare). We should remember that *interventions breed more interventions*; that is, if the government lowers the price of milk, it will next have to lower the price of feed for cattle, then of farm equipment, and so on until it ends up in complete socialism (like telling bigger lies to explain the previous ones—reality keeps catching up with you). See *Socialism*.

**Justice** is defined by God's law. Any deviation from His commandments—even in the name of "love" or "compassion"—is not justice, but injustice. Our view of right and wrong must always come from the Bible. The Bible, rather than Plato, Marx, or Keynes, defines right and wrong.

**John Maynard Keynes** [Canes] was an advocate of price inflation as a remedy for unemployment. He reasoned that if there is more paper money and credit, it will be easier to employ more people—even though the actual purchasing power of the money will be lower. Laborers will accept lower real wages (fewer goods and services), so employers will hire them. He figured that working people who didn't have degrees in economics wouldn't notice the difference. Lord Keynes died in 1946. He has been receiving his proper wages ever since. (Keynes was a homosexual who delighted in low-wage Tunisian boys. It was his way to fight unemployment in an underdeveloped nation.)

**Labor unions** are gangs of legalized thugs. They do not believe in allowing employers and employees the freedom to make contracts. They do not allow non-union people to sell their labor at lower wages; thus they create institutional unemployment for they are also strong advocates of minimum wage laws. By forcing employers to raise wages above the free-market price, they raise production costs, which means two more things: *lower production* and *higher consumer prices*. There is nothing wrong with workers bargaining with employers about wages. What is wrong is when unions are able to get the government behind them. This means that bargaining is done at gunpoint. The fact that government backs them also means that unions can usually threaten, terrorize and even kill those who oppose them, without facing punishment from the state. Their *opponents* are not employers but *rival workers* who are willing to work for wages lower than union members want for themselves.

**Laissez-faire** means "let things alone." It is a synonym for the free market, which government should let alone. The market does have civil laws surrounding it: the Bible doesn't allow just anything to be done simply because someone is willing to pay for it. It should be illegal, for example, for homosexuals to buy sexual favors from children in exchange for heroin. But, in general, the function of the government is to protect people and to punish crime. The government must enforce God's law. Apart from this, the government must "let things alone."

**Land reform** is a socialistic euphemism for government stealing land from some people and giving it to others. Calling theft by another name doesn't change the fact that it's theft.

**Liberation** is supposed to mean "giving people freedom." But socialists use it to mean a revolution that leads to state control of everybody. In plain translation, *liberation* is *tyranny* and *dictatorship*. "Liberation theology" is a current version of this revolutionary perspective.

**Libertarianism** is the name for a philosophy which teaches much that is biblical about economics and politics. But those who call themselves libertarians usually don't care much for Christianity or the laws of the Bible; they just want government off their backs. They realize that the biblical system of free enterprise without government intervention works well, but they don't like the biblical laws which go along with it. So while they say a lot that is economically accurate, their basic principle is one of anarchy and antinomianism. For example: they want government to stop controlling prices (correct); but they don't want the government to punish homosexuals, adulterers, and abortionists (incorrect).

**Market** is the meeting of people for buying and selling. It exists wherever any exchange of goods or services takes place. The *free* market means that people are free to make exchanges. If Jack wants to sell his cow for a handful of beans, he should be allowed to do so without government intervention. But Jack is not permitted to use his beanstalk to trespass on the giant's property and steal his possessions. God's law protects everyone's property, even rich, unpopular giants.

**Marxism** is the philosophy of Karl Marx (1818-1883), who wrote *Das Kapital*, perhaps the most famous unread book in the world, except possibly for Darwin's *Origin of Species*. Marxism teaches that everyone who gets rich does so at the expense of the poor. Marxism teaches that labor is the only source of value. Marxism teaches that the lower classes are always exploited by the upper classes. Marxism teaches that landowners should be dispossessed, and that all property should be held in common, jointly "owned" by all. Marxism teaches that people should have only what they need. By now, some of these ideas may sound suspiciously familiar.

**Mercantilism** was popular during the 16th and 17th centuries. It was the theory that if one nation gains, it must be at the expense of another nation. Mercantilists felt that if any exchange benefitted a person, he must have ripped off the other guy. So they said the government should intervene to make things *fair*—by favoring one group over another. This way, no one would benefit except the government and those who receive government handouts. They seldom used out-of-context Bible verses to support their case for state intervention. Unfortunately, some modern mercantilists do. This tends to confuse people. Nevertheless, it sells books.

**Minimum wage laws** prohibit employers from paying their workers below a certain amount. Thus, such laws "help" many poor people by making it illegal for unskilled workers to get jobs. Anyone who sees the logic in this can qualify as a roving editor for *theOtherSide*, and will be invited to give chapel lectures to seminary students. See *Institutional unemployment* and *Surpluses*.

**Money** is a *commodity*, a real thing which people value. It is the *most marketable commodity*. In the Bible, money is always gold and silver. Money makes exchange much easier, because people can trade their goods for money and use the money to buy other things they want. Money also helps people calculate the market worth of their products, and enables them to figure out their profits and losses. Paper money initially is not money. It is a *substitute* for money, and is useful because it is difficult to fold coins into a wallet. But if paper money is honest, it will always be backed by a specific amount of real, "hard" money, and redeemable at any time. It should be a true "warehouse receipt." The paper money you have right now is not backed by anything except the government's promise that it is good—which is why, compared to the purchasing power of the 1932 dollar, each dollar you have today is worth less than a nickel. Many optimistic economists think the dollar will not be entirely destroyed until 1990. Many optimistic economists are also involved in college pension programs. Many optimistic economists will soon receive a first-rate economics lesson. Isn't education wonderful?

**Monopoly** means a situation in which one person or group has exclusive control over something that other people want. A monopoly exists when the government controls the market and forbids people to exchange according to their own wishes. In a free market, anyone who is making huge profits will attract competitors, and those competitors will compete by offering a comparable product for a lower price. The only way to keep competition away from a successful enterprise is to have government make competition illegal. *Monopolies are always created by government.* A monopoly cannot possibly exist in a free market, unless consumers just don't think it's worth shopping for an alternative product. Example: Arm & Hammer's 99% share of the baking soda market in the United States. "So what?" you ask. Correct.

**Nationalization of industry** is what socialists call it when government steals a private business. Since Ronald Sider is an important theologian, he has probably heard of the Ten Commandments, which tell us not to covet or steal. He has revised the eighth commandment: "Thou shalt not steal, except by majority vote."

**Nazi** is the popular term for one who belonged to Adolph Hitler's *National Socialist German Workers Party.* Nazis believed that capitalism is an unfair system of exploitation; that government should manage the economy; that price controls and minimum wage laws are good; and that credit expansion can make a country prosperous. You would be amazed at how popular these ideas still are.

**Presuppositions** are the ideas we have *before* we think—for instance, when you think about a problem, you have already *presupposed* that you are able to think logically in the first place. Christians presuppose that the Bible is true, that God's word is the standard of truth for everything. They know that the fear of the Lord is the *beginning* of knowledge for every area. Non-Christians presuppose that man's would-be autonomous reason is the standard of truth. You can tell what a man's presuppositions are by observing how he deals with a problem. Does he begin from the Bible and work from there, or does he begin somewhere else? Does he try to align his thoughts with God's laws, or does he try to interpret God's laws according to another standard? To say that the Bible is God's word is really not worth much, if you also say that the Bible does not answer economic questions. Ronald Sider does not believe that the Bible gives us a "blueprint" for economics. This means that when he writes about economics, his suggested policies do not come from the Bible. Ultimately, there is only one *other* source.

**Prices** are determined by the demonstrated preferences of consumers. High prices are not set by producers; they indicate only that many people want high-priced items very much. No producer would be able to charge arbitrarily any price he liked, because if the price were too high, people would simply buy something else. Furthermore, someone else would begin producing the item at a lower price, in order to make profits by meeting the demands of consumers at a price they would be more willing to pay. In a free market, prices will be low enough to prevent permanent surpluses and high enough to prevent permanent shortages.

**Price controls** are government regulations which set either a maximum or a minimum price on certain items. (For some reason this practice is often called "fair trade," meaning that it is *unfair* for people to trade voluntarily.) The government is not allowed to do this by the Bible, and therefore price controls never work. A price set above the free-market price will result in *surpluses*, for few people will be willing to pay it. A price set below the market price will cause *shortages*, because producers will be unable to produce the goods. (If the government takes Ronald Sider's advice and imposes price ceilings, maybe they will start by pricing his book at 10¢. For the sake of the poor, of course.) Price controls only add to human misery. The main reason for price controls is not to alleviate poverty, but to increase the power of government. See *Statism*.

**Productivity** is the rate at which demanded goods are produced. Productivity can rise only by investing to increase the factors of production devoted to producing what consumers want. What consumers want is indicated by the prices in a free market. If this information is distorted by price controls or monetary inflation, it is impossible for producers to make accurate decisions about what to produce. High productivity can be achieved only in a free society, where producers have a personal, direct incentive to meet consumer demand.

**Profit** is the goal of everything we do. It is the *net satisfaction* we get from doing something successfully. This is why both buyers and sellers profit in any exchange: both get what they want in exchange for what they give up. Both are buyers, and both are sellers. When a businessman makes a high profit, this means that he has been able to satisfy consumers by providing them with what they want at a price they are willing to pay. When other businessmen see his profits, they will begin competing with him because they want profits too. The only way to compete successfully is by offering something better or cheaper. If the competing goods are better, the first businessman will try to get more people to buy his goods by either lowering his prices or improving the quality of his products. The consumers are thus faced with many producers competing for profits by low prices and high quality. In this way, high prices end up serving the consumers by creating goods that are constantly improving. And as production increases, the profit margin will tend to come down.

**Psychic income** has nothing to do with the wages of fortune-tellers. It refers to the personal, subjective *feelings* of people in having achieved some end, not always monetary in nature. People often prefer working in a beautiful environment with friendly associates, or doing a a particular kind of work, more than making lots of money.

**Real wages** are wages measured not in terms of dollars, but in terms of "purchasing power" (how much those wages will really buy). For instance, the average worker in 1967 earned $5,000 per year. Ten years later he earned twice as much, measured in dollars—but measured in ability to *buy*, his *real* wages did not increase at all. His tax bills did, however: higher tax brackets. On the other hand, real wages can increase even if money wages do not. As productivity rises, and more goods become available, prices fall; and the same amount of money will buy more goods. Our concern must be with *raising real wages*, and this is possible only by generating more production of desired goods. See *Capital*.

**Saving** means storing wealth for future use—accumulating it in order to provide for the future. This requires the ethic of *deferred gratification*: foregoing benefits in the present in order to have more benefits later. The only way to raise future production is to limit present consumption, gathering capital for investment. Socialists do not understand this, so they have another word for saving: *hoarding*. Notice Sider's complete ignorance of the concept of saving when he says: "Capital need not be given away. But all income should be given to the poor after one satisfies bare necessities" (*Rich Christians*, p. 172). Where does he think *replacement* capital comes from? Capital doesn't just drop out of the sky. It is the result of *saving income* above and beyond one's bare necessities. Sider is really saying that all present capital should be consumed, and that there should be no subsequent production at all, except "bare necessities" produced with men's bare hands.

**Shortages** are always the result of price controls. A free-market price ensures that goods will go where they are in highest demand—where people are most willing to sacrifice their other purchases to get the product. For example: in 1977, the government controls on natural gas prevented people in freezing weather from paying high prices in order to get fuel. Higher prices would have motivated producers to deliver gas to people who desperately needed heat, while those in warmer climates would have cut down their buying because they did not need the fuel enough to justify paying high prices. But because of the price control, the people who needed the gas the most were unable to compete for it by bidding up the price. The price stayed at a "fair" level, and so people froze to death. However, they had saved 20% on their fuel bills, a government-produced benefit.

**Simple living** is Ronald Sider's term for living on a bare-subsistence income. As I have pointed out in the book, the concept is an entire fraud, because while he presents it as a voluntary lifestyle, he really intends to have the government enforce it on everyone. There is also another reason why socialists want us to live "simply." They really know that socialism cannot produce economic progress, and that a socialistic economy is nothing but a managed stagnation, except when the economy is contracting or collapsing. Thus, in preparing us for the Workers' Paradise, they want us to get in the habit of "doing without." For when socialist principles are fully implemented, that's *all* we'll be doing. There will be permanent shortages of everything except starvation, death, and official forms in quadruplicate.

**Sin** is defined in the Bible as "lawlessness" (I John 3:4). This means that sin is doing what God's law doesn't allow, or disobeying what God's law commands. Concerning the subject of this book, it is crucial to recognize that the Bible commands government to punish criminals and protect law-abiding people. When our rulers do not obey these commands they are sinning. And the Bible does not allow government to manage the economy or intervene into the market. When our rulers do these things they are sinning. Ronald Sider's program is in reality a call for more disobedience. His book is premised on the notion that sin is beneficial.

**Socialism** is governmental control—or outright ownership—of the means of production. This means that the state monopolizes everything in the market, determining what will be produced, who will produce it, how it will be produced, who will be able to get the product, and how it will be used. All interventionist practices have socialism as their logical outcome, since you cannot fully control one part of the economy without controlling all the other parts. Of course, none but God can control the economy, and true socialism is therefore an impossibility. Socialism's ultimate objective is complete government domination over everybody. See *Sin* and *Statism*.

**Statism** is the practice of giving the government progressively unlimited powers. It is a violation of God's law, when rulers attempt to play god by controlling the lives and activities of their subjects. God has severely limited the powers of the state, and when the state transgresses these limits it is making a claim to deity, "to be as God." Statism is the applied theology of Ronald Sider and the "Christian" socialists. For the answer to practically every problem in life, they do not look to God and the law-order He provides. They look instead to the all-powerful state. Statism includes all forms of interventionism and socialism. See *Sin* and *Curse*.

**Structural change** is Ronald Sider's term for changing the laws of the nation. Usually, it refers to government interventions that are outlawed by the Bible. Mostly, it is left vague, thereby producing greater guilt among the readers while avoiding sounding like a Marxist. No blueprints, please! Safety first! See *Interventionism*.

**Supply** is the *willingness* and *ability* of producers to sell goods. This is determined by the demand of competing consumers, revealed in the price system of the free market. Those products that are most wanted by consumers will be produced. An outstanding characteristic of capitalism is that goods are supplied for the wants of the common man. Visit the house of any ordinary worker in this country, and you will find that almost all of his possessions have been supplied by "big business." What makes big business big is the simple fact that it is efficiently supplying the needs of the masses. Mass production, low profit margins per sale, and a mass markets produce big fortunes. If you believe that certain goods — gothic novels, for instance — should not be produced, you must not try to stop the *supply* of them but the *demand* for them. And the only biblical — and effective — means of stopping the demand for them is by changing the hearts of people through the gospel. The people will then stop reading escapist literature and begin reading good books. The supply will shrivel up because of the lack of demand due to changed values. (Of course, this will necessarily mean that people will stop reading the more damaging kinds of escapist fiction, and Ron Sider will have to find another line of work.) See *Demand*.

**Surpluses** occur when the government sets a price that is higher than the market price. When a price is too high, people will not buy the product. On the other hand, high prices lure sellers into the market. An obvious example of this is the minimum wage, which is a state control of the price of labor. Labor is so expensive that producers will not hire workers whose productivity is worth less than the cost of hiring them. This creates a "surplus of labor," which we call *unemployment*. There are millions of these surplus workers who would be able to find jobs if the price control were abolished. Surpluses are always caused by price controls. See *Price controls* and *Shortages*.

**Tariffs** are a form of legalized theft. The government taxes imported goods, raising their prices in order to allow home industries to "compete" with foreign products. Tariffs encourage international inefficiency. Protected industries are not forced by the market to improve their products or reduce their costs. Tariffs hurt consumers by making them spend more money for products of a lower quality than would be available on a free market. Exporters are hurt because foreigners cannot gain access to as many dollars, and therefore they must reduce their consumption of American goods. This, of course, helps protect inefficient *foreign* producers. Consumers everywhere lose.

**Value** is the judgment each person makes of what different things mean to him. We place importance upon things according to our personal scales of value, and these scales of value are reflected in the way we act. It is necessary to remember that *values are not in goods or services but in the minds of men*. We all value things differently. This does not mean that everything is relative, or that it doesn't matter what we value. We all will face God to be judged for our thoughts and actions, and He has determined the ultimate values of everything in the world. But the point about value being *subjective* is that we cannot arbitrarily set prices as if the market values of things are definite and permanent. Values change as people change, as individuals rearrange their scales of value in terms of what they feel they need or lack. For example: someone living in Anchorage would probably place a higher value on snowshoes than would someone living in San Diego; a trapper in Anchorage would probably value them higher than would a banker living in the same city; and a trapper who needs a new pair would probably value them higher than would another trapper who has just gotten three pairs for Christmas. To repeat: *Value is not intrinsic. Value is imputed by men*. There are no fixed economic relationships in a world of constant change.

# SELECT BIBLIOGRAPHY

The following books have been chosen for two reasons: (1) they are important for understanding the issues dealt with in this book, and (2) they are relatively easy to read. Not all the authors listed are Christians, but their basic perspective stems from the biblical foundations of our culture. Furthermore, even professedly Christian writings must be tested in terms of Scripture. *Note*: All titles followed by an asterisk (*) may be obtained from the Foundation for Economic Education (FEE), 30 South Broadway, Irvington-on-Hudson, NY 10533. FEE publishes a monthly journal, *The Freeman*, which contains extremely helpful articles and reviews on free-market economics. U.S. subscriptions are free upon request.

Bahnsen, Greg L. *Theonomy in Christian Ethics*. Nutley, NJ: The Craig Press, 1977.

Banfield, Edward C. *The Moral Basis of a Backward Society*. New York: The Free Press, 1958.

———. *The Unheavenly City Revisited*. Little, Brown and Co., 1974.

Bastiat, Frederic. *Economic Sophisms*.* FEE, 1968.

———. *The Law*.* FEE, 1950.

———. *Selected Essays on Political Economy*.* FEE, 1968.

Bauer, P. T. *Dissent on Development*. Cambridge: Harvard University Press, 1976.

————. *Economic Analysis and Policy in Underdeveloped Countries*. Durham: Duke University Press, 1957.

————. *Equality, The Third World and Economic Delusion*. Cambridge: Harvard University Press, 1981.

Bauer, P. T. and Basil S. Yamey. *The Economics of Underdeveloped Countries*. University of Chicago Press, 1957.

Billington, James H. *Fire in the Minds of Men: Origins of the Revolutionary Faith*. New York: Basic Books, Inc., 1980.

Brown, Susan Love, *et al. The Incredible Bread Machine*.* San Diego: World Research, Inc., 1974.

Campbell, Roderick. *Israel and the New Covenant*. Tyler, TX: Geneva Divinity School Press, 1982.

Carson, Clarence B. *The World in the Grip of an Idea*.* New Rochelle: Arlington House, 1979.

Chodorov, Frank. *Fugitive Essays*. Indianapolis: Liberty Press, 1980.

Davidson, James Dale. *The Squeeze*. New York: Summit Books, 1980.

DeMar, Gary. *God and Government: A Biblical and Historical Study*. Atlanta: American Vision Press, 1982.

Friedman, Milton. *Capitalism and Freedom*.* Chicago: The University of Chicago Press, 1962.

Friedman, Milton and Rose. *Free to Choose: A Personal Statement*. New York: Avon Books, 1981.

Gilder, George. *Wealth and Poverty*. New York: Basic Books, 1981.

Greaves, Bettina B. *Free Market Economics: A Basic Reader*.* FEE, 1975.

————. *Free Market Economics: A Syllabus*.* FEE, 1975.

Greaves, Percy L., Jr. *Mises Made Easier: A Glossary for Ludwig von Mises' HUMAN ACTION*.* Dobbs Ferry, N. Y.: Free Market Books, 1974.

————. *Understanding the Dollar Crisis*.* Boston: Western Islands, 1973.

Harper, F. A. *Why Wages Rise*.* FEE, 1957.

Hayek, Frederick A. *The Road to Serfdom*.* University of Chicago Press, 1944.

Hazlitt, Henry. *The Conquest of Poverty*.* New Rochelle: Arlington House, 1973.

————. *Economics in One Lesson*.* New Rochelle: Arlington House, 1979.

————. *The Inflation Crisis, and How to Resolve It*.* New Rochelle: Arlington House, 1978.

Herbert, Auberon. *The Right and Wrong of Compulsion by the State*. Indianapolis: Liberty Classics, 1978.

MacKay, Thomas, ed. *A Plea For Liberty: An Argument Against Socialism and Socialistic Legislation.* Indianapolis: Liberty Classics, 1981.

Mises, Ludwig von. *The Anti-Capitalistic Mentality.** South Holland, IL: Libertarian Press, 1978.

––––––. *Bureaucracy.** New Rochelle: Arlington House, 1969.

––––––. *Economic Policy.** South Bend, IN: Regnery/Gateway, Inc., 1979.

––––––. *Liberalism: A Socio-Economic Exposition.* Kansas City: Sheed Andrews and McMeel, 1978.

––––––. *Planned Chaos.** FEE, 1961.

––––––. *Planning for Freedom.** South Holland, IL: Libertarian Press. 1980 (4th edition).

––––––. *Socialism: An Economic and Sociological Exposition.** Indianapolis: Liberty Classics, 1981.

North, Gary. *How You Can Profit from the Coming Price Controls.* Indianapolis: American Bureau of Economic Research, 1980.

––––––. *An Introduction to Christian Economics.** Nutley, NJ: Craig Press, 1973.

––––––. *Successful Investing in an Age of Envy.* Sheridan, IN: Steadman Press, 1981.

––––––. *The Dominion Covenant:Genesis.* Tyler, TX: Institute for Christian Economics, 1982.

––––––. ed. *The Journal of Christian Reconstruction* (back issues available from Fairfax Christian Bookstore, 11121 Pope's Head Road, Fairfax, VA. 22030; $5.00 per issue, $9 per year). The issues most relevant to the subject of this book are:
Vol. II, No. 1: Christian Economics
Vol. II, No. 2: Biblical Law
Vol. III, No. 2: The Millennium
Vol. V, No. 1: Politics
Vol. V, No. 2: Puritanism and Law
Vol. VI, No. 1: Puritanism and Progress
Vol. VI, No. 2: Puritanism and Society
Vol. VII, No. 1: Inflation
Vol. VII, No. 2: Evangelism
Vol. VIII, No. 1: Social Action

Potter, David M. *People of Plenty: Economic Abundance and the American Character.* Chicago: The University of Chicago Press, 1954.

Reisman, George. *The Government Against the Economy.** Thornwood, NY: Caroline House, 1979.

Rogge, Benjamin A., ed. *The Wisdom of Adam Smith.** Indianapolis:

Liberty Press, 1976.

Rose, Tom. *Economics: Principles and Policies*. Milford, MI: Mott Media, 1977.

Rose, Tom, and Robert Metcalf. *The Coming Victory*. Memphis: Christian Studies Center, 1980.

Rothbard, Murray. *America's Great Depression*.* Kansas City: Sheed and Ward, (1963) 1975.

———. *Man, Economy, and State*.* New York University Press, (1962) 1975.

———. *What Has Government Done to Our Money?*.* Santa Ana: Rampart College. 1974.

Rushdoony, Rousas John. *The Institutes of Biblical Law*. Phillipsburg, NJ: Presbyterian and Reformed Publishing Co., 1973.

———. *Law and Society: Vol. II of the Institutes of Biblical Law*. Vallecito, CA: Ross House Books, 1982

———. *God's Plan For Victory*. Fairfax, VA: Thoburn Press, 1977.

———. *Law and Liberty*. Fairfax, VA: Thoburn Press, 1977.

———. *The Myth of Overpoulation*. Fairfax, VA: Thoburn Press, 1973.

———. *Politics of Guilt and Pity*. Fairfax, VA: Thoburn Press, 1978.

———. *Tithing and Dominion*. Vallecito, CA: Ross House Books, 1979.

Schaeffer, Francis A. *A Christian Manifesto*. Westchester, IL: Crossway Books, 1981.

Schoeck, Helmut. *Envy: A Theory of Social Behaviour*. New York: Harcourt, Brace & World, Inc., 1970.

Schoeck, Helmut, and James W. Wiggins, eds. *Central Planning and Neomercantilism*. Princeton: D. Van Nostrand, 1964.

Schuettinger, Robert, and Eamonn Butler. *Forty Centuries of Wage and Price Controls: How Not to Fight Inflation*. Thornwood, NY: Caroline House, 1979.

Sennholz, Hans F. *Age of Inflation*.* Belmont, MA: Western Islands, 1979.

———, ed. *Gold Is Money*.* Westport, CT: Greenwood Press, 1975.

Sowell, Thomas. *Knowledge and Decisions*. New York: Basic Books, Inc., 1980.

Taylor, E. Hebden. *Economics, Money and Banking*. Nutley, N. J.: The Craig Press, 1978.

Templeton, Kenneth S., ed. *The Politicization of Society*. Indianapolis: Liberty Press, 1979.

Weber, James A. *Grow or Die!* New Rochelle: Arlington House, 1977.

# NOTES

## PREFACE TO THE SECOND EDITION

1. Joseph Schumpeter, *Capitalism, Socialism and Democracy* (3rd ed., New York: Harper Torchbook, [1950] 1962), p. 161. Schumpeter was a distinguished professor of economics at Harvard University until his death in 1950. He was a contemporary of Ludwig von Mises, and in fact was an intellectual rival. Both studied under one of the founders of the "Austrian School of economics," Eugen von Böhm-Bawerk, in the early 1900's. He was not a socialist, but he believed that socialism was winning by default—not because of the economic "failure" of capitalism, but, on the contrary, because of its incomparable economic success. See his essay, completed just before he died, "The March into Socialism" (1950), reprinted as an appendix in the third edition of *Capitalism, Socialism and Democracy*.

2. See Appendix A of my book, *The Dominion Covenant: Genesis* (Tyler, Texas: Institute for Christian Economics, 1982): "From Cosmic Purposelessness to Humanistic Sovereignty."

3. For a satirical view of the modern seminary's quest for academic respectability, see my essay, "A Letter to St. Paul," *The Journal of Christian Reconstruction*, II (Summer, 1975).

4. See my essays, "Who Should Certify Competence?" *Biblical Economics Today*, Vol. IV (Feb./Mar., 1981): "Academic Compromise," *Christian Reconstruction*, I (Nov./Dec., 1978); "Humanism's Accomplices," *Christian Reconstruction*, III (March/April, 1979); "Subsidizing One's Opponents," *Tentmakers*, I (Nov./Dec., 1978). These are all publications of the Institute for Christian Economics.

5. I personally heard him tell an audience of enthusiastic university students that he had given the following spiritual counsel to a black parishoner as the man was about to go on a theft spree during a late-1960's race riot in Milwaukee: "Don't get caught, Joe; don't get caught!" The crowd cheered.

6. For an account of one such visit, see "Father Groppi At Calvin College," *The Standard Bearer*, XLVI (June 1, 1970).

7. R. J. Rushdoony, *Politics of Guilt and Pity* (Fairfax, Virginia: Thoburn Press, [1970] 1978).

8. Martin Luther, "Against the Robbing and Murdering Hordes of Peasants," (1525), in *Luther's Works* (Philadelphia: Fortress Press, 1967), Vol. XLVI. See also Luther, "An Open Letter on the Harsh Book Against the Peasants," (1525), *ibid.*, pp. 63-85. John Calvin was also hostile to the revolutionary

Anabaptists. See Willem Balke, *Calvin and the Anabaptist Radicals* (Grand Rapids: Eerdmans, [1973] 1981).

9. Cited in "Anabaptism," *Cyclopedia of Biblical, Theological, and Ecclesiastical Literature,* edited by John McClintock and James Strong (New York: Harper & Bros., 1894), I, p. 210. Reprinted by Baker Book House, 1981.

10. A good account of the revolutionary Anabaptists is found in Norman Cohn's book, *The Pursuit of the Millennium: Revolutionary Millenarians and Mystical Anarchists of the Middle Ages* (rev. ed.; New York: Oxford University Press, 1970).

11. John W. Robbins, "Ronald Sider *Contra Deum*," *The Trinity Review* (March/April, 1981). Copies available on request: The Trinity Foundation, P. O. Box 169, Jefferson, MD 21755.

12. Henry Manne's study, "The Political Economy of Modern Universities" (1971), has been printed in several places. I am using the version that appeared in *The Journal of Christian Reconstruction,* VI (Summer, 1977). The comments on trustees appear on pages 159-60. The comments on university presidents appear on pages 161-63.

13. David Joravsky, *The Lysenko Affair* (Cambridge, Mass.: Harvard University Press, 1970).

14. Gary North, *Unconditional Surrender: God's Program for Victory* (Tyler, Texas: Geneva Divinity School Press, 1981), pp. 213-14.

15. Cornelius Van Til, *Christianity and Barthianism* (Philadelphia: Presbyterian & Reformed, 1962).

16. David Chilton, "The Case of the Missing Blueprints," *The Journal of Christian Reconstruction,* VIII (Summer, 1981).

17. Ronald Sider, "Living More Simply for Evangelism and Justice" (mimeographed), Keynote Address, International Consultation on Simple Lifestyle (March 17-21, 1980), p. 17.

18. Sider, *Rich Christians,* p. 216.

19. *Idem.*

20. Sider, "Ambulance Drivers and Tunnel Builders" (Philadelphia: Evangelicals for Social Action, no date), p. 4.

21. Augustine, *City of God,* XVIII:40.

22. See Appendix C of my book, *The Dominion Covenant: Genesis:* "Cosmologies in Conflict: Creation vs. Evolution."

23. R. J. Rushdoony, "The Society of Satan," *Biblical Economics Today,* II (Oct./Nov., 1979). Copies available from the Institute for Christian Economics.

## INTRODUCTION

1. James H. Billington, *Fire in the Minds of Men: Origins of the Revolutionary Faith* (New York: Basic Books, Inc., 1980), p. 41.

2. *Ibid.*, p. 257.

3. *Ibid.*, p. 252.

4. *Ibid.*, p. 316.

5. *Ibid.*, p. 258.

6. G. Groen van Prinsterer, *Unbelief and Revolution: Lecture XI* (Amsterdam: The Groen van Prinsterer Fund, 1973), p. 10.

7. *Ibid.*, *Lecture IX* (1975), pp. 73f.

8. *Ibid.*, *Lecture VIII* (1975), pp. 29f.

9. See Otto Scott's *Robespierre: The Voice of Virtue* (Ross House Books, P. O. Box 67, Vallecito, CA 92521). This enlightening and thoroughly terrifying book is must reading for those who wish to study the rise and progress of revolutions.

10. Ronald J. Sider, *Rich Christians in an Age of Hunger: A Biblical Study* (Downers Grove, IL: Inter-Varsity Press, 1977); referred to in following references as *Rich Christians.*

11. Sider, *Living More Simply: Biblical Principles & Practical Models* (Downers Grove, IL: Inter-Varsity Press, 1980).

12. Sider, *Cry Justice: The Bible Speaks on Hunger and Poverty* (New York: Paulist Press; Downers Grove, IL: Inter-Varsity Press, 1980).

13. The best expositions of this view are in Greg L. Bahnsen, *Theonomy in Christian Ethics* (Nutley, NJ: The Craig Press, 1977), and Rousas John Rushdoony, *The Institutes of Biblical Law* (Nutley, NJ: The Craig Press, 1973).

14. Sider, "Words and Deeds," *Journal of Theology for Southern Africa* (December, 1979), p. 40.

15. Sider, "Resurrection and Liberation," in Robert Rankin, ed., *The Recovery of Spirit in Higher Education* (New York: The Seabury Press), pp. 170f.

16. *Ibid.*, p. 164.

17. Clarence B. Carson, *The World in the Grip of an Idea* (New Rochelle, NY: Arlington House, 1979).

18. John Chamberlain, *The Roots of Capitalism* (Princeton: D. Van Nostrand Company, Inc., 1959; revised 1965), p. 46.

19. See Helmut Schoeck, *Envy* (New York: Harcourt, Brace & World, Inc., 1970).

20. Sider, *Rich Christians,* pp. 120ff. Italics added.

21. *Ibid.*, p. 125.

22. *Ibid.*, p. 178.

23. *Ibid.*, p. 118.

24. *Ibid.*, p. 117.

25. *Ibid.*, p. 172.

26. *Ibid.*, p. 173.

27. See Arnold A. Dallimore, *George Whitefield: The Life and Times of the Great Evangelist of the Eighteenth-Century Revival* (Westchester, IL: Cornerstone Books, 1980, 2 vols.), 2:68ff.

28. Sider, *Rich Christians,* p. 200.

29. Otto Scott, *James I* (New York: Mason/Charter, 1976), p. 13.


**CHAPTER 1**

1. Sider, *Rich Christians,* p. 115.

2. *Ibid.,* p. 205.

3. *Ibid.*

4. "Door Interview: Ron Sider," *The Wittenburg Door* (Oct./Nov. 1979, No. 51), p. 16.

5. A much more complete discussion of this text is found in Greg Bahnsen's *Theonomy in Christian Ethics,* pp. 39-86.

6. Sider, *Rich Christians,* pp. 115, 210, 218.

7. *Ibid.,* p. 209.

8. *Ibid.,* p. 214.

9. *Ibid.,* p. 145, 207, 218ff.

10. *Ibid.,* p. 212.

11. *Ibid.,* p. 220.

12. *Ibid.,* pp. 160, 218.

13. *Ibid.,* pp. 165, 211f.

14. *Ibid.,* pp. 212, 218.

15. *Ibid.,* pp. 214, 218.

16. *Ibid.,* p. 145.

17. George Reisman, *The Government Against the Economy* (Ottawa, Ill.: Caroline House Publishers, Inc., 1979), p. 151.

18. Ludwig von Mises, *Planning For Freedom* (South Holland, Ill.: Libertarian Press, 4th ed., 1980), p. 135.

19. Tom Rose and Robert Metcalf, "Inflation is Immoral," *The Journal of Christian Reconstruction,* VII (Summer, 1980).

20. Ludwig von Mises, *Human Action* (New Haven, Conn: Yale University Press, 1949), ch. 20.

21. Sider, *Rich Christians,* p. 213.


**CHAPTER 2**

1. Cited in *The Alan Stang Report,* July 23, 1979.

2. Sider, *Rich Christians,* p. 212.

3. Auberon Herbert, *The Right and Wrong of Compulsion by the State* (Indianapolis: Liberty Classics, 1978), pp. 179f.

4. *Ibid.,* p. 77.

5. Sider, *Rich Christians,* pp. 175ff.

6. *Ibid.*, p. 182.

7. See below, pp. 178f.

8. Murray Rothbard, *Man, Economy, and State* (New York: New York University Press, [1962] 1975), p. 818.

9. *Ibid.*, p. 931.

10. Sider, "Words and Deeds," p. 38.

11. *Ibid.*, p. 49. Cf. *Rich Christians*, pp. 60f.

12. For a fascinating history of an important aspect of this, see *Forty Centuries of Wage and Price Controls*, by Robert Schuettinger and Eamonn Butler (Thornwood, NY: Caroline House Publishers, Inc., 1979).

13. The best exposition of the biblical slavery laws is in James B. Jordan, *Slavery and Liberation in the Bible* (Tyler, TX: Institute for Christian Economics, forthcoming).

14. James B. Jordan, "Slavery in Biblical Perspective," term paper, Westminster Theological Seminary, 1979, p. 44f.

15. Herbert, pp. 65f.

16. Sider, *Rich Christians*, p. 73; *Cry Justice*, pp. 31, 203, 210.

17. See Sider, *Rich Christians*, pp. 114f.

18. Cited in Schuettinger and Butler, *Forty Centuries of Wage and Price Controls*, p. 73. Italics added.

19. Hilaire Belloc, *The Servile State* (Indianapolis: Liberty Classics, 1977), p. 168.

20. F. A. Hayek, *The Road to Serfdom* (The University of Chicago Press, 1944), pp. 145f. Italics added.

## CHAPTER 3

1. Sider, *Rich Christians*, pp. 60f.

2. *The Wittenburg Door*, p. 27.

3. Sider, "Resurrection and Liberation: An Evangelical Approach to Social Justice," in Robert Rankin, ed., *The Recovery of Spirit in Higher Education: Christian and Jewish Ministries in Campus Life* (New York: The Seabury Press, 1980), pp. 154ff.

4. Sider, "An Evangelical Theology of Liberation," *The Christian Century* (March 19, 1980), p. 318.

5. Sider, "Words and Deeds," *Journal of Theology for Southern Africa* (December, 1979), p. 318.

6. Otto Scott, *The Secret Six: John Brown and the Abolitionist Movement* (New York: Times Books, 1979), pp. 295f.

7. *Ibid.*, p. 251.

8. Cf. in this regard Sider's praise of Jonathan Blanchard's perfectionism, in "Words and Deeds," pp. 155f.

9. Otto Scott, *Robespierre: The Voice of Virtue*, p. 195.

10. Scott, *The Secret Six*, p. 15.

11. *Ibid.*, pp.319f.

12. *Ibid.*, p. 303.

13. Bennet Tyler and Andrew Bonar, *The Life and Labours of Asahel Nettleton* (Edinburgh: The Banner of Truth Trust, 1975), p. 449. On Finney's Pelagianism, see Benjamin B. Warfield, *Perfectionism* (Philadelphia: Presbyterian and Reformed Publishing Co., 1958), pp. 125-215.

14. Scott, *The Secret Six*, p. 202. This was before Keynes and inflation!

15. *Ibid.*, p. 212.

16. Sider, "A Call for Evangelical Nonviolence," *The Christian Century*, (September 15, 1976), p. 753ff.

17. Sider, *Cry Justice*, p. 214.

18. See pp. 31, 35 above.


**CHAPTER 4**

1. Sider, "An Evangelical Theology of Liberation," pp. 314f.

2. See, e.g., Sider, *Rich Christians*, pp. 59-85.

3. *Ibid.*, pp. 66f.

4. *Ibid.*, p. 73. Italics added.

5. *The Wittenburg Door* Interview, p. 27. Italics added.

6. *Karl Marx: Essential Writings*, Frederic L. Bender, ed. (New York: Harper and Row, 1972), p. 272.

7. Billington, p. 417.


**CHAPTER 5**

1. Carson, p. 439.

2. Sider, *Rich Christians*, pp. 33ff.

3. Carson, p. 446f.

4. Sider, *Rich Christians,* p. 163.

5. *Ibid.*, p. 164.

6. P. T. Bauer, *Dissent on Development* (Cambridge, Mass.: Harvard University Press, 1972), p. 46.

7. Cited in *ibid.*, pp. 32f.

8. Sider, *Rich Christians*, p. 40 and 45.

9. Bauer, p. 111.

10. Rothbard, p. 838.

11. Sider, *Rich Christians*, p. 218.

12. Bauer, p. 21.

13. *Ibid.*, p. 109f. Italics added.

14. Sider, *Cry Justice*, p. 2.

15. Sider, *Rich Christians*, p. 32.

16. See Bauer's extended discussion, pp. 55ff.

17. Sider, *Rich Christians*, pp. 18ff.

18. Ludwig von Mises, *Socialism: An Economic and Sociological Analysis* (London: Jonathan Cape, 1951), p. 131; see pp. 113ff. Reprinted by Liberty Press, 1981.

19. Reisman, pp. 63ff.

20. Thomas Watson, *The Beatitudes* (Edinburgh: The Banner of Truth Trust, 1971), p. 117.

## CHAPTER 6

1. Sider, *Rich Christians*, p. 207.

2. *Ibid.*, p. 206.

3. *Ibid.*, p. 205.

4. *Ibid.*, p. 217.

5. *Ibid.*, pp. 14-16.

6. *Ibid.*, p. 16.

7. *Ibid.* Italics added.

8. *Ibid.*, p. 15.

9. See Henry Hazlitt, *The Conquest of Poverty* (New Rochelle, NY: Arlington House, 1973), pp. 125ff.; cf. Schoeck, pp. 193ff.

10. See W. M. Curtiss, *The Tariff Idea* (Irvington-on-Hudson, NY: The Foundation for Economic Education, 1953).

11. Lawrence W. Reed, "The Case Against Protectionism," *The Freeman* (October, 1980), p. 580.

12. Sider, *Rich Christians*, p. 140.

13. *Ibid.*, p. 212. Italics added.

14. *Ibid.*, pp. 141ff., 212f.

15. *Ibid.*

16. See Gary North, *An Introduction to Christian Economics* (Nutley, NJ: The Craig Press, [1973] 1976), p. 190.

17. Bauer, p. 101. Italics added.

18. Sider, *Rich Christians*, p. 219.

19. Bauer, p. 97.

20. *Ibid.*, p. 112.

21. *Ibid.*, p. 115.

22. *Ibid.*, p. 124.

23. Thomas Sowell, *Race and Economics* (New York: David McKay Company, Inc., 1975), pp. 195f.

24. Schoeck, pp. 197f.; cf. 46ff.; see also Bauer, pp. 118, 120.


**CHAPTER 7**

1. Sider, *Rich Christians*, p. 18.
2. *Ibid.*, p. 21; cf. p. 130.
3. *Ibid.*, p. 218.
4. *Ibid.*, p. 153.
5. *Ibid.*, p. 54.
6. Bauer, p. 119. Italics added.
7. Robert L. Sassone, *Handbook on Population* (Santa Ana, CA, 1973), p. 174.
8. James A. Weber, *Grow or Die!* (New Rochelle, NY: Arlington House, 1977), p. 23.
9. Colin Clark, *Population Growth: The Advantages* (Santa Ana, CA, 1972), pp. 72f.
10. Weber, pp. 135ff.
11. R. J. Rushdoony, *The Myth of Overpopulation* (Fairfax, Virginia: Thoburn Press, [1973] 1969), pp. 1ff.
12. For a recent discussion of Christianity and its effect on the development of the environment, see René Dubos, *The Wooing of Earth* (New York: Charles Scribner's Sons, 1980).
13. Sassone, p. 53.
14. Cited in *ibid.*
15. *Ibid.*, p. 36.
16. Rushdoony, *The Myth of Overpopulation*, p. 5. Citation from E. Parmalee Prentice, *Hunger and History* (Caldwell, Idaho: Caxton, 1951), p. 6.
17. Bauer, p. 128.
18. Cited in Weber, p. 213.


**CHAPTER 8**

1. Sider, *Rich Christians*, pp. 160ff.
2. *Ibid.*, p. 162.
3. *Ibid.*
4. One of the best discussions of profit is in Ludwig von Mises, *Planning for Freedom*, pp. 108ff.
5. See Armen A. Alchian, *Economic Forces at Work*, (Indianapolis: Liberty Press, 1977), pp. 159ff., 251ff.


**CHAPTER 9**

1. Sider, *Rich Christians*, pp. 46f.

2. *Ibid.*, p. 47.
3. Mises, *Human Action*, p. 321.
4. Sider, *Rich Christians*, p. 47.
5. *Ibid.*, p. 49.
6. *Ibid.*

## CHAPTER 10

1. Samuel Willard, *A Compleat Body of Divinity* (New York: Johnson Reprint Corporation, 1969), p. 750.
2. Schoeck, p. 17.
3. Billington, p. 290.
4. Willard, p. 751.
5. Hazlitt, *The Conquest of Poverty*, p. 126.
6. See, e.g., Mises, *Socialism*, pp. 436, 457ff., 531.
7. Sider, *Rich Christians*, p. 54.
8. *Ibid.*, p. 153.
9. *Ibid.*, p. 73.
10. *Ibid.*, p. 77.
11. *Ibid.*, p. 84.
12. *Ibid.*
13. Billington, p. 6. Italics added.
14. Sider, *Rich Christians*, p. 208.
15. *Ibid.*, pp. 208f.
16. *Ibid.*, p. 160.; cf. p. 218.
17. *Ibid.*, pp. 161f.; cf. his demand for "nationalization," p. 145.
18. Charlotte Mann in *The Christian Century* (June 11-18, 1975), p. 596.
19. Randall Basinger, "One Father's Prayer," *theOtherSide* (December, 1980), p. 20.
20. *Ibid.*, pp. 21f.
21. Sider, *Rich Christians*, pp. 14ff.
22. *Ibid.*, p. 18.
23. *Ibid.*, p. 210.
24. *Ibid.*, p. 151.
25. *Ibid.*, p. 156.
26. *Ibid.*, p. 158f.
27. *Ibid.*, p. 153, 162.
28. *Ibid.*, p. 132f.
29. *Ibid.*, p. 159.
30. *Ibid.*, p. 161.
31. *Ibid.*, p. 162.

32. *Ibid.* Italics added.

33. *Ibid.*

34. *Ibid.*, p. 148. Italics added.

35. *Ibid.*, p. 139. Italics added.

36. *Ibid.*, p. 174.

37. Edward C. Banfield, *The Moral Basis of a Backward Society* (New York: The Free Press, 1958); see esp. pp. 83-101.

38. George Gilder, *Wealth and Poverty* (New York: Basic Books, Inc., 1981), p. 99.

39. Willard, pp. 750, 752.

## CHAPTER 11

1. Sider, *Rich Christians*, p. 223.

2. *Ibid.*, p. 88.

3. *Ibid.*, p. 129.

4. *Ibid.*, pp. 114ff.

5. *Ibid.*, pp. 184ff.

6. *Ibid.*, p. 213.

7. *Ibid.*, p. 223.

8. *Ibid.*

9. Cf. *Ibid.*, pp. 216, 220, where he calls for unprecedented totalitarian powers to be granted to the United Nations; also his praise (though not by name) for the work of the Trilateral Commission, p. 23. (For further information on how this important group is working for "equality" around the world, see *Trilaterals Over Washington*, by Antony C. Sutton and Patrick M. Wood; Scottsdale, AZ: The August Corporation, 1979.)

10. *Ibid.*, p. 93.

11. *Ibid.*, p. 94.

12. *Ibid.*

13. *Ibid.*, p. 93.

## CHAPTER 12

1. Sider, *Rich Christians*, p. 209.

2. *Ibid.*, pp. 54, 90, 94, 95, 173, etc. (I didn't count them all.)

3. *Ibid.*, p. 88; cf. p. 90.

4. *Ibid.*, pp. 105f.

5. On communion, see Gary North's essay, "Family Authority vs. Protestant Sacerdotalism" (*The Journal of Christian Reconstruction*, Vol. IV, No. 2, Winter, 1977-78), esp. pp. 108ff.; on biblical church life in general, see Robert Banks,

*Paul's Idea of Community: The Early House Churches In Their Historical Setting* (Grand Rapids: William B. Eerdmans Publishing Co., 1980).

6. Sider, *Rich Christians*, p. 107.

7. Sider, "Living More Simply For Evangelism And Justice" (Keynote address for the International Consultation on Simple Lifestyle at Hoddeson, England, March 17-21, 1980), p. 9.

8. Sider, *Rich Christians*, p. 93.

9. *Ibid.*, pp. 96ff.

10. *The Christian Century* (June 8-15, 1977), pp. 560ff.

11. *Ibid.*, pp. 564f.

12. *Ibid.*, pp. 560, 563. Italics added. See also Sider, *Rich Christians*, p. 205.

13. Sider, *Rich Christians*, p. 107.

14. Sider, "Sharing The Wealth," pp. 564f. Italics added.

15. *Ibid.*, p. 564.

16. Sider, "Ambulance Drivers or Tunnel Builders," (Philadelphia: Evangelicals for Social Action, n.d.), p. 4.

17. Sider, *Rich Christians*, p. 214. Italics added.

18. Mises, *Socialism*, p. 458; cf. pp. 76ff.

19. Bauer, p. 72. Italics added.


## CHAPTER 13

1. L. P. Hartley, *Facial Justice* (Garden City, NY: Doubleday & Company, Inc., 1960), p. 7; see Schoeck, pp. 149ff.

2. North, *An Introduction to Christian Economics*, p. 226.

3. Sider, *Rich Christians*, p. 49.

4. *Ibid.*, pp. 114f.

5. Adam Smith, *The Theory of Moral Sentiments* (Indianapolis: Liberty Classics, 1976), p. 195.

6. *Ibid.*, p. 228.

7. *Ibid.*, p. 174.

8. Adam Smith, *The Wealth of Nations* (Chicago: The University of Chicago Press, two vols., 1976), vol. 2, p. 445.

9. Sider, *Rich Christians*, p. 41.

10. *Ibid.*, p. 84.

11. Sider, "Ambulance Drivers or Tunnel Builders," pp. 4f.

12. Hans Sennholz, *Age of Inflation* (Belmont, MA: Western Islands, 1979), p. 155.

13. Sider, *Rich Christians*, p. 214.

14. *US News and World Report* (February 20, 1978), p. 55; and *Time* (November 20, 1978), p. 84.

15. Bauer, p. 73.

16. *Ibid.*, p. 86.

17. Mises, *Planning for Freedom*, p. 17.

18. Smith, *Theory of Moral Sentiments*, pp. 380f.

19. Sider, "A Call for Evangelical Nonviolence"; see also "To See the Cross, To Find the Tomb, To Change the World," in *theOtherSide* (February, 1977), pp. 16ff.


**CHAPTER 14**

1. Edward J. Young, *My Servants the Prophets* (Grand Rapids: William B. Eerdmans Publishing Co., 1952), p. 82.

2. Meredith G. Kline, *By Oath Consigned: A Reinterpretation of the Covenant Signs of Circumcision and Baptism* (Grand Rapids: William B. Eerdmans Publishing Co., 1968), p. 52.

3. Some of the following material has been adapted from my "Studies in Amos" column, published in the *Chalcedon Report* (P. O. Box 158, Vallecito, CA 95251), from January through August 1980.


**CHAPTER 15**

1. David Howarth, *1066: The Year of the Conquest* (New York: The Viking Press, 1977), pp. 176ff.

2. John Meskill, *An Introduction to Chinese Civilization* (Lexington: D. C. Heath and Company, 1973), pp. 324ff.

3. Sider, *Rich Christians*, p. 172. Obviously, this means he is a legalist in the *first* sense of our discussion in Chapter One.

4. *Ibid.*, p. 205.


**CHAPTER 16**

1. Gustavo R. Velasco, *Labor Legislation from an Economic Point of View* (Indianapolis: Liberty Fund, Inc., 1973), p. 40.

2. Henry R. Van Til, *The Calvinistic Concept of Culture* (Philadelphia: The Presbyterian and Reformed Publishing Company, 1974), p. 39.

3. John Chamberlain, *The Roots of Capitalism* (Princeton: D. Van Nostrand Company, 1959; revised, 1965), p. 47.

4. Mises, *Planning for Freedom*, p. 202.

5. Bauer, pp. 78f.

6. *Ibid.*, p. 79.

7. *Ludwig von Mises, Notes and Recollections* (South Holland, IL: Libertarian Press, 1978), p. 115.

8. Edward C. Banfield, *The Unheavenly City Revisited* (Boston: Little, Brown and Company, 1974), pp. 61f.

9. *Ibid.*, pp. 234f.

10. *Ibid.*, p. 269.

11. Sider, *Rich Christians*, p. 187.

12. Arnold Dallimore, *George Whitefield: The Life and Times of the Great Evangelist of the 18th-Century Revival* (Edinburgh: The Banner of Truth Trust, 1970), I: 28.

13. J. C. Ryle, *Christian Leaders of the 18th Century* (Edinburgh: The Banner of Truth Trust, 1978), p. 14.

14. *Ibid.*

15. Mises, *Planning for Freedom*, p. 200ff.

## CHAPTER 17

1. J. Marcellus Kik, *An Eschatology of Victory* (Nutley, NJ: The Presbyterian and Reformed Publishing Company, 1971), p. 19.

For further study on the view of prophecy presented in this chapter, the following references are recommended, in addition to the book by Marcellus Kik (cited above): Loraine Boettner, *The Millennium* (Philadelphia: The Presbyterian and Reformed Publishing Co., 1957). Iain Murray, *The Puritan Hope: A Study in Revival and the Interpretation of Prophecy* (Edinburgh: The Banner of Truth Trust, 1971). David Chilton, *The Future of the Planet Earth* (A 16-tape exposition of the Book of Revelation and other prophetic passages; available from Geneva Tape Enterprises, P. O. Box 6975, Tyler, TX 75711).

2. *Ibid.*, p. 202.

3. Belloc, p. 72.

4. Kik, p. 250.

5. Benjamin Breckenridge Warfield, *Biblical and Theological Studies* (Philadelphia: The Presbyterian and Reformed Publishing Company, 1968), pp. 518f.

6. Groen van Prinsterer, *Lecture XI*, p. 22.

7. Belloc, p. 200.

# INDEXES

## NAME & SUBJECT

# WHAT IS THE ICE?

by Gary North, President, ICE

The Institute for Christian Economics is a non-profit, tax-exempt educational organization which is devoted to research and publishing in the field of Christian ethics. The perspective of those associated with the ICE is straightforwardly conservative and pro-free market. The ICE is dedicated to the proposition that biblical ethics requires full personal responsibility, and this responsible human action flourishes most productively within a framework of limited government, political decentralization, and minimum interference with the economy by the civil government.

For well over half a century, the loudest voices favoring Christian social action have been outspokenly pro-government intervention. Anyone needing proof of this statement needs to read Dr. Gregg Singer's comprehensive study, *The Unholy Alliance* (Arlington House Books, 1975), the definitive history of the National Council of Churches. An important policy statement from the National Council's General Board in 1967 called for *comprehensive economic planning*. The ICE was established in order to *challenge* statements like the following:

*Accompanying this growing diversity in the structures of national life has been a growing recognition of the importance of competent planning within and among all resource sectors of the society: education, economic development, land use, social health services, the family system and congregational life. It is not generally recognized that an effective approach to problem solving requires a comprehensive planning process and coordination in the development of all these resource areas.*

The *silence* from the conservative denominations in response to such policy proposals has been deafening. Not that conservative church members agree with such nonsense; they don't. But the conservative denominations and associations have remained silent because they have convinced themselves that *any* policy statement of any sort regarding social and economic life is *always* illegitimate. In short, there is no such thing as a correct, valid policy statement that a church or denomination can make. *The results of this opinion have been universally devastating.* The popular press assumes that the radicals who do speak out in the name of Christ are representative of the membership (or at least the press goes along with the illusion). The public is convinced that to speak out on social matters in the name of Christ is to be radical. *Christians are losing by default.*

The ICE is convinced that conservative Christians must devote resources to create alternative proposals. There is an old rule of political life which argues that "You can't beat something with nothing." We agree. It is not enough to adopt a whining negativism whenever someone or some group comes up with another nutty economic program. We need a comprehensive alternative.

**SOCIETY OR STATE**    Society is broader than politics. The State is not a substitute for society. *Society encompasses all social institutions:* church, State, family, economy, kinship groups, voluntary clubs and associations, schools, and non-profit educational organizations (such as ICE). Can we say that there are no standards of righteousness—justice—for these social institutions? Are they lawless? The Bible says no. We do not live in a lawless universe. But this does not mean that the State is the source of all law. On the contrary, God, not the imitation god of the State, is the source.

Christianity is innately decentralist. *From the beginning, orthodox Christians have denied the divinity of the State.* This is why the Caesars of Rome had them persecuted and executed. They denied the operating presupposition of the ancient world, namely, the legitimacy of a divine rule or a divine State.

It is true that modern liberalism has eroded Christian orthodoxy. There are literally thousands of supposedly evangelical pastors who have been compromised by the liberalism of the universities and seminaries they attended. The popularity, for example, of Prof. Ronald Sider's *Rich Christians in an Age of Hunger,* co-published by Inter-Varsity Press (evangelical Protestant) and the Paulist Press (liberal Roman Catholic), is indicative of the crisis today. It has sold like hotcakes, and it calls for mandatory wealth redistribution by the State on a massive scale. Yet he is a professor at a Baptist seminary.

The ICE rejects the theology of the total State. This is why we countered the book by Sider when we published David Chilton's *Productive Christians in an Age of Guilt-Manipulators* (1981). Chilton's book shows that the Bible is the foundation of our economic freedom, and that the call for compulsory wealth transfers and higher taxes on the rich is simply *baptized socialism.* Socialism is anti-Christian to the core.

What we find is that laymen in evangelical churches tend to be more conservative theologically and politically than their pastors. But this conservatism is a kind of *instinctive conservatism.* It is *not* self-consciously grounded in the Bible. So the laymen are unprepared to counter the sermons and Sunday School materials that bombard them week after week.

It is ICE's contention that *the only way to turn the tide in this nation is to capture the minds of the evangelical community,* which numbers in the tens of millions. We have to convince the liberal-leaning evangelicals of the biblical nature of the free market system. And we have to convince the conservative evangelicals of the same thing, in order to get them into the social and intellectual battles of our day.

In other words, *retreat is not biblical,* any more than socialism is.

**BY WHAT STANDARD?**   We have to ask ourselves this question: *"By what standard?"* By what standard do we evaluate the claims of the socialists and interventionists? By what standard do we evaluate the claims of the secular free market economists who reject socialism? By what standard are we to construct intellectual alternatives to the humanism of our day? And by what standard do we criticize the social institutions of our era?

If we say that the standard is "reason," we have a problem: Whose reason? If the economists cannot agree with each other, how do we decide who is correct? Why hasn't reason produced agreement after centuries of debate? We need an alternative.

It is the Bible. The ICE is dedicated to the defense of the Bible's reliability. But don't we face the same problem? Why don't Christians agree about what the Bible says concerning economics?

One of the main reasons why they do not agree is that the question of biblical economics has not been taken seriously. Christian scholars have ignored economic theory for generations. This is why the ICE devotes so much time, money, and effort to studying what the Bible teaches about economic affairs.

There will always be some disagreements, since men are not perfect, and their minds are imperfect. But when men agree about the basic issue of the starting point of the debate, they have a far better opportunity to discuss and learn than if they offer only "reason, rightly understood" as their standard.

**SERVICES**   The ICE exists in order to serve Christians and other people who are vitally interested in finding moral solutions to the economic crisis of our day. The organization is a *support ministry* to other Christian ministries. It is non-sectarian, nondenominational, and dedicated to the proposition that a moral economy is a truly practical, productive economy.

The ICE produces several newsletters. These are aimed at intelligent laymen, church officers, and pastors. The reports are non-technical in nature. Included in our publication schedule are these monthly and bi-monthly publications:

> *Biblical Economics Today* (6 times a year)
> *Christian Reconstruction* (6 times a year)
> *The Biblical Educator* (12 times a year)
> *Tentmakers* (6 times a year)

*Biblical Economics Today* is a four-page report that covers economic theory from a specifically Christian point of view. It also deals with questions of economic policy. *Christian Reconstruction* is more action-oriented, but it also covers various aspects of Christian social theory. *Tentmakers* is aimed specifically at church officers, seminarians, and other people who are responsible for handling church funds.

*The Biblical Educator* is different: a four-page report written by several educators, and aimed at the Christian school market. It offers suggestions for better teaching, curricula revisions, and a biblical approach to school-state relations. Of course, the report stresses careful management of resources.

The purpose of the ICE is to relate biblical ethics to Christian activities in the field of economics. To cite the title of Francis Schaeffer's book, "How should we then live?" How should we apply biblical wisdom in the field of economics to our lives, our culture, our civil government, and our businesses and callings?

If God calls men to responsible decision-making, then He must have *standards of righteousness* that guide men in their decision-making. It is the work of the ICE to discover, illuminate, explain, and suggest applications of these guidelines in the field of economics. We publish the results of our findings in the newsletters.

*The ICE sends out the newsletters free of charge.* Anyone can sign up for six months to receive them. This gives the reader the opportunity of seeing "what we're up to." At the end of six months, he or she can renew for another six months.

Donors receive a one-year subscription. This reduces the extra trouble associated with sending out renewal notices, and it also means less trouble for the subscriber.

There are also donors who pledge to pay $10 a month. They are members of the ICE's *"Reconstruction Committee."* They help to provide a predictable stream of income which finances the day-to-day operations of the ICE. Then the donations from others can finance special projects, such as the publication of a new book.

The basic service that ICE offers is education. We are presenting ideas and approaches to Christian ethical behavior that few other organizations even suspect are major problem areas. *The Christian world has for too long acted as though we were not responsible citizens on earth,* as well as citizens of heaven. ("For our conversation [citizenship] is in heaven" [Philippians 3:20a].) *We must be godly stewards of all our assets,* which includes our lives, minds, and skills.

Because economics affects every sphere of life, the ICE's reports and surveys are relevant to all areas of life. Because *scarcity affects every area,* the whole world needs to be governed by biblical requirements for *honest stewardship* of the earth's resources. The various publications are wide-ranging, since the effects of the curse of the ground (Genesis 3:17-19) are wide-ranging.

What the ICE offers the readers and supporters is an introduction to a world of responsibility that few Christians have recognized. This limits our audience, since most people think they have too many responsibilities already. But if more people understood the Bible's solutions to economic problems, they would have more capital available to take greater responsibility—and prosper from it.

**FINANCES**    There ain't no such thing as a free lunch (TANSTAAFL). *Someone has to pay for those six-month renewable free subscriptions.* Existing donors are, in effect, supporting a kind of intellectual missionary organization. Except for the newsletters sent to ministers and teachers, we "clean" the mailing lists each year: less waste.

We cannot expect to raise money by emotional appeals. We have no photographs of starving children, no orphanages in Asia. We generate ideas. *There is always a very limited market for ideas, which is why some of them have to be subsidized by people who understand the power of ideas — a limited group, to be sure.* John Maynard Keynes, the most influential economist of this century (which speaks poorly of this century), spoke the truth in the final paragraph of his *General Theory of Employment, Interest, and Money* (1936):

*. . . the ideas of economists and political philosophers, both when they are right and when they are wrong, are more powerful than is commonly understood. Indeed, the world is ruled by little else. Practical men, who believe themselves to be quite exempt from any intellectual influences, are usually the slaves of some defunct economist. Madmen in authority, who hear voices in the air, are distilling their frenzy from some academic scribbler of a few years back. I am sure that the power of vested interests is vastly exaggerated compared with the gradual encroachment of ideas. Not, indeed, immediately, but after a certain interval; for in the field of economic and political philosophy there are not many who are influenced by new theories after they are twenty-five or thirty years of age, so that the ideas which civil servants and politicians and even agitators apply to current events are not likely to be the newest. But, soon or late, it is ideas, not vested interests, which are dangerous for good or evil.*

Do you believe this? If so, then the program of long-term education which the ICE has created should be of considerable interest to you. What we need are people with a *vested interest in ideas,* a *commitment to principle* rather than class position.

There will be few short-term, visible successes for the ICE's program. There will be new and interesting books. There will be a constant stream of newsletters. There will be educational audio and video tapes. But the world is not likely to beat a path to ICE's door, as long as today's policies of high taxes and statism have not yet produced a catastrophe. We are investing in the future, for the far side of humanism's economic failure. *This is a long-term investment in intellectual capital.* Contact us at: **ICE, Box 8000, Tyler, TX 75711.**

Institute for Christian Economics
P. O. Box 8000
Tyler, TX 75711

Gentlemen:

I read about your organization in David Chilton's book *Productive Christians in an Age of Guilt-Manipulators*. I understand that you publish several newsletters that are sent out for six months free of charge. I would be interested in receiving the following:

- ☐ **Biblical Economics Today** *and* **Christian Reconstruction**
- ☐ **The Biblical Educator** *(edited by David Chilton)*
- ☐ **Tentmakers** *(church financial planning)*

Please send any other information you have concerning your program.

_____name

_____number & street

_____city, state, zip

☐ *I'm enclosing a tax-deductible donation to help defray expenses.*

---

Geneva Divinity School
708 Hamvassy Road
Tyler, TX 75701

Gentlemen:

I read about your school in David Chilton's book *Productive Christians in an Age of Guilt-Manipulators*. I would like to find out more about the school. I understand that you sell audiotapes, workbooks, and textbooks that are part of a home-study course leading to various degrees in theology. Please send further information.

- ☐ *Send information on your summer institute for college age students*
- ☐ *I would like to receive your monthly newsletter,* **Calvin Speaks**
- ☐ *I would like to receive your free monthly newsletter,* **The Geneva Papers**

_____name

_____number & street

_____city, state, zip

☐ *I'm enclosing a tax-deductible donation to help defray expenses.*